Transforming Thinking

Essential reading for anyone who seeks to prepare active citizens for the twenty-first century, this long-awaited book considers Philosophical Inquiry, an empowering teaching method that can lead to significant improvements in confidence and articulacy, and produce positive effects in other school activities and in interactions in the wider world.

Readers are guided through the creation of a Community of Philosophical Inquiry (CoPI) in the kindergarten, the classrooms of primary and secondary schools, the community centre and beyond, with practical ideas to make CoPI work. With examples ranging from 5-year-old children to underachieving teenagers, and even senior citizens, the book shows how participation in a CoPI develops:

- the skills of reasoning, critical and creative thinking;
- concept formation and judgement;
- the virtues of intellectual honesty and bravery.

Including chapters on the theory and development of Philosophical Inquiry, the creation of a community, and using CoPI with groups of different ages, this book is essential reading for teachers, professionals and community workers.

Catherine C. McCall is President of Stichting SOPHIA: The European Foundation for the Advancement of Doing Philosophy with Children, and a member of the Advisory Committee of the International Council for Philosophical Inquiry with Children (ICPIC). Her Philosophical Inquiry with six-year-old children was featured in the 1990 BBC documentary 'Socrates for Six Year Olds'. She currently trains teachers and other professionals in implementing Philosophical Inquiry at Strathclyde University, and delivers professional development through CoPI for a diverse range of groups.

Transforming Thinking

Philosophical Inquiry in the primary and secondary classroom

Catherine C. McCall

Routledge
Taylor & Francis Group

LONDON AND NEW YORK

First published 2009
by Routledge
2 Park Square, Milton Park, Abingdon, Oxon OX14 4RN

Simultaneously published in the USA and Canada
by Routledge
270 Madison Ave, New York, NY 10016

*Routledge is an imprint of the Taylor & Francis Group, an informa
business*

Typeset in Bembo by
Keystroke, 28 High Street, Tettenhall, Wolverhampton
Printed and bound in Great Britain by
CPI Antony Rowe, Chippenham, Wiltshire

British Library Cataloguing in Publication Data
A catalogue record for this book is available from the
British Library

Library of Congress Cataloging-in-Publication Data
McCall, Catherine.
   Transforming thinking : philosophical inquiry in the primary and
secondary classroom / Catherine McCall.
      p. cm.
   Includes bibliographical references.
   1. Philosophy–Study and teaching. 2. Children and philosophy.
3. Inquiry-based learning. I. Title.
   B52.M38 2009
   107.1–dc22   2008042127

ISBN10: 0–415–047668–2 (pbk)
ISBN13: 978–0–415–47668–3 (pbk)

To the memory of Keith and Olivia,
who personified 'the examined life'

Contents

Acknowledgements

I would like to thank my friend and colleague Mary Haight, whose enthusiasm for Community of Philosophical Inquiry (CoPI) has supported me over many years, and especially for reading and commenting upon the manuscript of this book. Needless to say, all errors of style and substance herein are my own. My thanks also to Christine Steverson, Radmila Sutton, Anton van Deursen, Goedele De Swaef, Ed Weijers and Carol Price for reading and commenting upon different chapters. Thanks too to Russ and Allen for their support and understanding during the writing of this book. I am most grateful to all my teachers, colleagues and students who have supported my CoPI work over the last thirty years.

Many people have contributed to the development of CoPI over the years, and I am sorry not to be able to mention them all by name. However, I owe special thanks to Mr Howie, my physics teacher, who encouraged the metaphysical speculation of a 10-year-old schoolgirl and set me on the road that led here; Professor David Berman, my supervisor in the Philosophy Department at Trinity College, Dublin University, who supported my auditorship of the Metaphysical Society of Dublin University in which I first experimented with what was to become the CoPI method; Dr David Lamb, Hegelian philosopher extraordinaire and my Ph.D. supervisor at Manchester University, who taught me how to be a scholar and encouraged me to continue applying practical philosophy in all settings; Dr Matthew Lipman, my colleague at Montclair State University, for his pioneering work and creative leadership; Mrs Connie Bowsher, first grade teacher at Tuscan School, whose belief that even young children could philosophise made possible the experimental research in CoPI with young children; Professor Sir Drummond Bone (Vice-Chancellor of Liverpool University 2002–8), who, while Dean of the Faculty of Arts at Glasgow University, established and supported the postgraduate Centre for Philosophical Inquiry with courage and far-sighted wisdom; Keith Hammond, for his enthusiastic support for CoPI as a student, postgraduate and lecturer at Glasgow University; all the M.Phil. and Ph.D. degree students from the Centre for Philosophical Inquiry at Glasgow University, who made personal sacrifices to study and then implement CoPI in schools and in the community, including special thanks to Dr Claire Cassidy of Strathclyde University, who has kept the CoPI flame burning for many years; and, last but not least, all the Tuscan School first grade children from 1984 to 1990, whose joy in participating in CoPI was inspirational.

Finally, I wish to acknowledge the late Professor E. J. Furlong, Fellow of Trinity College, Dublin University, for his wise and invaluable advice.

I would like to acknowledge and thank the Herald & Times Group and The Big Issue Scotland for granting permission to quote material contained in the three examples to be found in the Afterword.

Example 1: the 1992 'Empowerment through Philosophical Dialogue' project on pages 190–191 is reproduced with the permission of the Herald & Times Group

Example 2: the 'Hawthorn' project on pages 193–194 is reproduced with the permission of The Big Issue Scotland

Example 3: the 'Philosophy is Fun' project of 1994–1995 on pages 194–196 is reproduced with the permission of The Big Issue Scotland

Preface

We had been sitting in a circle for an hour and a half, engaged in a fascinating dialogue that began with investigating the nature of persons,[1] and had moved to inquiring into the similarities and differences between artificial intelligence and human thinking when James put forward his argument that there are concepts which we know that we *cannot* know, although we can speak about them. He was disagreeing with Robert's argument that while it was (empirically) impossible for one person to know everything, if we pooled all human knowledge it would be (logically) possible to know everything. Countering Robert's optimistic view, James argued that we know that there are things which we cannot know, not because we are ignorant, but because of the unknowable nature of these things. To illustrate his point, James said, 'There is no last number!' Following this insight, our session had to finish, for although everyone wanted to continue, we were over time.

Earlier, while considering the nature of persons, different members of the group put forward arguments for a number of properties that they thought were essential for an entity to be considered a person.

Joy had thought that while existence is a necessary condition of being a person, there are also sufficient conditions to be satisfied – that to be a person, it is not enough just to exist.

David had initially suggested that one of the necessary conditions of personhood would be that to be 'counted' as a person, an entity must have the capacity to have sensory perceptions – to see, to feel, to hear, etc. However, the status of this characteristic as a necessary condition was challenged on the grounds that people who have some limitation on their sensory perceptions are still people; Joy claimed that even when someone is dead they are still in some sense a person.

Karen and Mark put forward a more inclusive condition: that in order to be a person, one must be a biological entity.

Being a biological entity is a very broad category (including animals, bacteria, etc.), so Mark refined the criteria by suggesting that one of the unique characteristics of persons is that they are owed moral consideration – you cannot hurt a person. (These considerations are not only abstract questions; they can become crucial, literally a matter of life and death, when for example an individual is in a 'vegetative' state and decisions must be made about whether they should be kept alive by artificial means.)

Later, Mark suggested that a further condition of personhood was that persons possess free will: they can decide for themselves what they will do (and not do).

While these characteristics appeared to be important aspects of personhood, they would arguably include animals, which also have the characteristics that had so far been suggested as determining personhood – because animals also:

- exist;
- have sensory perception;
- are biological entities;
- are owed moral consideration;
- appear to have a kind of free will.

There was a further characteristic, which the group thought was paramount:

- that in order to be a person, an entity had to be able to think.

However, Robert disagreed that the ability to think would by itself identify an entity as a person, as it might be possible to create an entity, say a robot, that would use artificial intelligence (AI) to think.

While Karen argued that robots would be denied the status of personhood on the grounds that they are not owed moral consideration, the suggestion that robots *could think* stimulated the group to consider whether there were any differences between the kind of thinking generated by AI and human thinking. The group suggested that there are several important differences, including a truly original philosophical insight from Mark:

- unlike AI systems, people forget!

Many modern writers appear to fall into what I would describe as a 'metaphorical fallacy', in which they use the term 'memory' for the artificial intelligence system's storage of data and processes. They then draw implications for human cognition from AI systems. However, as Mark correctly claimed, human memory is not like AI storage: to have the capacity to remember actually entails having the capacity to forget!

While 'chairing' this ninety-minute dialogue, during which members of the group proposed, argued for, defended, criticised, synthesised and often transcended so many theories and ideas, which echoed classical theories in the philosophy of personhood that they had never read, I could not help but compare the group to a philosophy class I had recently been teaching at university. I remembered how hard it had been to get the university students (who had the advantage of having read the classical philosophical theories) to talk and to think for themselves. What a contrast to this group, who did not want to stop talking and thinking!

But this was not a philosophy class, and these were not university students. These were 5-year-old children.

And they were not being taught philosophy. They were practising a method called Community of Philosophical Inquiry (CoPI) through which the children generated ideas and reasoned about them in dialogue with each other.[2]

This is a book about the method that enabled 5-year-olds to philosophise better than university students. It is a book about a specific method of Community of Philosophical Inquiry: how it was developed, what it is, what it achieves and how to create a 'Community of Philosophical Inquiry'.

Chapter 1

Introduction

The core of this book is a transcript of a ninety-minute philosophical dialogue with 5-year-old children,[1] which illustrates many of the features of the Community of Philosophical Inquiry (CoPI) method.[2] This philosophical dialogue was part of a five-year research project designed to demonstrate that, given the right environment, even young children could engage in philosophical reasoning.

When the research project began, almost no one would believe that young children had the capacities that would be required to engage in the kind of philosophical reasoning which occurred in CoPI sessions; it was commonly held that that young children could neither think in abstract terms nor engage in logical reasoning about philosophical concepts. Influenced by Piagetian[3] theories of cognitive development, most education professionals[4] took it to be *a fact* that young children could think only in 'concrete' terms. One of the few theorists to question this widely assumed view was Gareth Matthews,[5] who questioned the very concept of 'stages' in cognitive development.[6] However, because most of the 'experts' held that young children could think only in 'concrete' terms, education curricula had largely been stripped of abstract ideas and ambiguity. And so from the 1960s onwards, young children generally had no experience with, or practice in, thinking and reasoning about difficult abstract ideas, ambiguities, contradictions and inconsistencies.

Because they had had no experience with abstract thinking, it is not surprising that young children 'failed' in this skill when they were tested. And research results which showed that young children were unable to perform complex abstract thinking tasks served to entrench the idea that children were *incapable* of so doing.

However, being unable to do something does not mean that one does not have the capacity to do it. For example, I cannot speak Russian and would fail any test of my Russian language skills, but that does not mean that I am incapable of learning Russian. It would most likely be very difficult but not impossible for me (and quite possible for a 5-year-old) to learn Russian. I have the capacity to learn Russian. This is not to say that practising CoPI is like learning Russian; analogies only go so far! Rather, it is to say that to be proficient in any activity or skill, one needs to be exposed to the activity and to practise it. For example, a child or adult who has never been in water will not be able to swim. There is a lot involved in learning how to swim, and many human beings cannot swim, but all have the *capacity* to swim.[7] It is even possible to teach a lot about swimming without going into water, and some swimming coaches do this prior to their students going into the water, but no matter how much one knows *about it*, one cannot be said to know how to swim without actually being able to swim in water.

Similarly, although many adults and children do not practise philosophising, they all have *the capacity* to do so. And philosophising is not the same as learning about philosophy. One can learn a lot about philosophy without actually philosophising, but to engage in philosophising for oneself requires practice.

The 5-year-old children described in the Preface[8] had already spent fifty-six hours philosophising through the practice of CoPI, whereas the university students had spent sixty hours listening to lectures about philosophy. So, perhaps it should not be surprising that the group who had spent fifty-six hours engaged in the practice of philosophising for themselves were better at philosophising than the group who had listened to lectures about, and learned the results of, someone else's philosophising. What did surprise (then and still today) was that 5-year-old children could philosophise.

The children knew nothing of Plato, Aristotle, Hume, Hegel, Wittgenstein, and so on, so one could say they did not know philosophy. But they could juggle with epistemological and metaphysical ideas, and make ethical distinctions and meta-ethical distinctions. In short, they could philosophise.

The next chapter begins by describing how the idea of CoPI arose out of a mixture of academic philosophy and improvisational theatre techniques. It continues by describing the development of CoPI as a method of eliciting philosophical dialogue from groups of people in a non-academic setting, and the way in which CoPI was then adapted to its current form initially to use with 5-year-old children.

Chapter 3 looks at the theoretical landscape in which CoPI was first implemented. The chapter describes background theories in cognitive psychology that have influenced both education and school curricula for many years. This chapter presents some examples that show 5-year-old children reasoning correctly with hypothetical syllogisms and with set relations as a result of their immersion in CoPI, and analyses the logical structures that underlie their reasoning.

Chapter 4 presents the transcript of the CoPI session with 5-year-old children (referred to in the Preface), with comments and explanations about the role of the Chair (teacher): what the Chair is actually doing in this session; what is philosophically important in the thinking of the 5-year-olds in the session; what is startling in the cognitive skills and emotional intelligence skills of the 5-year-olds in this session; and an analysis of the underlying logic within the children's dialogue.

Chapter 5 explains the nature of the Community of Philosophical Inquiry, illustrated with examples from the transcript of the 5-year-olds in Chapter 4.

The chapter gives a simple, understandable explanation of the philosophical theory of realism that underlies the CoPI method, and how that philosophy is instantiated in the practice. It describes the role of the Chair in creating the CoPI, and the different levels at which the Chair works.

Chapter 6 gives an outline of different methods of eliciting philosophical dialogue, describing first Leonard Nelson's Socratic dialogue method and Matthew Lipman's P4C programmes. In an accessible and easily understandable way, it explains the different philosophical theories that underlie different methods, and how those theories are instantiated within the different practices. It describes, too, the actual practices – what a teacher does in the classroom when using each method. The chapter continues by giving an outline of two methodologies designed specifically for the classroom: the SAPERE approach to Philosophy for Children,[9] and the Guided Socratic Discussion series. The chapter compares and contrasts all four methods with the CoPI method.

Chapter 7 gives a longer exposition of what the teacher needs to know in order to create a CoPI in the classroom, as well as an outline of the philosophy and logic that it is desirable for an aspiring CoPI Chair to know. Illustrated with transcripts from the classroom, the chapter describes features of CoPI that are distinct from other kinds of pedagogy.

Chapter 8 outlines features that are specific to implementing CoPI with younger children in primary school and with younger and older teenagers in secondary school. Illustrated with transcripts of beginning CoPI sessions in both primary and secondary classrooms, this chapter looks at the similarities and differences that a teacher is likely to find when beginning to implement CoPI in either primary schools or secondary schools.

Chapter 9 explores the purpose of philosophising with children. The chapter first outlines the individual benefits of philosophising for the future life chances of children of all ages and backgrounds, including the academic benefits of the raising of achievements in subjects such as mathematics and language, the development of both moral virtues and cognitive skills through the practice of CoPI, and the positive changes in behaviour that are induced through the practice of CoPI. Second, the chapter explains how the practice of CoPI benefits society through the development of the skills and disposition required for children to become active, effective citizens within a democracy. The way in which CoPI develops those skills and dispositions is illustrated with transcripts of CoPI dialogue.

Chapter 10 develops the explanations given in Chapter 9 about the way in which the CoPI practice creates active citizens. This chapter gives expanded examples of three different projects, which involved both adults and children who practised CoPI out with the education system, and explains how these projects changed their lives and their communities. The chapter also describes how the CoPI practice follows in the tradition of the philosophy clubs of the Scottish Enlightenment, and makes a case that the re-emergence of philosophising outside academia could transform society in the twenty-first century.

Chapter 2

The origins and development of 'Community of Philosophical Inquiry'

When I went to university, I made a tremendous discovery: that there was a name for the kind of thinking I had been doing all my life. It was called philosophy, and moreover it had a 2,000-year history.

I had always been fascinated by questions about the nature of reality; how we know what is true and what is 'correct'; what makes some actions and decisions fair or just; the nature of good and bad; and why some things are beautiful. As a young child I would ask my teachers, but I never seemed to get replies that answered the questions I was asking; it seemed as though these were the wrong questions. The teachers at the local village primary school were (mostly) kind and caring. They thought I was a 'dreamer', and they probably thought these were fantastical childish questions, which were distracting me from class work. Gradually they 'weaned me off' asking – but I never stopped wondering.

Then, when I was 10 years old, we had the good fortune to have a wonderful science teacher. When I asked Mr Howie whether 'power' was real in the same way as objects were real, he did not treat it as a 'silly' question. We were learning about electrical circuits, and another teacher might just have been annoyed at the distraction, but he responded by giving me books on theoretical physics. For the first time I encountered serious thinking about the nature of reality and of the world, and the possibility that there was more than one answer, and that the answer had to be argued for and demonstrated. It seemed to me that there could be nothing more important! Although theoretical physics did not address questions of morality or aesthetics, it did raise questions of metaphysics and also of epistemology. (Of course, at the time, I did not know the names for these kinds of questions, or even that they had names.) Later, in a new school and studying algebra, I was trying to fathom what 'tending to infinity' meant. There was no Mr Howie to ask. An exasperated teacher told me that it didn't mean anything; it was just how you describe this graph, and this part of the equation. If anything, that answer made the concept even more puzzling.

In encountering the discipline of philosophy at university, I found the home for all these questions. It was a revelation and a kind of liberation. It felt as though a great secret had been kept from us all through our childhood and teenage years. It wasn't because here were the answers to all the questions; rather, it became clear that this kind of thinking was important and fundamental. All my classmates seemed to feel the same way: we were all excited about the topics and we spent hours discussing philosophical puzzles in the coffee bar. But after a year or so we began to feel something was missing. We were learning the canon of philosophy, and every week we wrote essays putting arguments for and against the theories of great philosophers but not about our own thoughts. Then one week we were given the option of writing a modern philosophical dialogue instead of the usual essay. We all chose this option, thinking it would be easier – just like a record of our coffee bar discussions. But we were wrong. Writing a philosophical dialogue was much more difficult. We learned that a dialogue is not a discussion. As in a play script, the dialogue had to develop, it had to have tension and it had to have variety, and there had to be character development shown through the dialogue itself. But a philosophical dialogue had to do more: it had to show a development in philosophical ideas as well. Sitting in the library trying to write such a dialogue was not productive, so I decided to try a theatrical technique to get my classmates to improvise a philosophical dialogue.[1] This was the beginning of what would develop over time into the Community of Philosophical Inquiry method.

The most challenging aspect of improvising or writing a philosophical dialogue was how to create the development of the philosophical ideas within the dialogue. We had no guidance as to how to do this; in fact, we had no guidance in how to write a philosophical dialogue beyond the advice to look at Plato. However, there was one philosopher who wrote about the development of thought: Hegel. So, for the purposes of the improvisation exercise I asked my classmates to use a (simplified) Hegelian structure. The first speaker should put forward a thesis; the second should put forward an antithesis; the third should then offer a synthesis of the thesis and antithesis; the fourth should regard the synthesis as a new thesis; the fifth should then offer a new antithesis; and so on.

It was extremely difficult to accomplish, but it was fun to try and we did manage to achieve a kind of development of ideas. There was a problem with the final result of our written dialogues: they all looked similar, and partly because of this we received very low marks. Of course, the essays were bound to be similar because they were the product of a collaborative exercise. Setting aside the fact that they were all similar, the written dialogues were not very good and the task was never set again. However, I was fascinated by the fact that the written dialogues did not reflect the energy that had been generated in the improvisation, and nor did they reflect the work everyone did or the delight that was produced when someone managed to find a new antithesis or synthesis. I decided it was worth pursuing because this way of working was so much more interesting than listening to lectures or having discussions or writing essays. The opportunity to continue practising this improvising dialogue arose a few months later.

During my third year at university I had joined the Metaphysical Society,[2] only to find that no one attended the lectures. I offered to produce posters and 'fly-post' around the college, as we did for theatre productions, in order to attract an audience. By virtue of this I was seconded on to the committee as 'Social Secretary'. The next year I was the only committee member left, and by default became the Auditor (Chair). The society had a large budget and no members.

I had no experience of committees or running a society,[3] but I knew what attracted students: free wine! Taking Plato[4] as the model (and who could be better?), I persuaded my classmates and friends to come to 'Symposia'. We would sit round a huge oval table and have philosophical dialogues with wine – just like Socrates!

However, having enticed an audience through the door with the prospect of free wine, we needed something more to keep them, and listening to philosophy lectures was not something most students would choose to do in their free time. So, I decided to try the improvised 'Hegelian' dialogue that we had used to produce our written dialogues for class. We wrote to various philosophers and explained that we wanted to try a new type of programme for the Metaphysical Society: a short paper followed by a dialogue. To our surprise, they all agreed. It turned out that they also preferred to have a dialogue rather than give a lecture in *their* free time. The dialogues were always rather clumsy, but they improved with practice, and they were fun for everyone.

All university societies had access to funds for field trips (though the Metaphysical Society had not taken advantage of this). So, we applied for funds to send two of us students on a field trip to observe professional philosophers in one of their natural habitats: a philosophy conference. We wanted to see how philosophers 'did' philosophy when they were not lecturing. So we set off to the Northern Universities Conference, and there we found something wonderful: a group of Northern Universities philosophers engaging in dialogue with each other. The dialogues were similar to the Metaphysical Society Symposia, but were much more sophisticated and smooth. Of course, the professionals did not use the somewhat rigid structure of thesis, antithesis and synthesis; their dialogues were more fluid and more varied. Moreover, the philosophers were using underlying logic that they all understood without having to make it explicit, whereas the students and others who attended the Metaphysical Society Symposia had not internalised logic and needed some kind of external structure.

Not all of the sessions at the conference included dialogue; some of them were more like listening to lectures followed by a short question–and–answer session. However, in some sessions the paper would be followed by fascinating dialogue in which the structure looked something like this:

1 Smith gave his paper explaining a new theory.
2 The Chair then asked the audience for any questions.
3 Five philosophers raised their hands to indicate that they had a question.
4 The Chair selected Brown to ask a question.
5 Brown asked a question about one of the claims put forward in the paper.

6   The Chair called on Smith to speak.
7   Smith then responded by restating the claim (x), giving an argument (i) to support it.
8   The Chair then called on Carerra, who took the argument (i) and showed that it led to a different conclusion (y).
9   The Chair then called on Davids, who came in and gave an example (a) which contradicted (y) and supported (x).
10 The Chair called Evelyn, who offered a counter-example (b), which weakened the support for (x) but suggested a new theory (z).
11 The session continued with the Chair calling on different philosophers to enter the dialogue.
12 Smith took the new theory (z) and examined whether it was consistent with his original claim (x), using new arguments (ii) and (iii) to show that (x) was stronger than (z).
13 Fredericks then contributed a new argument (iv), which demonstrated that Smith's original theory (x) had to be altered.

And so it continued.

The dialogue proceeded with contributions from different philosophers, critical but constructive. While there was a variety of different papers at the conference, those sessions in which dialogue occurred seemed to have some features in common. The 'dialogue-stimulating' papers had a kind of 'human interest': you could see their relevance for everyday life, compared with what could be described as technical papers. For example, one of the 'dialogue-stimulating' papers concerned children's rights,[5] and because many of the audience were parents, their examples and arguments came from personal experience.

Perhaps a more important factor that distinguished the dialogue sessions from the more traditional sessions was the skill of the Chair. The philosophers all knew each other and knew each other's work, and some of the Chairs seemed to be able to call on individual respondents in a sequence that furthered the dialogue. One Chair[6] was exceptionally skilled at this; she would ask for comments from particular philosophers at particular times, appearing to have some knowledge as to the kind of argument they would make and how it would 'play' within the dialogue. Observing these features,[7] I decided to try to incorporate them into the Metaphysical Society Symposia upon our return.

As Auditor, one of my duties in the Metaphysical Society was to chair the meetings, so I tried to reproduce what we had observed on our field trip: to ensure that the philosophers whom we invited would give papers that had obvious application in everyday life – human interest – and to chair the Symposia in a way that would help the flow of dialogue, which included eliciting contributions from participants and trying to do so in an order that would enable different ideas and examples to come forward.

However, the Metaphysical Society was not the same as the Northern Universities group of philosophers.

First, the members of the Northern Universities group were all professional philosophers, whereas, while there were some philosophy students within the Metaphysical Society, most of the members were drawn from students in other disciplines and the general public. This meant that while the content of the dialogues at the Northern conference was entirely philosophical, this could not be assumed within the Metaphysical Society.

Second, the Northern philosophers were already familiar with the work of the philosophers who gave the 'stimulating' papers – they had read and responded to each other's papers in the past – whereas the work of the visiting philosophers at the Metaphysical Society was known to only a few of the participants. This meant that while the Northern philosophers entered their dialogues from an equal knowledge base, in the Metaphysical Society some participants had much more background knowledge than others, so the group was not equal in this respect. In order to have a balanced dialogue, I had to find a way to begin with 'an even playing field'.

Third, the Northern philosophers had known each other for a long time – they were already a community – whereas (apart from the six philosophy students) the members of the Metaphysical Society were strangers to each other.

Fourth, the way in which the Northern philosophers knew each other was unusual: they knew each other through their philosophical work. This became more apparent outside of the sessions: at mealtimes and, most amazingly, when they played charades[8] in the evening![9] In playing charades they were not engaged in philosophical dialogue with each other, but they appeared to use an understanding of the minds of the players both in the acting of the title and in guessing. This had been one of the most wonderful and fascinating experiences of the conference – seeing a community of philosophers at play. It seemed that this unique characteristic of the community was somehow the result of their collaborative philosophical work.[10]

Given these differences, just copying the format of the Northern Universities dialogues was not going to produce the same result. We needed strategies to help create conditions that would produce something similar, but not identical. We could begin with a philosophy paper in the same way as the Northern Universities dialogues began. But then we would have to proceed differently. So, in order to create a more equal 'playing field', I decided that participants should not be allowed to cite their previous knowledge of the topic, or to use 'technical' philosophical terms that would be unfamiliar to other Symposia participants. While this requirement was devised with the philosophy students in mind, it also worked more broadly, for other participants had their own specialist knowledge, of genetics, say, which would also introduce an inequality within the group.

So, the Symposia dialogues would have two new features: the dialogues had to be spoken in ordinary, everyday language without any specialist terms being used; and participants were asked to refrain from using their previous specialist knowledge and to think afresh at the moment about the topic rather than citing experts or research.

The problem of how to keep the Symposia dialogues philosophical when many of the participants did not have knowledge of philosophy was more difficult. In the Northern Universities sessions, the dialogue would emerge from a question, but one of the keys to stimulating dialogue was the Chair's selection of the first questioner. The Chair knew the five philosophers who indicated that they had a question and she chose the one who would be most contentious and/or fruitful, using her judgement and prior knowledge of that philosopher's work. In the Symposia, I would not know the questioners, or know what kind of question they might ask, so how could I make a similar judgement and pick the best question? The solution was to take a list of questions and then choose the one that seemed to have the most potential to stimulate philosophical dialogue.

Having selected what I thought would be the best question, I still had a problem in how to ensure that the following dialogue kept to a philosophical path. The triadic Hegelian structure, which we had already been using, helped to achieve this. But it was not enough on its own. The Northern Universities Chair had called in contributions in a particular order, so one of the strategies I used was to call upon the philosophy students in the group to bring in a philosophical argument at particular times. I could also call upon the speaker to help with this task. Since the visiting speakers were all philosophers and mostly also lecturers, they were happy to help. And they found this role to be useful too. For example, in a dialogue about ethics, several different types of ethical theory were under consideration: a type of utilitarian ethics; a variation upon Kantian ethics; and a kind of 'egoistic' ethics.[11] One of the participants told a story of a decision he had to make when he discovered that a fellow student was cheating in an exam. In order to tie this story into the dialogue, I called upon the visiting speaker to give a kind of philosophical analysis of the example and show how it related to the previous contributions and the question under consideration. The speaker benefited from this procedure because it would reveal aspects of her or his paper that might need more explanation or argument and it would supply examples that could illustrate these.

Our dialogues became less clumsy, and began to look more like the Northern Universities dialogues we had observed.

The Metaphysical Society Symposia provided the space, which as students we had felt was missing, for developing our own philosophical thinking. And they did more: they reignited a passion for philosophical *wonderment*, which we had begun to lose under the weight of weekly essay writing and examinations. They also created a unique bond among the participants. Something important was happening, to do with the activity of philosophising collaboratively. Thinking through fundamental ideas for ourselves, developing new insights, changing our mind about important questions – all had a cumulative and profound effect upon the participants.[12] It seemed like an important thing to do, an important thing for everyone to do, but where could one find a place for this to flourish? We were leaving university; we all had to earn a living now.

Some years later I found myself teaching an extramural class at another university. I had prepared a standard introductory course on the philosophy of mind, but the class was composed of such a variety of students (a university fellow, an unemployed 18-year-old, a judge, a couple of 'home-makers', etc.) that a traditional course could not be 'pitched' so that all students would both understand and be interested in it. Wondering what to do, I remembered the Metaphysical Society; there had been a similarly wide range in the participants attending the Symposia. So, I decided to try the dialogue exercise with this class. Without having recourse to philosophers to come and give papers, we had to use texts that would be accessible to the 18-year-old, would be interesting to the judge, and would stimulate philosophical thinking for everyone. In order to stimulate dialogue, the texts had to raise philosophical questions and puzzles, but not answer them. Finding such texts proved to be a difficult task. In the end we used a mixture of newspaper articles, poems, selections from Lewis Carroll's *Alice's Adventures in Wonderland* and *Through the Looking Glass*,[13] parables from the New Testament and Kohlberg's moral dilemmas.[14]

There was another difference between this class and the Metaphysical Society: we did not have the resource of either a visiting speaker or the philosophy students to call upon when the dialogue was moving away from the philosophical themes. The content of dialogue was intended to be composed of the participant's ideas and reasons, and it would undermine this aim if the lecturer were to step in and 'insert' those ideas directly. Direct intervention was more likely to undermine the dialogue within this class than in the Metaphysical Society Symposia because students in a class expected lecturers to 'give the answer', as this was what they were accustomed to. Even in seminars where students were expected to talk, the lecturer was still the authority. Within philosophy teaching I did not know of any way to 'refocus' a dialogue towards philosophical arguments without introducing new content.

However, I did have experience within professional theatre work[15] that might help. When working with young actors at the Royal Court Theatre, I had learned how to elicit performance through indirect suggestion, finding an aspect of the actor's performance that we could develop in a new direction – for example, by eliciting from the actor what he or she thought were the underlying motivation(s) of the character he or she was playing in order to bring this motivation into the performance of the actor. Using this experience, I experimented with analysing the philosophical assumptions that underlay the contributions of participants and finding questions that would bring this underlying philosophy to the forefront. I tried to work with what was already potentially present in the contributions, rather than introducing new ideas and arguments.[16]

The process worked and, equally important, it seemed to generate the same kind of community bonds as we had experienced in the Metaphysical Society

– without the free wine. This seemed like a possible route to applying philosophy: a way of enabling people to philosophise without having to learn the discipline of philosophy, which is time-consuming and difficult, and not something for which the opportunity could realistically be made available to everyone.

Towards the end of the course, while looking for stimulating material to use as a starting point for the dialogues, I came across a reference to Matthew Lipman,[17] who had developed a programme called Philosophy for Children (P4C) in the United States.[18] Thrilled at this discovery, I wrote to Professor Lipman immediately, describing the kind of philosophical dialogue I had been developing – for surely here was the place where the idea that philosophising was for everyone (including children) could flourish.

Within months I was in the United States, invited to create and deliver graduate courses for teachers, which included some teaching of philosophy and logic with the training in delivering the P4C programmes. Arriving into a new culture, a new country and a new university system, I made a mistake that was to prove fortuitous. As professors at the Institute for the Advancement of Philosophy for Children (IAPC) we had the task of registering graduate students for the P4C courses. The courses were available to teachers of fourth grade and up (children aged 10 and older). When registering the teachers for the courses, I failed to check which grades they taught, and was later disconcerted to find that first, second and third grade teachers had registered. There were no programmes for these younger children, but the teachers had paid their fees![19] I discussed this problem with the teachers, and we reckoned that we could use the first P4C programme, *Pixie*,[20] with third grade. But what could we do with first and second grade? The first grade children could not read, but the teachers nevertheless begged me to do something for them.[21]

With the only alternative being to 'de-register' teachers, which did not seem fair since I had made the mistake, we decided instead to experiment with a dialogue approach for the young children.[22] We needed to have an activity that was entirely oral and also simple enough for very young children. Having argued theoretically against Piaget's stage theories, and made the theoretical claim that even young children could reason and use abstract ideas,[23] I was now faced with the practical reality of how to 'do' philosophising with young children. So, I decided to see whether we could adapt the Metaphysical Society Symposia practice to work with young children.

The key was to make it as simple as possible while conserving the 'logical' structure, which would make sure that we had dialogue rather than discussion. Thinking about what were the most basic elements that differentiated philosophical dialogue from discussion, there seemed to be five. A philosophical dialogue should have:

- philosophical content;
- two or more different philosophical ideas;

- contrasting philosophical ideas;
- arguments given to support the ideas;
- a movement or development of ideas and arguments.

The first challenge was how to ensure the philosophical content. In the Symposia the philosophical content and the questions had been suggested by a philosophical paper; in the extramural classes we had used a variety of texts. Fortunately for the young children, we had the wonderful resource of a Lipman novel, *Pixie*. Although the young children could not read, we could read episodes aloud to them. Here there were philosophical topics in a simple story that would intrigue the children. We would follow the Symposia practice by having a text, which would stimulate questions, read aloud.

The next step was to ask the children whether they had any questions. In practice the children had lots of questions, but not all of them would in themselves stimulate philosophical thinking.[24] So, following the Symposia practice, the Chair would select those questions that were most likely to lead to philosophical dialogue.

The next challenge was how to ensure that there were at least two contrasting ideas put forward in the dialogue. The dialogue followed the question, so we needed a method that would make sure that the children could contribute contrasting ideas. Without such a contrast we could have a discussion but it would not be a dialogue. The Symposia used two 'tools' to ensure contrasting ideas. First, during the dialogue the Chair would try to call on people who would contribute different ideas or theories or arguments, and would try to sequence the contributions so that they produced a clash of ideas. Second, the participants in the Symposia used a thesis, antithesis and synthesis structure that provided a development of ideas. Working with young children, the Chair could still use her or his skills in eliciting different ideas and sequencing them, but the structure of thesis, antithesis and synthesis would have to be simplified.

The Symposia triadic 'Hegelian' structure had been complicated to use, and it also took quite a long time for participants to master. So, with the young children, we[25] decided to try a much simpler way of generating different ideas: to ask the children to say whether they agreed or disagreed with what had been said before. Every contribution would be prefaced with:

> **'I agree with** _____ (the name of the child with whom the speaker was agreeing)'

or

> **'I disagree with** _____ (the name of the child with whom the speaker was disagreeing).'

This would ensure that:

1   different and contrasting ideas would come forward;
2   the children had to listen to each other;
3   as well as thinking about the content of their own idea, the children had to think about the relationship between their idea and the ideas of other children who had spoken previously;
4   in order to do (3), the children had to understand the ideas and reasons put forward by other children;
5   the children could then make explicit the relationship between their idea and the idea of another child.

Moreover, the Chair could use the structure as a tool to bring in different ideas or examples without having to make direct suggestions of content him- or herself, through intervening to bring in a new contribution by asking a particular child whether they agreed or disagreed with anything.

The next challenge was to ensure that the children did not just put forward their opinions, but gave arguments. To make an argument, one needs to put forward at least one supporting premise; to give a reason that supports the conclusion.

To help the children to give an argument, they had to give a reason for the point they were making. In order to ensure that the children would not only give reasons but *think* about the reasons for each point before they put it forward, I added the requirement to give a reason to the basic structure. So the final structure was:

'**I agree with** _____ (the name of the child with whom the speaker was agreeing) **because** _____ (give a reason)'

or

'**I disagree with** _____ (the name of the child with whom the speaker was disagreeing) **because** _____ (give a reason).'

In the Symposia dialogues (and also in the Northern philosophers dialogues) the participants would also give examples and counter-examples. I considered how to incorporate that aspect of the dialogue into this method, but decided that it would be too complex.[26] Within this structure there was already a multiplicity of possibilities for the children to respond to. The first child who speaks (let's say Clare) gives an idea and a reason. The second child (José) immediately has four options. He can:

A   agree with the idea (x) and the reason (i);
B   disagree with the idea (x) but agree with the reason (i);

C   agree with the idea (x) but disagree with the reason (i);
D   disagree with the idea (x) and disagree with the reason (i).

If José chooses option B, C or D, he will introduce at least one new element that can be agreed or disagreed with. If he chooses D, disagreeing with both idea (x) and reason (i), he will give a new idea (y) and a new reason (ii).

Moreover, every child who is listening is also thinking about whether they would choose option A, B, C or D. And potentially there will be as many new ideas and reasons as there are children participating.[27]

So, if José chooses option D, then immediately the third child (Anya) has sixteen options (see Table 2.1). Every option except 1 and 11 in Table 2.1 will generate a new idea. So, the structure immediately generates multiple possibilities. (Of course, only one is chosen at each juncture in the dialogue.) To add another 'variable' such as the giving of examples and counter-examples would render the structure too difficult to follow. So, rather than incorporating the element of giving examples into the basic structure, the Chair would take on the role of asking for examples and counter-examples where these were needed.

Table 2.1 Anya's sixteen options

	Agree with J idea (x)	*Disagree with J idea (x)*	*Agree with J idea (y)*	*Disagree with J idea (y)*
Agree with J reason (i)	1	2	3	4
Disagree with J reason (i)	5	6	7	8
Agree with J reason (ii)	9	10	11	12
Disagree with J reason (ii)	13	14	15	16

With a Chair using the structure of agreeing and disagreeing and giving reasons, a children's dialogue would look something like this:

Idealised CoPI dialogue
1   The Chair would begin by reading aloud from a specially written philosophical novel.
2   The Chair would then ask the children for any questions.
3   Children would raise their hands and ask questions.
4   The Chair would write the questions on a board or flip chart paper.
5   The Chair would choose a question to begin.
6   The questioner, Lauren, would say what she thought about the question she asked (x).
7   Children would raise their hands if they had an agreement or a disagreement with what Lauren said (x).
8   The Chair would call on one of the children, David, to speak.
9   David would say he disagreed with Lauren (x) because (i).
10 The Chair would call on Clare to speak.

11 Clare would agree with Lauren's point (x) but for a different reason (ii).
12 The Chair would call on Robin to speak.
13 Robin would say that she agreed with the reason (i), but she also disagreed with the point (x) because the reason (i) led to a different idea (y).
14 The Chair would call on Peter to speak.
15 Peter would say that he agreed with Robin's point (y) for the new reason (iii).
16 The Chair would call on Ayisha to speak.
17 Ayisha would agree with Peter's reason (iii), but disagree with Robin's point (y) and offer a new idea (z).
18 The Chair would ask Ayisha if she could give an example of (z).
19 Ayisha would give an example (a) of the idea (z).
20 The Chair would call on James to speak.
21 James would disagree with Ayisha's example (a) and give a counter-example (b) that supported Robin's idea (y).
22 The Chair would call on Simon to speak.
23 Simon would agree with Robin's idea (y) and Lauren's original idea (x), but add a new overarching idea (w), giving new reasons (v) and (vi).
24 The Chair would call on Ayisha to speak again.
25 Ayisha would say that she disagreed with herself (z) and agreed with Simon (w) for reason (v), and she had an example (c).

And so on.

The final challenge was how to ensure a movement or development within the dialogue. In the Symposia there had been an inbuilt mechanism to ensure this progression through the triadic structure, the resource of the visiting speaker and philosophy students to help with this process, as well as the role of the Chair in working to juxtapose people and ideas so that the dialogue flowed. In the extramural class I had used a method of eliciting the underlying philosophical assumptions to focus the dialogue and keep it moving forward. With the young children, these tasks would fall to the Chair: to try to bring in children and ideas when the dialogue needed to move forward, and to refocus the dialogue using the elicitation techniques from the extramural class.[28]

It seemed as though this new method might enable young children to engage in philosophical dialogue: we had a text that would stimulate philosophical thinking and questions; a structure which would ensure that different and contrasting ideas and also arguments were put forward; and the role of the Chair.[29] But it had never been done before, so now we had to see if it would work.

I remembered wondering about philosophical questions as a young child myself, and I disagreed with the stage maturational theories which would preclude young children from being able to philosophise, but I had no experience of working with young children. However, I was encouraged by Gareth Matthews, who had been philosophising with children as young as 8 (in

St Mary's Music School in Edinburgh) two years earlier. Matthews believed that all children had a natural talent for philosophising similar to their talent for art. He also believed that, like artistic talent, children's ability and desire to philosophise began to disappear at around the age of 11.[30] His view contrasted with that of Lipman, who regarded the ability to reason philosophically as *beginning* at around the age of 10. Theoretically I could see no reason why children (and adults) of all ages would be unable to philosophise – given an environment that 'taught' them how to!

However, theory is not the same as practice, so the 'experiment' to see whether philosophising with 5-year-olds was possible in practice began in September 1984 with one first grade class.

We were soon surprised at the ability of the children to follow the reasoning structure. They did not find it difficult to understand, and with practice they learned patience as well as how to reason. At first the children were concerned with articulating their own ideas and defending them, but soon they began to be fascinated by the ideas of other children.[31] And they were delighted to change their minds after hearing a new argument. The children invented the phrase 'I disagree with myself because . . .'; they thought it was important to articulate when and how they had changed their minds.

Two features of this new 'method' became apparent very quickly: its generative power and the complexity of the role of the Chair. The children's dialogues could move into unknown territory very quickly: there was no way to foresee which philosophical themes would 'catch' the children's minds. So, the Chair had to make instant analysis of all the potential directions in which a dialogue *might* go forward, while at the same time trying to remember (with the children) all the ideas and arguments that had already been put forward. At times the children would remember and refer to an argument that had been made weeks before.

Using this new method with young children had some surprising results. The first was that when we engaged them in philosophical dialogue, the children would sit for up to ninety minutes! No one expected this. The most optimistic expectation had been that 5-year-old children could sit and concentrate for fifteen minutes. Sitting for such a long time, usually on the floor, became physically uncomfortable and the children would wriggle and move around, but they would be listening. The Chair needed to ignore the physical squirming.

The second delightful surprise was that the 5-year-olds could master the reasoning structure easily. Later, adults who engaged in this method of Philosophical Inquiry found it more difficult to master the reasoning structure than the young children. As the year progressed, many of the children were able to use the reasoning structure in complex ways. However, at this time the sessions rarely comprised ninety minutes of 'pure' philosophical dialogue; for some of the time, the discussion would comprise reiteration rather than a developing dialogue, as can be seen in Chapter 4, which will examine a transcript of the dialogue mentioned in the Introduction.

A further feature of this new CoPI method was remarkable. Over time the classes changed from being groups of children who happened to be together in a class into communities of children who respected each other, helped each other and knew each other in an unusual way. Their behaviour changed, both in school and elsewhere. Parents noticed the changes in their own children. For example, in an interview for the regional newspaper,[32] one 5-year-old explained how he used his philosophy when his mum and dad were 'fighting', in order to help them get on better. Inside schools, teachers and librarians[33] noticed changes. In most schools there were three classes in each grade level. Those classes that practised Philosophical Inquiry were quite different from the other classes in their grade. When the children were redistributed in the following year, teachers noticed the differences between the children from CoPI classes and their peers.

Moreover, the 'academic' performance of the CoPI children improved. As predicted by the first grade teacher who had fought to have some philosophy provision for her children, tests showed that the CoPI children were scoring 60 per cent higher in language comprehension and 30 per cent higher in mathematical computation.[34] The results were so remarkable that one school district began a new practice of integrating children with special educational needs into those first grade classes that were practising CoPI.

Practising Philosophical Inquiry with children over the course of a year created a Community of Philosophical Inquiry in each class. And although every community was different, they all had a similar 'feeling' to the kind of community created with adults in the Metaphysical Society in the previous decade.

Most communities develop among groups of people because they share the *same* views, interests, beliefs or perspectives. But the Communities of Philosophical Inquiry were different: their members did *not* share the same views, interests, beliefs or perspectives. In fact, they delighted in holding different views and perspectives. Through the practice of Philosophical Inquiry, both adults and children developed not only a tolerance of different views and ideas but a *delight* in encountering views and ideas that contradicted and/or challenged their own. This delight grew from the enjoyment of discovering and creating new ideas and theories.

Over time, participants in CoPI moved from being personally invested in their own views and wishing to defend them to being able to differentiate between their own personal worth and their views and opinions. This ability developed at different times for different people: some could lose their personal investment in their views more quickly than others. And it happened much more quickly for most children than for most adults – most likely because children are more flexible, they are still creating their worldviews, whereas adults have often built their identity partly on these views.

Once participants were able to make this distinction, they were able to make a further distinction between *thinking* about an idea or concept and *holding an opinion* about the idea or concept. If they wished, they could use their own thinking to examine their opinions. It should be noted that CoPI participants are not required to articulate their personally held opinions: they are free to keep them private if they wish. What participants are required to contribute to CoPI is their *thinking*.

The Communities of Philosophical Inquiry were created out of the participants' joint activity of inquiring into basic and foundational concepts and ideas. Guided by a CoPI Chair, participants were able to use their own thinking and the thinking of others to examine the concepts and theories that underlie the topics under inquiry. The *purpose* of this Philosophical Inquiry was not to investigate the thinking of the participants – the participants were not 'under the microscope' themselves – but rather to use the tools of thought to reach a deeper understanding of questions that interested them.

There are many elements involved in creating a Community of Philosophical Inquiry, and Chapter 5 will begin to examine these.

Chapter 3

The theoretical landscape

The Preface described some 'highlights' of the main topics in a particular Philosophical Inquiry session with 5-year-old children. Chapter 4 is a transcript of the original film of a whole dialogue with comments explaining the role of the CoPI Chair in the dialogue, the philosophy that underlies the children's contributions in the dialogue, and the reasoning and sensitivity demonstrated by the children in the dialogue. However, before we look at the dialogue, it is worth reviewing the kinds of theory that dominated the fields of both education and psychology at the time the dialogue took place – the 'landscape' that made it particularly difficult to persuade educators, psychologists and even philosophers that, given the right environment, young children had the capacity to engage in philosophical reasoning.

These theories are still taught in teacher training colleges and used as the basis for education curricula materials for young children. Most influential are Piaget[1] and those psychologists who developed his original work about cognitive stage development. Piaget posited that cognitive development progresses in roughly four stages:[2]

1 **From 0 to 2 years old: the *sensorimotor stage***
   Where children experience the world through movement and senses.
2 **From 2 to 7 years old: the *preoperational stage***
   In this stage, children are unable to use logical thinking; they use 'magical thinking'. Children are also 'egocentric'; that is, they cannot understand that other people think and experience differently from themselves.
3 **From 7 to 11 years old: the *concrete operational stage***
   Children can 'reason' only using concrete objects; they cannot understand abstract ideas and concepts.
4 **From 11 years old and up: the *formal operations stage***
   Children can understand abstract concepts and use logic.

One of the reasons why his stage theories were so powerful (and remain influential today) is that the experiments which Piaget and his followers designed gave 'robust' results; that is, when experiments were carried out with children in different parts of the world and from different cultures, they yeilded the same results. However, there was a problem with Piagetian experiments (and with other applied psychological research): experiments were designed in order to confirm hypotheses. When Piaget and his followers found results that contradicted the hypothesis, or were inconsistent with the hypothesis, those results were discarded. It is considered completely respectable to discard a certain percentage of results within this research method. So, for example, some of the children's responses were discarded as 'fantasising'. But it could be argued that those responses represented philosophical thinking and reasoning.[3]

Margaret Donaldson[4] was one of the few psychologists who had recognised a problem with Piaget's results: that they did not conform to her experience of young children. So, she sought to explain why the results of Piagetian experimental research were so consistent.[5] She examined the design of the experiments and concluded (roughly) that the results had been obtained partly because the children failed to understand the instructions they were given by the researchers and partly because of the children's desire to please the adult researchers.

As famously shown in the Milgram (1963) experiments,[6] even adults will try to help a researcher in psychological experiments. How much more likely is it that children will try to work out what the adult wants and try to do that?

Example I

If a child is shown two jars, one tall and thin and filled with coloured water and the other short and fat, and then the adult pours the water from the tall, thin jar into the short, fat jar and asks, 'Which jar has more water?', then the child is likely to think:

- that one of the jars *must* hold more water, or else why does the adult ask the question?
- that the adult knows the answer.

This is a kind of trick question! If the child has logical thinking abilities, he or she will recognise *correctly* that there is an assumption in the experimenter's question 'Which jar has more water?', and that the assumption is that 'one jar holds more water'. Even if the child really thinks, 'It is the same amount of water', he or she may assume that the experimenter must be right and he or she is wrong, because the experimenter is an adult and the child has been taught that adults know better than children. So, to please the adult and give the answer the child thinks the adult wants, the child might identify one of the jars as holding more water when he or she does not really think that. But when children behaved in this way in similar experiments, such as 'incorrectly' identifying one jar as holding more water, Piaget and his followers concluded that the children were unable to 'conserve'.

Having seen that in other everyday situations children were able to 'conserve' (and showed other cognitive abilities 'denied' by Piagetians), Donaldson designed a series of experiments to test the same cognitive abilities in young children but with differently worded instructions to the children and using different tasks. She created a way to gain the information from children without asking 'trick questions', and she obtained different results.

Most mothers of young children know that even 3-year-olds understand what is in fact abstract logical reasoning in statements such as that given in Example 2.

Example 2

'If you go out in the snow without your mittens, your fingers will freeze!'

The above sentence involves hypothetical reasoning about a situation that is not present, and in that sense is abstract. This is the kind of reasoning which according to Piagetian stage theories should be understood only by children of 11 years old plus. But 3-year-olds understand this kind of statement, so Piagetian stage theory cannot be correct.

Basic logic tells us that only one counter-instance is enough to prove a universal statement false.[7] So, finding one 3-year-old child who can understand hypothetical reasoning should be enough to tell us that there cannot be 'stages', which are universal *by definition*, in cognitive development.

Nevertheless, Piagetian theories were so dominant that the nursery and school curricula in many countries were based upon these stages. It was taken as *fact* that young children could not use abstract reasoning.[8]

Some psychologists, such as Donaldson, questioned the Piagetian results, but few academics questioned the whole concept of 'stages' in cognitive development. Because there are stages in physical development, the lure of the analogy led many to accept a parallel concept of stages in cognitive development. One exception was Gareth Matthews, a philosopher from the University of Massachusetts, who questioned the assumption that 'stages' were applicable to cognitive development at all.[9]

Having held philosophical discussions with his own children when they were young, and then noted the diminution in his children's interest in philosohical puzzles as they grew older, Matthews came to believe that children's philosophical abilities were similar to their abilities in art: all children have an interest in and an ability in art when they are young, but few maintain this interest and ability into the teenage years and adulthood. Matthews' theory is more or less the opposite of Piaget's: that far from developing the ability to reason with abstract ideas only after the age of 11 or so, children have this ability when young but lose it as they grow older. That younger children do have the ability to philosophise was confirmed by Matthews in his research project with children in St Mary's Music School in Edinburgh in 1982. On the basis of his first-hand experience of young children philosophising, Matthews was able to show that Piagetian theories could not be correct. Furthermore, he argued that the basic notion that there are stages in cognitive development is itself a philosophical assumption, not a fact.[10]

This major idea, that there are stages in cognitive development, was further popularised by Kohlberg.[11] Following Piaget, Kohlberg hypothesised that there are three levels and six stages in the development of moral reasoning, roughly as follows:

Level 1, Pre-conventional

- Stage 1: Obedience and punishment orientation. Children and some adults do what is right only for fear of the direct consequences for themselves of being punished.
- Stage 2: Self-interest orientation. Children and some adults do what is right only if it is in their self-interest ('if you scratch my back, I'll scratch yours').

Level 2, Conventional

- Stage 3: Conforming to the expectations of others. Teenagers and some adults do what is right only because it is expected by others, who would disapprove of their 'wrongdoing'.
- Stage 4: The need to maintain order in society through laws. Teenagers and some adults do what is right only because it is necessary to follow society's laws in order to maintain society. Following the law is right.

Level 3, Post-conventional

- Stage 5: Social contract. Mostly, adults do what is right for utilitarian reasons: what is right is what benefits the greatest number.
- Stage 6: Universal moral principles – deontological ethics. The highest level of moral development is where people follow universal rules because they are right, irrespective of social approval or laws or self-interest. (In empirical studies, Kohlberg found that almost no one operated under deontological ethics.)

According to Kohlberg,[12] people must progress through each stage in sequence in order to reach the highest stage of moral reasoning: they cannot jump from, say, stage 1 to stage 3, or stage 4 to stage 6.

There are many problems with Kolberg's theory, not least that he assumes without any empiricial reason that deontological ethics represents the highest form of moral reasoning. Each of Kohlberg's stages actually represents a classic philosophical school of thought in ethics and/or meta-ethics. There is no justification for placing, say, Kant's deontological ethics[13] 'above' utilitarian ethics, as first suggested by Hume[14] and later developed by Mill[15] and James.

Moreover, critics have noted that several ethical theories are missing from Kohlberg's stages, for example the ethical theory known as 'the ethics of caring'. The psychologist Carol Gilligan claims that women tend to use 'the ethics of caring' where men use rule-based ethics.[16]

I do not question that empirical psychological research has tended to confirm the theories of Piaget, Kohlberg and Gilligan. However, so much of what children are *able* to do depends upon what they have *learned* to do, whether through being taught or through learning from their environment. For example, I have seen children as young as 7 years old working by themselves as street traders.[17] Those children were completely competent in mental arithmetic: they could add and subtract; and multiply and divide, when converting currencies. They were able to communicate with tourists in English, French, German and Spanish. They could navigate traffic without adult supervision and find their own way around busy cities. Those children did not go to school; they learned either by themselves from their environment or from older children. If one had tested, say, British children on any of these competencies, they would probably have 'failed', not because they did not have the capacity for complex mental arithmetic, or to communicate in five languages, or to cross the road by themselves, but rather because they had not learned any of these competencies.

Similarly, when they are 'taught' how to reason philosophically, the results prove that children of both genders are not bound by 'stages' in cognitive development or in moral reasoning. Nor are they divided by gender in the kind of reasoning they employ. Experimental CoPI work with 5-year-old children from 1984 onwards has shown that:

- They use 'formal operations'.
- They reason about abstract philosophical concepts.
- They operate with utilitarian ethics, virtue ethics and deontological ethical theories, interchangeably.
- Both boys and girls can choose to use rule-based ethical theories in their moral reasoning.
- They demonstrate an ability to place themselves in the position of other people and reconstruct the thinking of other children.
- They can understand and reconstruct thinking that is different to their own thinking and with which they disagree.
- Their ability to perform complex reasoning and sophisticated under-standing combined with their phenomenal memory for what has been said previously is better than that of many adults.

Chapter 4 will demonstrate in full the sophisticated philosophical reasoning in a dialogue with 5-year-old children. However, it is worth highlighting here some of the examples of the 5-year-old children using 'formal operations' in their reasoning, because these examples clearly demonstrate that the 'Piagetian' claims that young children (1) are incapable of formal operations, (2) must develop through maturational cognitive stages, and (3) cannot place themselves in the viewpoint of others are all *incorrect*.

The following examples demonstrate that when children are guided in the practice of CoPI, many are capable of the same kinds of logical reasoning about abstract concepts as are adults.[18]

In the dialogue in Chapter 4, among other topics,[19] the children are examining these issues simultaneously:

- the ontological status of both robtos and persons; that is, 'what kind of entity is a person?' and 'what kind of entity is a robot?';
- the epistemological questions of 'how can we know what a robot is?' and 'how can we know what a person is?';
- the ethical questions of 'what ethical duty do we owe to a person?' and 'what ethical duty do we owe to a robot?'

Early in the dialogue, several children put forward the idea that one cannot distinguish a person from a robot just by looking at the entity's behaviour, because a robot could look like a person and walk and talk and even think like a person. So, Robert uses hypothetical reasoning in a manner similar to that used in experimental scientific method to suggest a test one could use to distinguish a robot from a person:

Robert   [Y]ou could tell a robot from a person because you could – What you could do to the robot was like you could like, you could – Well, you could throw a needle at it.
Mc   And?
Robert   And if it doesn't go through, then it would be a robot!

Example 1: the logical structure of Robert's hypothetical reasoning test

When one formalises the logical structure of Robert's argument, it looks like this:

Robert's argument takes the form of modus ponens (or the affirmation of the antecedent):

If A then B
A
Therefore B

If A *(you throw a needle and it does not go through)* then B *(it is a robot)*
A *(you throw a needle and it does not go through)*
Therefore B *(it is a robot)*

ROBERT'S ARGUMENT: LOGICAL STRUCTURE

> Where   N stands for 'the needle doesn't go through'
>   A stands for 'it'
>   R stands for 'a robot '

Logical structure:

> $N \rightarrow (A \text{ is } R)$
> N
> $\underline{A \text{ is } R}$

Although Robert's 'scientific' test would 'work', Mark intervenes at several points in the dialogue to point out that it would be unethical even to consider doing such a test, so Robert's test is not a 'proper' test:

Mc   Could you tell whether it was a robot or a person?

Mark   Yeah, you could because if. If you like, maybe like, just – Well, no! Because if, **if** it looks just like a person then you wouldn't be able to. Because you can't, you can't rip off – you can't like do something to it because what if it's a real person? You never know which, if it's a real person or not, because.

Mc   Now that's an interesting thing you said, Mark! You could do something to it if it was a robot, but you couldn't do something to it if it was a person?

Mark   Yeah! You can't like rip stuff off of it. Because then, because then, because **if** it was a real person you'll hurt it. You'll hurt the person then.

. . .

Mark   I agree with Chloe. Because if you, if you, if you throw a ro- if a robot – if somebody walked in the door, right, and someone – and we thought it was a robot, we wouldn't, we wouldn't be able to know. And if you threw, **if** you threw – and if you threw a needle at it, the pers- and **if** it was a real person, wherever you threw it, it would start bleeding. And, and if it was a rusty needle – if it was a rusty needle it could, it could, it could hurt then 'cause it would have rust on it and everything.

Mc   Karen?

Karen   Well, I, I think that that's not really a good idea to find out how it works because if it was a real person it would hurt very badly and the person could get hurt. I think that you **could**, that it's pretty good, but you **shouldn't** do it. You should pick a different way to disc- . . . to, to find out!

Example 2: the logical structure of Mark's hypothetical moral arguments

When one formalises the logical structure of Mark's argument, it looks like this:
    Mark's argument takes the form of modus ponens (or the affirmation of the antecedent):

> If A then B
> A
> Therefore B

> If A *(throwing needles is a test to see if the entity is a robot and throwing needles would harm a person)* then B *(the 'throwing needles' test should not be used − it is not a proper test)*
> A *(throwing needles is a test to see if the entity is a robot and throwing needles would harm a person)*
> Therefore B *(the 'throwing needles' test should not be used − it is not a proper test)*

MARK'S ARGUMENT: LOGICAL STRUCTURE

> Where: T stands for 'throwing needles is a test'
>   H stands for 'throwing needles would harm a person'
>   P stands for 'throwing needles is a proper test '
> $(T \ \& \ H) \rightarrow \daleth P$
> $(T \ \& \ H)$
> $\underline{\daleth P}$

And at a later part of the dialogue we can see an example of Clare using some complex hypothetical reasoning:

[Karen has earlier established that

Karen   [a] ro- a robot isn't a person because it's − it's a robot, it's not a person.]

. . .

Clare   If you're thinking, you must be for real.
Mc   Why?
Clare   Because, because it − when I'm thinking I'm for real. But you might have brain surgery and you're still for real, but if you're thinking, you must be for real.
Mark   Oh, oh, oh!
Clare   [To Mark] Wait. And robots can think and so − and robots can think and they're for real. So I kind of disagree with that.

Here:

- Clare presents a hypothetical: IF you are thinking, THEN you must be a real person.

- She then emphasises that the implication is one-way; you might be a real person and not be thinking (after brain surgery).
- Then she discovers a counter-example: that robots think.
- So either the hypothetical is false – denial of the consequent – or robots are persons.
- But it has been established by Karen earlier in the dialogue that robots are not persons.
- So she now disagrees with her initial hypothesis.

Example 3: the logical structure of Clare's hypothetical arguments

When one formalises the logical structure of Clare's argument, it looks like this:

1 The first stage in her argument takes the form of modus tollens (or the denial of the consequent):

> If A then B
> Not B
> Therefore Not A

2 The second stage in her argument takes the form of modus ponens (or the affirmation of the antecedent):

> If A then B
> A
> Therefore B

CLARE'S ARGUMENT: LOGICAL STRUCTURE

Clare's initial assumption is that all thinkers are persons.

> Where: T stands for 'a thinker'
> P stands for 'a person'
> R stands for 'a robot'

Logical structure:

1)

> ((R are T) & (T are P)) → (R are P)
> ¬R(are P)
> ¬R((are T) & (T are P))

2)

> ¬R((are T) & (T are P)) ≡ (R are T) → ¬T(are P)
> (R are T)
> ¬T(are P)

So, Clare's argument shows that her initial assumption that 'all thinkers are persons' is wrong, as her argument shows that not all thinkers are persons, and so she then disagrees with her initial assumption.

In another part of the dialogue, the children's ability to think in terms of class relationships is demonstrated. Initially, David explains the origin of the question that he has raised about whether you could think and dream at the same time.

> *David*   Well, what I think was interesting about it is, um, even though it didn't say that . . . Elfie thought and dreamed at the same time – it's just that she said, 'I don't have fancy dreams', but she never said that she didn't have dreams. But she also said that she thought.

Here David differentiates between 'dreams' as a class of events and the subset of 'fancy dreams'. His use and understanding of class relations enables him to make a correct deductive inference: that the claim 'I don't have fancy dreams' does not exclude the possibility of having other dreams that are not members of the subset of 'fancy dreams'.

According to David, the character's claim in the text (which the children read) – that she does think and that she doesn't have fancy dreams – does not exclude the possibility of both thinking and dreaming at the same time. He is interested in this possibility.

Example 4: the logical structure of David's argument using set relations

David is asking whether it is possible to have thoughts inside of the set of dreams, thoughts that do not overlap with the set of fancy dreams (Figure 3.1). David operates correctly with class relations. Moreover, he operates with the relations that can logically hold between classes of difficult abstract concepts.

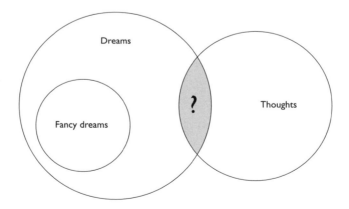

Figure 3.1

Joy also shows this ability with class inclusion using abstract concepts. She offers a solution that has the logical form of a hypothetical: IF thinking is a subset of dreaming, THEN you can think and dream at the same time:

Joy   ... like you can if you're dreaming and then you're thinking **in** your dream ...

To repeat: IF thinking is a subset of dreaming, THEN you can think and dream at the same time.

Example 5: the logical structure of Joy's argument using set relations

Mark then offers a different way to construct the relationship between thinking and dreaming:

Mark   ... Because when you're not thinking and you're dreaming, your imagination is thinking. So your imagination is thinking sometimes but your brain is thinking with it.

But David sees a logical flaw in Mark's construction. According to David, Mark's claim – when you're not thinking and are dreaming, your imagination is thinking – amounts to an exclusive disjunction: either you are thinking in your imagination or you are dreaming in your imagination, but not both. (And because of this problem, correctly identified by David, it is not possible to represent Mark's argument visually here.)

David's *solution* to the problem he sees in Mark's construction makes use of the idea of the unity of consciousness as providing a superset. He disagrees with Mark's apparent classification of 'imagination' as being a separate class to 'you'. Then, following Joy's hypothesis, he suggests that the problem could be resolved if 'you' is taken to be the superset, which includes as one of its elements the set of 'dreaming events', which, according to Joy, includes a subset of 'thinking'.

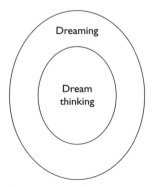

Figure 3.2

David   I agree with Mark and I disagree with Mark. Because you control your imagination. So if you were dreaming – Some people say that your dreams are in your imagination, and some people say you don't – But if your dreams **are** in your imagination, then how could you **think** in your imagination while you're **dreaming** in your imagination? But you could think in your dream while you're in your imagination!

Example 6: the logical structure of David's 'solution' using set relations

Not only is David operating with the relations between classes of abstract concepts, but his disagreement with Mark is based on his analysis of the classificatory logic which Mark uses!

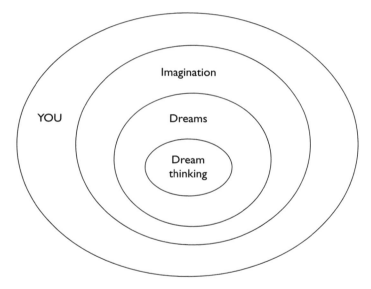

Figure 3.3

It can be seen from the transcript of the dialogue in Chapter 4 that the children are engaging in logical reasoning (itself formally and structurally sophisticated) about philosophical ideas – ideas that involve abstract concepts such as dreams, thought, truth, the nature of reality, etc. It is very unusual for children to use such sophisticated reasoning procedures and, as many cognitive tests bear out, when tasks that require logical procedures are presented to children, they usually fail.

But it is not only children who fail to perform or perform 'incorrectly'. Empirical work by cognitive psychologists (such as Wason and Johnson-Laird, and Nisbett[20]) has shown that adults also fail on tasks that require logical reasoning. In one famous task devised by Wason and Johnson-Laird,[21] only 5 per cent of 128 university students were correct in a task involving hypothetical reasoning.

What differentiates the 5-year-old children's dialogue from an adult dialogue is not the sophistication of the philosophical reasoning, but rather their lack of vocabulary. They struggle to express their ideas with the limited vocabulary they have learned. This phenomenon – the gap between the children's vocabulary and their philosophical ideas – lends weight to the idea that thinking is not primarily verbal. It is clear that the children have ideas and arguments that they are then trying to put into words. Those ideas have not originated in language that they have heard.[22]

Chapter 4

Philosophising with 5-year-olds

The dialogue that follows in this chapter is not identical in structure to the idealised form of dialogue explained in Chapter 2; it is a real dialogue. However, the overall structure is similar. Moreover, the interrelationships between the different ideas and reasons offered by the children are more complex than the idealised model outlined in Chapter 2.

In general, the responsibility of a CoPI Chair is to create the conditions for philosophical dialogue to emerge. Through the practice of philosophical dialogue, children (or adults) are transformed from a group (who may or may not know each other) into a Community of Philosophical Inquiry. The role of the CoPI Chair is complex:

- She or he must balance the requirements for the discussion to follow philosophical lines with providing opportunities for everyone to participate.
- She or he uses the CoPI reasoning structure to help ensure that different arguments are presented.[1]

So, in the early phase of a developing Community of Philosophical Inquiry, the CoPI Chair teaches the participants how to use the reasoning structure – reminding them to give reasons and to agree and disagree.

Using the reasoning structure alone does not produce dialectical movement.[2] The Chair must intervene to help contrasting points of view come forward. She or he can do this in several different ways. One way to achieve this is to analyse the philosophical assumptions that underlie different participants' contributions and, making informed 'guesses' as to the kind of argument they might contribute, call in specific participants at specific times – in the hope that their contributions will contrast with each other. By juxtaposing what she or he predicts will be contradicting or contrasting arguments, the CoPI Chair creates the conditions for the philosophical tension that drives the dialogue forward. Another way to create these conditions is to analyse and then highlight the key philosophical junctures for the children. This is done as subtly as possible, and whenever possible by repeating the children's own comments (often as a question), and/or by articulating what is implicit in the children's contributions. This action, of calling on specific children at specific junctures in order to build philosophical tension, cannot be seen in the transcript that follows (pp. 35–77).

There are junctures within any CoPI session where a particular line of inquiry begins to dry up. Often, participants will begin to 'echo' earlier contributions without adding any substance to what has already been argued. The CoPI Chair needs to be aware of this and be ready to move to a new question.

During every CoPI session there are stretches of discussion that are not philosophical dialogue at all. The intellectual work being done during the periods of CoPI is very tiring, and groups need to have 'rest' periods between the intense periods of Philosophical Inquiry. So, the CoPI Chair needs to be aware of 'pacing': of having periods where the discussion relaxes before 'tightening up' again into the more intense Philosophical Inquiry. This is not the same as a particular topic drying up; children and adults in a CoPI session can suddenly become tired, and no Philosophical Inquiry on *any* topic can be sustained until after they have had a break.

These tasks are not easy; the speed at which the dialogue moves means that the CoPI Chair is engaged in instant and complex analysis while the participants are speaking. Children often struggle to present some sophisticated ideas without the language that would enable them to articulate those ideas. And it can be hard to follow their live reasoning because they change their thinking as they speak. The children offer logically complex arguments that are difficult to analyse 'on the spot'. So, a CoPI Chair needs a background in both philosophy and logic to be able to do the instant analysis that is required to structure the dialogue.

This CoPI session was filmed for American public television in 1988, and there are some gaps where the cameraman ran out of film and had to change cartridges (the TV producer had not expected to be filming a class of 5-year-olds in dialogue for ninety minutes!). The children[3] had been practising CoPI for approximately an hour a day, four days a week for several months when the film crew came. At the beginning of the year none of the children could read, but by this point some of them were beginning to do so, and all of them wanted to read. So, we would 'read together', which in practice amounted to me reading and the children following half a beat behind – most of them actually repeating what they had heard, rather than reading from the page. But they felt as though they were almost reading and were very proud of this!

CoPI sessions do not have to begin with reading. They can begin with looking at an image, or a video, or listening to a poem, or with a topic, or a question – anything that will serve as a stimulus to philosophical thinking. However, the development of philosophical thinking is aided by using a text, such as one of Matthew Lipman's P4C novels, which is specifically written with the purpose of stimulating philosophical wonderment and puzzles.

The exercise of 'reading aloud' also serves:

1   to prepare individual children in the physical act of using their voices in the following dialogue;

2   to prepare individual children psychologically to take part in a dialogue;
3   to prepare the group for their engagement in a joint group activity of dialogue, by sharing a group task of reading aloud;
4   to give the children a sense of joint ownership in the activity, which will transfer to the following dialogue.

Every CoPI session begins with a stimulus: reading a text, looking at an image, etc. Following the contemplation of the stimulus, the CoPI Chair asks for questions from the group.

When we look at this dialogue, it is worth noting the kind of questions the children ask:

• If she wasn't a real person, how can she think or talk?
• How could she have dreams and think at the same time?
• How come he thinks at the same time?
• Why did she touch her eyes?
• Why did he say to himself, 'Dummy, if you can wonder, you must be thinking'?
• Why did she say, 'Maybe I don't talk that much'?
• Why did she say that maybe some people can go to sleep with their eyes open?
• Why did Seth say 'Elfie hardly ever talks. Maybe she's not for real. That just shows how wrong he can be'?
• Why did she think she was asleep when she was really awake?

Note: The children are not sure of the name of the character. They are not sure whether the character is a boy or a girl. They are not sure whether the character is a human being.[4] But they do not ask whether it is a boy or a girl, or what the name is, or where the character lives! Their questions are mostly concerned with puzzles and ideas in the story. When we began the year, children did ask textual 'comprehension' questions, or questions about the likes and dislikes of characters. But by this time the children want to discuss *ideas*.

In the dialogue that follows, some of the children remember the text, but many of them are interested only in the ideas and reasons being put forward by other children.

The transcript is laid out with some comments[5] in shaded boxes to explain aspects of the dialogue concerning:

• what the children are doing within the CoPI session;
• the philosophical dimensions of the CoPI session;
• the logical structure of elements of the CoPI session;
• how the CoPI session is chaired.

Speaker   Dialogue

Mc   OK, now children, ignore this, don't look at this at all [indicating large sound boom swinging above children's heads]. All right? You're going to be looking at whomever is speaking and just ignore whatever else is going on. Pretend the camera isn't there. All right? So. We're going to begin today by reading aloud on page two.

> *Comments*
>
> Many children were intimidated by the presence of a large camera, a swinging sound boom and two six-foot strangers sitting among the children in the circle. However, as the session progressed, most, though not all, of the children became so involved with the dialogue that they ignored what had been obstacles for them.

Child   Two?
Mc   Page two.
Child   Four.
Mc   Four! Page four, I beg your pardon. And we will all read together. OK?
Child   Yeah, that's good.
Mc   We'll read together aloud.
Child   And then to the next page?
Mc   And then to the next page. Four and Five. And then we'll stop, and I'll ask you if there was anything interesting or puzzling that you want to talk about. And then we'll write it down. And then we'll have our discussion. All right, everyone ready? Follow it in the book if you don't want to read aloud. OK? So –

> *Comments*
>
> The philosophical topics are frequently presented in the text in such a way as to intrigue children. Since they also find character descriptions and plot lines interesting (though not puzzling), it is useful to ask them what they found puzzling. Using the term 'puzzling' usually brings out more philosophical topics.

Class   [Reads] 'Today, Seth said, Elfie hardly ever talks. Maybe she's not for real. That just shows how wrong he can be. Maybe I don't talk that much, but I think all the time. I even think when I sleep. I don't have fancy dreams. I just think when I'm asleep about the same things I think about when I'm awake. Last night I woke up in the middle of the night and I said to myself, Elfie, are you asleep? I touched my eyes and they were open. So I said, no, I'm not asleep. But that could be wrong. Maybe a person could sleep with her eyes open. Then I said to myself, at this moment am I thinking? I really wonder. And I answered myself,

Dummy, if you can wonder, you must be thinking. And if you're thinking, then no matter what Seth says, you're for real.'

Mc What was puzzling or interesting in that part?

> **Comments**
>
> Almost the whole class raise their hands.

Mc Maggie?[6]

Maggie If. If she wasn't a real person she wouldn't − be − if she wasn't a real person how can she think or talk?

> **Comments**
>
> Maggie's response here questions the foundation of scepticism. Underlying this response is a notion of the inherent inconsistency of Cartesian doubt: that is, that doubt about whether one is real or doubt about the existence of the external world cannot be expressed without involving one in absurdity.

Mc If she wasn't a real person, how could she think or talk? [Writes while talking] OK, let's put E., for Elfie, wasn't a real person how could she think or talk?

> **Comments**
>
> The CoPI Chair begins by writing the children's questions on a flip chart or board, followed by the name of the child who asked the question.

Mc David?

David How could she have dreams and − How could she have dreams and think at the same time?

> **Comments**
>
> The text seems to suggest that dreaming is thinking in your sleep. David is questioning this explanation of dreaming.

Mc [Writes while talking] How could she have dreams and think at the same time?

> **Comments**
>
> The second question is written on the flip chart.

Mc	Fern?
Fern	How come he thinks at the same time?

> **Comments**
>
> The third question is written on the flip chart.

Mc	[Writes while talking] How come – How come she thinks at the same time? Let's put your name up here, Fern, because that's adding to David's question.

> **Comments**
>
> Fern's response may not actually add to David's question, but prior to this discussion Fern rarely entered into the dialogue, so crediting her with adding to David's question encourages her to participate.

Mc	Mark?
Mark	Oh! Oh! Why did she touch her eyes?

> **Comments**
>
> The fourth question is written on the flip chart.

Clare	Because to see if they were open.
Mark	Why couldn't she touch something else?
Mc	Well . . .
Joy	Yeah!
Mc	. . . let's discuss that when we have our discussion. That's an interesting question. [Writes while talking] Why did she touch her eyes?

> **Comments**
>
> Children often want to begin a discussion immediately about what interests them. However, experience has shown that if we stop at this stage, the children forget the other points of interest that they would have wished to discuss.

Mc	Karen?
Karen	Why did he say to himself, 'Dummy, if you can wonder, you must be thinking'?

> **Comments**
>
> Karen's response raises a question about the nature of wondering.

Mc   [Writes while talking] Why did she say to herself, 'Dummy, if you can
          wonder, you must be thinking'?

> Comments
>
> The fifth question is written on the flip chart.

Mc   Sheena?
Sheena   Why did Pixie – did she say, 'Maybe I don't talk that much'?

> Comments
>
> The sixth question is written on the flip chart.

Mc   OK. [Writes while talking.] Why did sh- . . .
Sheena   I mean Elfie.
Mc   OK, I'll just put 'she' say, 'Maybe I don't talk that much.'

> Comments
>
> Although Sheena has adjusted her question, I try to write the
> original formulation of the question. This is done because often
> when children (and adults) reformulate their questions, the new
> question is less original than the first formulation.

Child   Maybe –
Mc   Chris?
Chris   I'm interested in David's question.

> Comments
>
> Usually, in a CoPI session, many children have their hands raised
> with questions they wish the group to discuss. In the initial couple
> of sessions, children would be disappointed if someone else asked
> 'their' question. The change from disappointment to recognition
> such as shown by Chris here demonstrates a feature of the com-
> munity in action wherein the children are more concerned with the
> content of the questions and are less competitive.

Mc   All right. Let's put your name up here.
Mark   You could put a little star.

Comments

Often many children are interested in the same topic, in which case I will put an asterisk next to the question, rather than list up to fifteen names. This saves time and also serves to indicate that the topic is important to the group.

Mc   Clare?

Clare   Why didn't she say that? I mean why did she say that she – some people – maybe some people can go to sleep with their eyes open?

Comments

The seventh question is written on the flip chart. Clare is struggling with her point. She wants to raise a more specific aspect rather than leave an 'open' why question, so she changes the articulation of her response halfway through. This is a typical occurrence in dialogue. The children often 'think aloud', and change what they started to say as they see problems with the way they have phrased something. They try hard to put their thoughts into words accurately. Here Clare wants to question the test of being asleep suggested in the text.

Blake   Yeah, oh man! [Clutches his head in his hand.]

Comments

Blake was thinking about the same question.

Mc   Robert?

Robert I want to know why they said may – that just – Why did Seth say that just shows how wrong he can be?

Mc   How wrong Seth could be?

Comments

Children often have difficulty giving the correct names of the characters in the text, and can be sidetracked from their original question by this problem. So, I question Robert to make sure we have his question accurately phrased.

Robert Yeah!

Mc   What did Seth say?

Robert He's [points at text] right.

Mc   Seth said . . .?

Robert	Seth says that [reading] 'Elfie hardly ever talks, maybe she's not for real. That just shows how wrong he can be.'
Mc	OK, shall we put up 'Why is Seth wrong?'

> **Comments**
>
> Here I tried to paraphrase Robert's question. This is something a CoPI Chair *should not do*. One cannot do the thinking for the children and then expect them to think for themselves. Even paraphrasing what they say in order to help them will, if practised, result in the children being more passive and relying on the CoPI Chair to think for them.

Robert	No. Why did Seth say that Elfie hardly ever talks. Maybe she's not for real . . .
Mc	OK.
Robert	That just shows how wrong he can be?
Mc	[Writes while talking] Elfie hardly ever talks, maybe she's not for real. That just shows how wrong he can be. OK, we have room for one more.

> **Comments**
>
> The eighth question is written on the flip chart. In the practice of CoPI, we stop taking questions usually at an arbitrary point, such as when the end of the paper is reached or the board is full.

Mc	Joy?
Joy	Why did she think she was asleep when she was really awake?
Mc	[Writes while talking] Why did she think she was asleep when she was really awake? OK.

> **Comments**
>
> The ninth question is written on the flip chart.

GAP IN TAPE

Mc	Let's look at Maggie's question, number one, 'If Elfie wasn't a real person, how could she think or talk?' What do you think about that?
Mc	Sheena?
Sheena	Well, I have a question to ask Maggie.
Clare	Maggie?
Maggie	What?
Sheena	Well, like why, I mean like how – when did – how did you – I mean how did you think of that question?

Maggie   Well, that's a toughie, because, um, it says in the story she may be notbe alive if she didn't talk. [Clare hands Maggie a book to help her find what it said.] Or she couldn't like think, or something. And it made me like – it came up to my head and I thought it would be a good question.

> ### Comments
>
> Maggie's response assumes that one criterion for being 'real' is to be alive. It seems that she is puzzled by the suggestion that in order to be alive one must talk and think.

Mc   So, how would you know if something was a real person or not?
Mc   David?
David   If, if she – if Elfie wasn't real, then, then she wouldn't be able to – She'd be able to talk because then she might be what we were discussing yesterday. [We were discussing 'real', 'fake', 'artificial' and – 'imaginary'.] But if she wasn't real, then she wouldn't be able, she wouldn't be able to think. And she wouldn't, she wouldn't be able to move every part of her body and stuff like that!

> ### Comments
>
> David explains the basis of Maggie's question – 'If Elfie wasn't a real person, how could she think or talk?': that while non-persons may in fact talk, existence is a necessary condition for thinking. There is an inherent absurdity in the Cartesian position hinted at in the text, that a non-existing being could do anything.

Mc   Fern?
Fern   I agree with David 'cause if you're not there you can – you can't do anything. You, you won't be able to think and move and stuff, and learn stuff.

> ### Comments
>
> Fern clarifies and emphasises David's point that existence is a necessary condition for doing anything.

Mc   Chris?
Chris   [Softly] I agree with David because if you weren't real, you, you couldn't, you wouldn't – you'd be like – you'd just be a model and you wouldn't be able to hear and everything like that.

> *Comments*
>
> Chris is expanding the line of argument introduced by David. While existence is a necessary condition of being a person, there are also sufficient conditions to be satisfied. An object such as a mannequin fulfils the condition of existence, but is not a person. To be a person, one must also be able to hear, etc.

Mc   Chris, what did you say? What would you just be if you weren't real?

> *Comments*
>
> Chris had flu, and his voice was very quiet.

Chris   Well, if you weren't real, you'd just be a model and you wouldn't be able to hear and everything.

> *Comments*
>
> By this point the children are not discussing the story (text), but rather ideas that have been raised by other children.

Mc   You'd just be a model?

> *Comments*
>
> I check that I have heard correctly.

Chris   And you wouldn't be able to hear.
Mc   Robert?
Robert   Well, I disagree with David because of – well, he wouldn't – What do you mean he wouldn't like not be able to move any part of his body? Maybe – What if like it was a robot?

> *Comments*
>
> Robert's counter-example challenges one of the conditions of personhood presented thus far: that in order to be a person, one must not merely exist, like a mannequin, but be able to move any part of one's body. In Robert's example, a robot fulfils this condition, and yet is not a person.

Mc   Well, that's an interesting question!

Comments

I make this intervention in order to highlight for the children that Robert's question is an important philosophical move.

Robert	A robot can move every part of his body and a robot isn't real!
Mc	[To the class] Now, is a robot a person?

Comments

Robert's statement, that a robot isn't real, could have served to introduce an ontological philosophical theme about the nature of a robot. Here I might have asked him what he meant by 'real'. However, I chose not to for two reasons: first, because we had discussed the meaning of 'real' in the previous CoPI session (referred to earlier by David); and second, and more importantly, because the lines of argument advanced so far by the children concerned the definition of person and the nature of personhood. So, my question to the class was intended to draw attention to the implicit challenge to their conditions of personhood presented by Robert's counter-example.

Chorus	No. No!
Mc	Joy?
Joy	I agree with David because if you weren't real, then you couldn't talk. You would just be still, and you wouldn't be able to hear and talk and move at all.

Comments

Joy is referring back to David's original ontological argument about the nature of persons.

Mc	Mark?
Mark	Well if, if – I agree with . . . [Looks at Joy.]
Mc	Joy.
Mark	Joy. Because if, if you weren't real, you wouldn't be able to, to like move around. And you would be, you would – You wouldn't be able to think, you wouldn't be able to hear and you wouldn't be able to do anything!
Mc	Karen?
Karen	A ro- a robot isn't a person because it's – it's a robot, it's not a person.

Comments

Karen states 'the law of identity'.

Mc   Well, let's think about this for a minute. Supposing something came in through the door right now and it looked just like a person, and it talked and it moved, how would we know whether it was a real person?

> **Comments**
>
> The dialogue has reiterated David's original ontological argument, but has not moved forward philosophically. So, I intervene to suggest an epistemological 'line' of thinking. That is, rather than investigating the (ontological) question of what the entity is, I suggest an epistemological 'angle' of looking at how we can *know* what it is. If a robot could meet all the conditions so far presented for person-hood, how could we distinguish persons from robots?

Chorus Oh, oh!

Mc   Mark?

Mark Well, on this, on this movie this person, this par- . . . this father made a robot. But you always can put like materials over it to make it look like skin and make it look like a real person so it could go to school and everything. And then, and then its robot brain could learn so much it would be like a perfect robot.

> **Comments**
>
> Mark uses the film *AI* as an example.

Mc   Could you tell whether it was a robot or a person?

> **Comments**
>
> I intervene to give Mark a space to link his example to the epistemological question.

Mark Yeah, you could because if, if you like – maybe like, just – Well, no! Because if, if it looks just like a person then you wouldn't be able to. Because you can't, you can't rip off – you can't like do something to it because what if it's a real person? You never know which, if it's a real person or not, because – But you would know if, if it didn't have skin on it and everything. If it was just plain and you could see its parts and everything. Then you would know it's a robot.

> **Comments**
>
> Mark is thinking as he talks. He has ideas about physical tests, but rejects them as he speaks. Underlying Mark's contribution here is a

new and important condition that might differentiate persons from robots – that persons are beings to whom one owes moral consideration. One has a moral duty not to hurt persons. If you don't know whether it is a person or a robot, you cannot risk ripping off its skin in case it is a person. A robot is differentiated from a person by its constitution. If you could see its parts, you would not need to test it.

Mc   Now that's an interesting thing you said, Mark! You could do something to it if it was a robot, but you couldn't do something to it if it was a person?

Comments

I intervene here because I am sure that Mark intends an ethical meaning of 'you can't rip off – you can't like do something to it . . .' The tone of Mark's voice and the expression on his face indicate this (but do not come across in a transcript). Most of the children have not noticed this ethical consideration, which is a new element in the dialogue. However, I use the words 'could' and 'couldn't' deliberately here because 'could' and 'couldn't' retain the ambiguity in 'can't' between the meanings of 'being able to' and 'being morally allowed to'. The intervention signals that there is something important here, but attempts to stay neutral as to what it is.

Mark   Yeah. You can't like rip stuff off of it. Because then, because then, because if it was a real person you'll hurt it. You'll hurt the person then.

Comments

Mark gives his reason as to why you can't (shouldn't) rip the skin off the entity.

Mc   Clare?
Clare I agree with Mark on his first question and at the end. Because they, they have – you can't rip off the skin of a person, but as a robot you can. And . . .

Comments

Throughout the dialogue, the children are careful to use the CoPI reasoning structure to connect what they are saying to what has been said earlier. This shows that they are thinking meta-cognitively. They are not simply presenting their ideas, but thinking about those ideas and how they relate to what other children have said. They take care to show the structure of the dialogue as they speak. This also involves paying close attention to who has said what, remembering the content and the person who originated the idea, while also thinking of their own contribution. This is a complex cognitive task for anyone, and although they do make mistakes, it is surprising how often their recapitulation of the structure of the dialogue is accurate.

Mc Now one minute, Clare. Why could you not rip off the skin of a person, but you could for a robot?

> *Comments*
>
> I intervene to remind Clare to give her reason for why you 'could not' rip off the skin of a person, deliberately using 'could' again.

Mark Oh, because, oh!

> *Comments*
>
> Mark wants to reiterate his earlier ethical reason, as Clare has just said she agrees with him, but he thinks Clare is going to miss the ethical point.

Mc Chris?
Chris I agree with Mark, too. Because, because if you did make like a human robot and you sent it to school, it could, it could learn a lot. And it would be a good thing to have it.

> *Comments*
>
> Chris picks up on a point that Mark made earlier: that a robot could go to school and learn. A child will often put forward two (or more) ideas at a time. When this happens, a dialogue may develop which follows both themes.

Mc James?
James Well, see, I disagree with Mark because, see, if a robot was – came in or something you, you couldn't rip off its skin because – even, even though if it didn't have, have skin. They would probably – they could just paint it the colour of skin and then it, and then it's really metal so it looks like a human.

Comments

When Mark raised the moral objection to ripping the skin off a person, he used the verb 'can't'. Clare completed the description by adding 'but as a robot you can'. Here James uses the verb 'can' in the sense of 'being able to', and he raises a technical difficulty concerning what one is able to do (as opposed to what one *should* do).

Mark	Ooh, ooh!
Child	What?
Mc	OK, Mark, do you want to clarify what you meant?
Mark	No. But, but if you painted it you would see, you would see! Like – but they would have to put metal over it, over the parts. So when you paint it looks like a round arm and it would have to bend and everything.

Comments

Mark is saying that if the robot were painted metal, you would already know it was a robot because you could see it was (so you would not need to test it).

Robert	Yeah, but robots – Well, I agree with Mark because, well, you could tell a robot from a person because you could – What you could do to the robot was like you could like, you could – Well, you could throw a needle at it.

Comments

Robert continues the line of thinking about what one would be able to do by suggesting another test by which one could distinguish a person from a robot. His test is also concerned with the physical difference between a person and a robot.

Mc	And?
Robert	And, and if it, and if it, and if it – and if it like – and if the needle, and if it doesn't go through, then it would be a robot!
Mc	So, that would be a test so you could tell the difference between a robot and a person?

Comments

I intervene here to emphasise the epistemological dimension – that the test is concerned with knowing which kind of entity it is.

Mark   But, but . . .

> ### Comments
>
> Mark wants to reiterate his moral objection: that you *should not* use that test in a situation where you did not know whether the entity was a robot or a person.

Mc   You could throw a needle at it?
Child   No, but . . .
Mc   Supposing it was a person?

> ### Comments
>
> Here I am intervening to highlight Mark's earlier objection to doing invasive physical tests.

Child   No, but . . .
Mark   That's what I'm saying!

> ### Comments
>
> Mark still wants to reiterate his moral objection.

Mc   Chloe – supposing it was a person, could you throw a needle at it?

> ### Comments
>
> I ask Chloe this question in order to widen participation in the dialogue. Chloe rarely talks, although she follows the discussions closely. I continue to use the verb 'could' with the ambivalence in meaning.

Chloe   No.
Mc   Why, why couldn't you throw a needle at it?
Chloe   Because, because if it's – if it sticks you really deep then you would bleed. And to a robot it would – wouldn't bleed.

> ### Comments
>
> In her objection to the test suggested by Robert, Chloe introduces a more specific physical differentiation between robots and people: that people bleed. This introduces a specifically biological feature of persons.

Mark   I agree with Chloe. Because if you, if you, if you throw a ro- if a robot
        – if somebody walked in the door, right, and someone – and we
        thought it was a robot, we wouldn't, we wouldn't be able to know.
        And if you threw, if you threw – and if you threw a needle at it, the
        pers- and if it was a real person, wherever you threw it, it would start
        bleeding. And, and if it was a rusty needle – if it was a rusty needle, it
        could, it could, it could hurt them 'cause it would have rust on it and
        everything.

> **Comments**
>
> Mark is conscious of involving other children in the dialogue and
> crediting them. Although he is eager to emphasise his moral
> objection to physical tests that may hurt a person, he is gracious
> about the protocol of dialogue – that one shares thoughts and credits
> others. So, he includes Chloe's point about bleeding in a more
> comprehensive account. Considering that Mark is only five years
> old, his sensitivity towards another child's thought, both in terms of
> crediting her and incorporating and developing her idea, is both
> noteworthy and praiseworthy.

Mc   Karen?
Karen   Well, I, I think that that's not really a good idea to find out how it works
        because if it was a real person it would hurt very badly and the person
        could get hurt. I think that you could, that it's pretty good, but you
        shouldn't do it. You should pick a different way to disc- . . . to, to find
        out.

> **Comments**
>
> Karen clarifies the distinction between what one is able to do and
> what one may do, highlighting Mark's moral objection to harmful
> physical tests on persons. She stresses the difference between what
> you can do and what you should do. Karen is struggling to find the
> word 'discover'. The CoPI Chair must be careful not to help
> children in their articulation, as that help runs the risk of changing
> the child's meaning. Even though it may seem obvious which word
> the child is seeking, the CoPI Chair must wait and let the child find
> their own way to articulate their point.

Mc   Can you think of any way, any test that you could give it, to find out
        whether it was a robot or a real person?
Mark   I know, I know!
Mc   David?

David   Well, mm, well a way that you could do it is if you sended it to a doctor. If you put a nee- and if he put a needle in it, it'll – it would have, it would have – Well, blood would have to come out. And . . . [Tape runs out.]

> **Comments**
>
> David proposes a way of avoiding the moral problem of harming people. The implication is that doctors are exempt from the moral injunction that prevents us from sticking needles into people. His suggestion raises an interesting moral issue. In this example, sticking a needle into the person would hurt. (The Hippocratic Oath actually forbids a doctor from taking a knife to his patient!) Would it be OK for a doctor to take a blood sample from someone for other than medical purposes? David's suggestion also emphasises the biological nature of persons.

GAP IN TAPE

> **Comments**
>
> The dialogue continues with considering why it's OK for a doctor to stick needles into people but not for a regular person to stick needles into people. General opinion is that a doctor can do it without injuring (the rusty needle!). Children then consider other ways of testing that would not hurt if it were a person.

Clare   . . . about the fact. You could have like, um – stick, um – have something metal and put it on there and see if it sticks because metal against a magnet does stick.

> **Comments**
>
> Clare suggests a physical test that would not hurt a person. A robot is made of metal and so a magnet could be used to distinguish between human flesh and metal.

Mc   OK, let's think about this for a minute. Joy, supposing a person had a metal leg, are they still a person?

> **Comments**
>
> This question is designed to probe the physical distinction between persons and robots that the children are making – that persons bleed whereas robots do not. I call in Joy because she is often too shy to volunteer her ideas, but often has different arguments from other children.

Joy   Well, um, they are and they aren't. Because they are for the rest of their body, but they're kind of not for that part of their body, because it's not the same as the other parts of their body, it's not as soft as the other parts of their body and it wouldn't be – And you could feel it would be harder because of their bones.

> *Comments*
>
> Joy maintains that physical (flesh and blood) constitution is a property of persons.

Mc   So, do you think they wouldn't be a person?

Joy   Well, I think they would be a person but that leg would be a kind of a person, not really like us.

> *Comments*
>
> By maintaining that the person would still be a person although part of them would not be person-like, Joy is approaching a whole–part distinction, wherein a property of the whole is not necessarily possessed by the parts.

Mc   David?

David   Well, I agree with Joy and I disagree with her, because if something happened to the leg like if it got flattened and the doctor had to replace it? Then they would still be a human. But if it was like how Mark said – if it was a robot with fake skin there – then it wouldn't be a human.

> *Comments*
>
> Here David introduces a new condition of personhood: origin. (Once a person, always a person.) For David, it is not the physical distinction that is important (the person and the robot could both have metal legs), but the *origin* of the being. David also affirms the whole–part distinction implicit in Joy's response.

Mc   Sheena?

Sheena   Well, I was going to say something about the other thing we were talking about.

Mc   Let's hear what you have to say.

Sheena   Well, I disagree with everyone who said you could take it to the doctor. Because you would have to take it in the car, right?

Mc   Um.

Sheena   Well, if it was a real robot it might be able to break out of the car.

> **Comments**
>
> During CoPI sessions, children sometimes refer back to earlier parts of the dialogue, as Sheena does here. At this point, the CoPI Chair has several judgements to make, keeping in mind that his or her job is to chair the dialogue, which includes the development of lines of argument, as well as ensuring the children's ownership of the content of the dialogue. Often the points raised have a bearing on the current topic or issue being discussed, in which case the development of the idea or example will further the dialogue.

Mc   So, it might be difficult to do this test? All right, now let's think about this question . . .

Clare   Suppose the doctor lives next door to you?

Mc   Then that would be OK, wouldn't it? Let me ask you this: supposing a person had two metal legs, would they be a person then?

> **Comments**
>
> I intervene to refocus the dialogue.

Karen   They would be real because just because they have the metal – metal legs doesn't mean that they're not real, because they are still a person.

Mc   Mark?

Mark   I agree with Karen. Well, I, I, – because – um . . .

Mc   Did you forget your reason? [Nods head.] Well, we'll come back to you when you remember. Fern?

Fern   I agree with Karen Rego because if you have two metal legs, it doesn't mean that you're a fake person, it means that you're a real person. If you have had legs replaced, you would still be a person!

> **Comments**
>
> We discussed real and fake in an earlier dialogue.

Mc   David?

David   I agree with Karen because, as I said, maybe something happened to it like if it got flattened or something like that. Or if it got chopped off by an axe or something. [Chuckles.] Maybe they would need to replace it with false legs, but it would still be a human, the person would still be a human.

> ### Comments
>
> Karen, Fern and David all emphasise human origin as an overriding condition of personhood. Replacement of human parts with non-human parts does not affect personhood. Fern also introduces a distinction between fake and real. A real person can have fake parts. The condition of personhood is a condition or property of the whole, even though the parts may not be human.

Children Oh, oh, oh.
Mc So, they would have false legs, but Fern said it wouldn't be a fake person.

> ### Comments
>
> David has used the term 'false' legs, and Fern used 'fake' person – both interesting contrasts to 'real', so I highlight this.

Child Oh, oh. I want to say . . .
David Yes, it would still be a person.
Mc Mark?
Mark I disagree with David on part of what he said. And I agree with Karen because even if you had two metal legs, you'd still be a person because you'd still think like a person, you'd still have a human brain. And I disagree with David because if someone chopped both of your legs off with an axe, you'd be dead!

> ### Comments
>
> Mark is taking care to show the exact relations of what he is about to say to what other children have said previously. He introduces two new conditions of being a person: that one has to think like a person, and that one has to have a human brain. In his third point, he disagrees with David that if someone had their legs chopped off, they would still be a person; he states that they'd be dead. Implicit in this point is that one must be alive to be a person.

Mc James?
James I disagree with Mark because you wouldn't be dead because, see – if they saved other kinds of legs, they could sew it back on. Like if you get stitches if you have a crack in the head, they sew it back together. Well, you could like sew the other leg back on.
Mc Brian?

Brian	Um, well . . .
Mc	What do you think? If you had two metal legs, would you still be a person?
Brian	I, um, disagree with Mark 'cause Mark said – I mean I agree with Mark 'cause Mark said if you had two legs chopped off then you would be dead.
Mc	Well, what about the other part of what Mark said: that if you had a human brain, you would be a person? Even though you had metal legs. Do you agree with that?
Brian	Yeah!
Mc	Fern?
Fern	I agree with Mark if you did have like – if you did chop off your legs, you would be automatically dead. And if you had a real brain, you would be a person.
Mc	Supposing that you had a human brain but the rest of you was all metal, your eyes and your mouth and your nose and everything, would you be a person then?

Mc	Chris?
Chris	I agree with David because if your legs were chopped off, you could replace them with false legs because your heart wouldn't be damaged or anything.
Mark	Oh, I know, I know!
Mc	OK, Mark, then Joy.
Mark	Well, about the one that you just asked us to think about. That one. If you still had your human brain, you would be – you wouldn't be a person because – you said the rest of your body was metal?

Mc   Uh-huh.

Mark   Your heart would be chopped off so you wouldn't be alive! You wouldn't have any blood flowing through your body!

> *Comments*
>
> You wouldn't be a person because you wouldn't be alive. The implication in Mark's statement is that being alive is a more basic condition of personhood than human origin. Being alive would be a necessary condition of personhood.

Clare   Wait! I don't understand that.

Mark   Oh, I'll clarify It! Well, see, you know your heart it flows blood through your body? Well, if all your body was metal and your head was only left, it would be cut right here. [Demonstrates.] Then your heart wouldn't be there to flow blood through your brain. So, you wouldn't be a real person, you wouldn't even be alive!

> *Comments*
>
> What Mark clarifies is how he reasons that a person with a totally metal body could not be alive. (He states in his last sentence that you wouldn't be a real person if you were not alive, but he does not argue this point.)

Child   I don't agree with that.

Mc   So, Mark, are you saying that you have to be alive to be a real person?

> *Comments*
>
> I am highlighting the philosophical point in Mark's contribution.

Mark   Well, no. But, well, kind of. I don't know, but you can't live without a heart because it has to flow blood to your brain.

Robert   I disagree with Mark because if your heart was metal, the rest of your body would be metal except your brain. Your brain doesn't need blood. And . . .

Child   Yes, it does, it needs some blood!

Mc   Wait a minute. What do you want to say, Robert?

Robert   But your brain doesn't need blood, just the rest of your body does, and if the rest of your body is metal, your heart can be metal too. And now it doesn't matter because if you fell down, all the outside part of you would be metal and you wouldn't get hurt.

> *Comments*
>
> Robert seems to think that a person remains a person without blood. It is not clear whether his disagreement with Mark is about whether the brain (or the person) is still alive under these conditions, or about whether the human origin of the person is more important than the condition of being alive.

Mc	Would you still be a person, Robert?
Robert	Yes.
Mc	Joy?
Joy	I disagree with all the people who said if your legs got chopped off, you would be dead. Because the only way you would be dead if your heart stopped beating, or if your brain stopped working, or if they got – But just because your legs got cut off, you wouldn't be dead.
Mc	Would you be a person if you were dead, Joy?

> *Comments*
>
> The basis of this question concerns the limits of personhood. Mark's statements imply that one has to be alive to be a person. According to Joy, a person is still a person if they are dead. There is a philosophical 'glitch' in casting the problem in this manner. Strictly speaking, only that which has the potential to be alive can be dead. A biological entity is one that may be alive or dead. An artefact is neither. Furthermore, there are real problems in defining death, especially when it comes to persons. And there are different medical, legal, biological, religious, social and philosophical definitions and criteria.

Joy	You would be a person if you were dead, just you wouldn't be talking or hearing. And I agree with all the people who said you'd be alive with cut off legs, 'cause you could always get them replaced, you could get metal legs and everything.

> *Comments*
>
> Joy introduces a new consideration: that a person remains a person even when they are dead.

Mc	Karen?
Karen	Could James please clarify what he said before? 'Cause I was going to say something about it if only I could hear it. Oh yes, now I remember.

Um, I disagree with James when he said that like you could sew a part to a part. Well, that's not what stitches are. Stitches are if you hurt yourself really bad, they stitch it just to – up, but not if your legs are cut off or – that's not a way how you stitch something.

Mc   All right, we're going to look at the next question now, which is David's question. [Reads] 'How could she have dreams and think at the same time?' And there was David and Fern and Chris were all interested in that.

> ### Comments
>
> The CoPI Chair has a duty to keep the dialogue philosophical as well as maintaining the children's ownership of the content. So, judgements have to be made weighing up different criteria for intervention. Since the group have already discussed the nature of stitches, which does not lead directly to Philosophical Inquiry, I intervene here to move to a new question that does raise philosophical issues.

Children Oh, oh, oh, oh!

Mc   OK. Now, David, you asked the question, so could you explain what was puzzling about that? 'How could she have dreams and think?'

David Well, what I think was interesting about it is, um, even though it didn't say that, oh, she, um, Elfie thought and dreamed at the same time – it's just that she said, 'I don't have fancy dreams', but she never said that she didn't have dreams. But she also said that she thought. So that's why I said that.

> ### Comments
>
> The text says, 'I think all the time. I even think when I sleep. I don't have fancy dreams. I just think when I'm asleep about the same things I think about when I'm awake.' David is making a very sophisticated distinction between 'dreams' and 'fancy dreams'. He makes the correct logical point: that saying you don't have fancy dreams does not preclude having other kinds of (non-fancy) dreams.

Fern   Sometimes you can think and dream, sometimes, but mostly you can't. 'Cause like when you're thinking and dreaming – mostly you can't but sometimes you can because, because sometimes when you're thinking too hard and you dream at the same time – you really can't dream at the same time.

> *Comments*
>
> Fern suggests that dreams and thinking are different kinds of mental activity.

Mc Sheena?

> *Comments*
>
> Sheena is experimenting with closing her eyes.

Sheena Well, I agree with Fern because, um, you can dream at the same time and think. Because, um, see 'cause sometimes if you're dreaming – You can't dream without thinking!

> *Comments*
>
> Sheena suggests that thinking and dreaming are connected.

Mc You can't dream without thinking?

> *Comments*
>
> I highlight Sheena's point.

Sheena You have to think what you're going to dream!

> *Comments*
>
> Sheena states what the connection between dreaming and thinking is.

Mc You have to think what you're going to dream?

> *Comments*
>
> I repeat Sheena's point because stating that thinking and dreaming are necessarily connected is an important philosophical claim.

Mc Maggie?
Maggie See – What was the question again?
Mc [Reads] 'Can you think and dream at the same time?'
Maggie Well, sometimes. Because if you were . . . the live one can like . . . When I have a dream, I always thought about that. And um, when I have a

dream, I think about it and I said – one dream I thought about this dream, and like I'm remembering this question but then I forgot it. And I asked my mom if it was true, and she said, 'You might have a dream', and I said, 'I was thinking when I was sleeping.'

> *Comments*
>
> Maggie seems to be recounting an experience that she describes as thinking when she was sleeping, which her mother told her is dreaming. This supports the apparent identification of dreaming with thinking in one's sleep suggested in the text – the identification that David questions.

Mc Joy?

Joy I agree with Fern and Maggie because like sometimes you can think and dream, and sometimes you can't. Because like when you're dreaming – like you can if you're dreaming and then you're thinking *in* your dream. Sometimes it's hard to think and dream at the same time, especially if you're thinking about something else and you're dreaming about something else. Because then you might get mixed up. When you sleep you can also – when you are asleep you can also think and dream too.

> *Comments*
>
> Joy considers dreaming and thinking to be different mental acts. In answer to David's questions as to whether one can do both at the same time, she suggests that it is possible to think within a dream. This relationship between dreaming and thinking is completely different from the one suggested by Sheena (who claimed that thinking precedes dreaming).

Child Yeah, 'cause you have to dream.

Mc Mark?

Mark Well, um, I agree with Fern because, um, you can think and dream sometimes. Because when you're not thinking and you're dreaming, your imagination is thinking. So your imagination is thinking sometimes but your brain is thinking with it. So I agree with Fern.

> *Comments*
>
> Mark puts forward a third type of relationship between dreaming and thinking, suggesting that dreaming is an imaginative act whereas

thinking is a cognitive act. ('Dreaming' is your imagination thinking, and 'thinking' is your brain thinking.) Being qualitatively different kinds of acts, they can occur at the same time. He seems to be using a modular model of mental activity (similar to some artificial intelligence models), in which different functions are assigned to different modules or locations. (What Mark says does not agree with Fern's point.)

Mc David?

David I agree with Mark and I disagree with Mark. Because *you* control your imagination. So if you were dreaming – some people say that your dreams are in your imagination, and some people say you don't – but *if* your dreams are in your imagination, *then* how could you think in your imagination while you're dreaming in your imagination? But you could think in your dream while you're in your imagination!

Comments

David puts forward a fourth type of relationship between dreaming and thinking, including imagination: that you could be thinking inside your dream that is inside your imagination.

David also raises a major point here when he states that imagination is intentional. The structure of his argument is complex and one has to rely on the preceding dialogue to understand what he is saying. On the one hand, his entire analysis appears to be making a case for the unity of consciousness (which is a classic philosophical argument against the modular distributive functions model). Even if one distinguishes between imaginative and cognitive activity, it is the one person who is the mental actor. In this case, neither your imagination nor your brain is thinking; you are the entity who is thinking.

Moreover, he seems to be saying that, given that you control your imagination, you cannot be simultaneously but independently thinking and dreaming in your imagination. There is an assumed premise here, which seems to be that you can control only one thing at a time.

Mc Ooh! Sheena?

Sheena I agree with Fern in the way beginning because if you think too hard and you dream and you only could think, because if you, um, think really hard – a dream – you, you have to think, because there's only a little bit of dreaming.

Mc All right, what's the difference between thinking and dreaming? How would you know if you were thinking or you were dreaming?

> *Comments*
>
> The four different relationships between dreaming and thinking suggested by Sheena, Joy, Mark and David are so complex that they require further consideration. Unfortunately, asking two questions instead of one did not help make it clear.

Child	Could you clarify that?
Mc	OK, yes, I asked two questions. First, what's the difference between thinking and dreaming? And second, which is a different question, how would you know whether you were thinking or dreaming?

> *Comments*
>
> Most of the children have used the distinction between thinking and dreaming that was assumed by David's original response. So, these questions are designed to probe that distinction.

Child	That's hard! That's hard, yes. Because if you're dreaming and you are not thinking . . .
Sheena	Well, like I go to bed, I just fall right to sleep and I forget to think, but I still think at the same time. The other question was – would you repeat the other question?
Mc	How would you *know* whether you were thinking or dreaming?
Maggie	If you were dreaming and you were thinking, how could you think and dream at the same time? I know that question because if, um, you think at the same time and how can you like think . . . If you had your eyes open you can think, and if you had your eyes closed you can think too!
Mc	Karen?
Karen	I think that thinking and dreaming – um, dreaming is when you're asleep or, yeah, when you're asleep and um, then your imagination it starts. I think a dream is imagination and thinking is, um, I think thinking is, eh – I can't, I can't say what thinking is!

> *Comments*
>
> Karen makes the point that you dream when you are asleep, and that dreaming is imagination. She seems to suggest that (at least when sleeping) imagination is not intentional.

Mc	But you think dreaming is imagination?
Karen	Yeah.
Mc	Fern?

Fern   Well, um, sometimes it is, and sometimes it's not. Um. I sort of disagree with Maggie and I sort of do. Um, sometimes you can and sometimes you, um, can't. Well, the reason why I agree with Maggie is because sometimes you can think, you can think, um, at the same time as dreaming. The reason I disagree with Maggie because you can't sometimes. If you're thinking too hard, you mostly go to sleep and you don't know whether you're sleeping or dreaming yet.

Mc   You don't know? (OK, Brian, put that down.) David?

David   Could I answer my own question of what I said!

Mc   Uh-huh?

David   I mean I agree with Fern about disagreeing with Maggie. Because sometimes if you think too hard and then like you don't dream enough, sometimes you – sometimes you go – sometimes you just go into only thinking. And sometimes if you just dream too much, and then you – and then you're just thinking a little bit, sometimes you go right into all dreaming.

> ### Comments
>
> David makes explicit the relationship of his argument with the arguments that have been put forward by Fern and Maggie.

Mc   All right, how do you know . . .

      GAP IN TAPE

David   Um, can I tell why I disagree with my question?

> ### Comments
>
> The question under discussion concerns how one would know whether one was dreaming or awake. The children have been discussing whether pinching oneself could be a test for being awake.

Mc   Yes, sure.

David   I disagree with my question, it's because some – I do this a lot too – If I pinch myself when I'm, when I'm, I'm still dreaming and I don't pinch myself in the – in my dream sometimes, I wake up and I fall off my bed. But, and, and then, and then I try, and then I go back to bed. But then I keep on pinching myself in my dream. Then I pinch myself when I'm, when I'm still dreaming.

> ### Comments
>
> David is saying that you can pinch yourself while you are dreaming although not *in* the dream. Or you can 'dream-pinch' yourself within a dream.

Mc	So, can you tell you're dreaming? Is that how you know you're dreaming, David?
David	Yeah. When I, when I pinch myself – when I pinch myself and when I don't wake up when I pinch myself in my dream. And then when I, when I pinch myself and I, and I'm waking – and I woke up when I pinched myself, that's how I know if I was pinching in my dreams or if I wasn't pinching in my dreams.

> ### Comments
>
> When he 'dream-pinches' himself, he does not wake up. When he pinches himself from outside his dream, then he wakes up. This is how he knows whether the pinch was within the dream or not.

Mc	Right! Clare?
Clare	I have a question for you, David. How can you do that? How can you like, if you're on the middle of the bed, how can you just fall off and – pinch yourself in your dreams?
David	What I do, what I do to do that is: when I pinch myself I – Sometimes my sis- my sister pinches me or something and that's what, and that's what I do to – And that's what it feels like. So, and then what I do to – to not – for her to not pinch me is I roll, is I roll, is I roll to my mom and dad sometimes. It happened to me. I thought I was downstairs in my den and then when I pinched myself, I fell – I rolled and I fell off the bed.

> ### Comments
>
> At this point in the discussion, the class became suddenly tired. We had been talking for about an hour. No one could follow David's explanation of the difference between 'dream-pinching' within his dreams and deliberately pinching himself to make himself wake up.

Mc	OK, let's look at this question here. 'Why did she touch her eyes?' Mark, why did she touch her eyes, Mark?

> ### Comments
>
> As everyone is tired and needs a break, the next question provides an interlude before returning to a more philosophical question.

Mark	To see if she was awake. But if she touched her eyes, she could've hurt her eye or something. Because if she didn't cut her fingernails, but maybe she didn't – then if they were very sharp, they, they could've like – she could've pinched – she couldn't – she could've hurt her

eye. And why I was interested in that question is because she could have
– that, that's a weird thing to do, to pinch your eyes to see if you're
awake.

> *Comments*
>
> The next phase of discussion is not philosophical dialogue. Even
> though some of the children use the 'agree and disagree . . . because'
> structure, this is *not* Philosophical Inquiry. Hence it is italicised
> here.

Mc   *Aha, what's weird about it?*

Mark   *Well, see like when you're awake you usually like, like try and, like try and
move around and go and turn on the light or something so you can really see if
you're awake. And then, and then, and if you, and if you didn't have a light,
if, if, if they were – if you couldn't find them in the dark, you, you could at least
just, just like, go like to do something. I don't know.*

Mc   *You could go and do something?*

Mark   *Yeah, like get off . . .*

Child   *Go off the bed!*

Mark   *. . . get off the bed and go downstairs and if you, and if your mind already had,
already knew where the bathroom was already, you could go in the bathroom
and get a drink of water, or pour it on yourself.*

Mc   *Karen?*

Karen   *I, I disagree with Mark because – about touching your eyes. I think what they
mean by touching your eyes is when they close their eyes and they just wipe
theirs or like do this. [Demonstrates.] But not really touch the eye. But they just
mean something like that or something like. [Demonstrates.]*

Mc   *So why do you – why did she do that in the story, Karen?*

Karen   *Maybe because they say in the story like 'Are you awake?' So she did it just to
see if she was awake or not.*

Mc   *And do you think that's a good way to tell if you're awake?*

Karen   *Kind of.*

Mc   *James?*

James   *Well, Karen, because see I think what they meant by touching their eyes was
not poking their eyes with your fingernail. That's poking. [Demonstrates.] But
like doing this, touching the, the inside of my finger, like touch like that.*

Mc   *Would you do that? All right, let's – we've had a demonstration already. James,
would you do that to see if you were awake? David?*

David   *I'm adding on to Mark's question and I'm agreeing with him and I'm
disagreeing with him. Why couldn't she pinch herself like I did?*

Mc   *Do you think that would be the same kind of thing?*

Mark   *Yeah, 'cause then you would, then you would struggle. [Demonstrates waking
up with pinching.] You'd go, 'Aaagh!'*

David   *And the reason I disagree with Mark is, is – and I'm agreeing with James about that one part of the – like you went like this or you went like that. [Demonstrates.] But, and that's why I disagree with him is that I don't think she took her fingernail and just put it in her eye. And the reason I agree with Mark is because if, if she like poured the water – I – mean and why I still disagree with Mark is because if sh- If she didn't know if she was asleep or awake, how would she be able to wake, wake up if she was asleep, get out of bed, then go pour water on herself?*

> ### Comments
>
> Again, even though David makes the structure of his argument and the relations between his contribution and the contributions of other children very clear, and even though he uses the words 'agree', 'disagree' and 'because', this is not Philosophical Inquiry.

Mc   *If she didn't know?*
David   *Yeah.*
Mc   *OK.*
David   *How could she know? And how could she know if she was awake or if she wasn't?*
Mc   *How would she know if she was doing it or she wasn't, if she didn't know if she was awake or asleep?*
David   *She could've sleepwalked.*

> ### Comments
>
> David seems to think that pouring water on oneself is not an adequate test for discovering whether one is asleep or awake, because one could be sleepwalking. He wonders how Elfie would know whether she was sleepwalking or really awake.

Mc   *She could've sleepwalked?*
David   *Yeah.*
Mc   *Fern?*
Fern   *I agree with Mark. Well, when you like poke your eye and you haven't cut your nails, that would really hurt. And the reason why I agree with Mark if you like poke your eyes, it will really hurt. And, and when you like touch your eye, that, if you touch like your eyelash, that will, will not hurt.*

> *Comments*
>
> 'Health and safety' requires the CoPI Chair to move on from this topic, now — before eyes are poked or scratched, as children are about to try touching their eyes and/or eyelashes.

Mc   OK, let's look at the next question here. [Indicates.] Karen, 'Why did she say to herself, "Dummy, if you can wonder, you must be thinking"?' Let's go back a bit. What was it she was wondering about? Does anyone remember what she was wondering about? You can look at it if you don't remember. What was it she was wondering about? [Children look at the text.]

> *Comments*
>
> After an interlude of discussion with no philosophical dialogical movement, it is time to go back to more difficult philosophical topics. So, I intervene to move to a more philosophical question.

Maggie   She knew she was in doubt if you can — if she can sleep and think.
Mc   At the same time?
Clare   I know, I know!
Mc   Tell the whole class, Clare.
Clare   It says in the book that if you can't dream — if I can dream, I must be thinking. So she's re- really talking about dreaming and thinking. She's really talking about dreaming and thinking?

> *Comments*
>
> The text does suggest that thinking when you are asleep might be dreaming, and it also suggests that wondering is a kind of thinking. Clare has conflated these two suggestions, and comes up with the notion that if you can dream, you must be thinking. This suggests an interesting twist to the Cartesian dictum '*Cogito ergo sum*'. Crudely speaking, because of his difficulty in distinguishing dreams from reality, Descartes suggests that everything is open to doubt. But since doubting is a form of thinking, he cannot doubt that he thinks, and thinking implies a thinker. So, he concludes, 'I think therefore I am.' Using Clare's notion, Descartes might have avoided having everything open to doubt, by going straight from dreaming to thinking to existing.

Mc	David?
David	She was thinking about if she was real or not!
Mc	And so why did she say, 'If you can wonder, you must be thinking'?
David	I don't know why she said that. I don't know why she said that. But maybe she – maybe she said that because even though dreaming and thinking are not the same thing – But it could and it couldn't. Like if you're wondering, like what's in that – what's over that fence, and you're thinking, and then you could think, 'What's over that fence?' And why you can't think and wonder is you can't. You can't . . .

> **Comments**
>
> David is very careful to distinguish between what the text says and what he wants to say. His contribution here provides an example showing how wondering could be a kind of thinking – if one characterises the thought as a question.

Child	Wonder.
David	. . . Well, I don't have an answer for that.
Mc	All right, we'll come back to you a little bit later. Karen?
Karen	I don't think Clare heard what I said on this, because I meant the part 'Dummy, you can't – you can't . . .

> **Comments**
>
> Karen is concerned because Clare was talking about her own thoughts about the question, which were different from Karen's thoughts.

Clare	[Looking at book] At 'Dummy'?
Mc	Uh-huh.
Karen	'If you can wonder, you must be thinking' – that's what I was talking about!
Clare	[Reads] 'If you can wonder, you must be thinking'.
Karen	[To Clare] So you, so you really, so you didn't say what I really meant.

> **Comments**
>
> Karen is concerned that the question that she had in mind is not being addressed (Clare mentioned *dreaming* and thinking instead of *wondering* and thinking), although she does not now remember her puzzle.

Mc	What did you really mean, Karen?
Karen	That – I can't answer that. [Laughs.]
Mc	You don't know?
Karen	No. [Laughs.]
Mc	Maggie?
Maggie	What I . . .
Mc	[To Robert] Raise your hand.
Maggie	What is the question again?
Mc	All right, the question here. [Points to the flip chart.] Why did she say to herself, 'Dummy, if you can wonder, you must be thinking'?
Maggie	You can wonder and think at the same time. Only sometimes . . . whatever that thing is. You still can think and wonder at the same time because, say I was like, um, Mark. Kind of like you said 'Oh.' You, you – that was like, oh, you're wondering and you're, and too, what you're wondering or . . .
Mc	Would that be thinking? . . .
Maggie	Thinking!
Mc	. . . Maggie?
Maggie	Well, kind of.
Mc	Be a kind of thinking? All right. Clare?
Clare	Well, Karen, it says in the book that if you can wonder, you must be thinking.

> **Comments**
>
> Clare returns to the text to try to retrace what she thinks Karen may have wanted to ask.

Karen	I know, that's what I said. What do you mean?
Clare	I, I, I mean that in the book – You had a different answer, but in the book it said if you – and that –

> **Comments**
>
> Clare is trying to explain that what she thinks about the text is different to what Karen thinks about the text.

Mc	If you can wonder, you must be thinking?
Clare	Thinking!
Mc	Why was she interested in that? What else did she say?
Karen	Well, I was interested in . . .
Clare	She said [reading text], 'and if you're thinking, then I must be,' um –
Mc	[Points to text] 'you're for real'. What do you think she meant by that? 'If you're thinking, you're for real'?

Clare   If you're thinking, you must be for real!

Mc   Why?

Clare   Because, because it – when I'm thinking, I'm for real. But you might have brain surgery and you're still for real, but if you're thinking, you must be for real.

> **Comments**
>
> Clare makes the point that the implication is one-way. To say that if you're thinking, you must be real does not imply that if you're real, you must be thinking. If you had brain surgery and were incapable of thinking, you would still be real.

Mark   Oh, oh, oh!

Clare   [To Mark] Wait. And robots can think and so – and robots can think and they're for real! So, now, I kind of disagree with that.

> **Comments**
>
> Clare links this idea back to the earlier topic in the dialogue about robots. She repeats Karen's argument made earlier in the dialogue: that thinking is not a sufficient condition for being a real person. Robots fulfil this condition and are not real persons. Clare also performs a complex piece of reasoning: showing that her initial premise must be wrong. Where T stands for 'a thinker', P stands for 'a person' and R stands for 'a robot', her initial premise is that
>
>   (T are P)
>
> The logical structure of her argument is:
>
> $((R \text{ are } T) \ \& \ (T \text{ are } P)) \rightarrow (R \text{ are } P)$
> $\rceil(R \text{ are } P)$
> $\underline{\rceil(R \text{ are } T) \ \& \ (T \text{ are } P)}$
> $(R \text{ are } T)$
> $\underline{\rceil(T \text{ are } P)}$

Mc   You kind of disagree?

Mark   I, I agree with Clare because I'm thinking what to say and I'm for real right now! And I disagree with Clare is – Well, I agree with Clare on two things. Because if I'm, I'm thinking right now what to say – And the second thing she said, because robots, robots they're for real. Because they are real. But, but they don't – but they don't think how we do.

> *Comments*
>
> Mark also engages in complex reasoning. He agrees with the major premise that if you are thinking, you must be a real person. But he disagrees with Clare's second premise that robots are thinkers, because he claims that robots do not think in the way that humans do.
>
> So, he rescues the idea by essentially adjusting the major premise to all 'human-type thinkers' are real persons, and as robots are not human-type thinkers, it is consistent that they are not persons. So the (new) major premise is not contradicted.

Mc	They don't think how we do?
Mark	Because – They don't think how we do because, because they, they like have brains and they're made out of – Well, we have brains but they, they think a little bit different. But they think, they think somehow alike to us!

> *Comments*
>
> This modification suggests that a certain kind of thinking may be characteristic of persons, and that robots could be differentiated by the way in which they think.

Mc	Karen?
Karen	I don't understand what Clare said. What did you say? It, it wasn't anything about my question at all!

> *Comments*
>
> Karen doesn't understand Clare's thinking about the question (asked originally by Karen).

Clare	I know. But Dr McCall had said, 'What else was she saying?' And then I told her what else she was saying, from the book.
Karen	I don't know what I said!
Mc	OK, Karen, you don't understand what you said?
Karen	I don't know why I even said it!
Mc	You don't remember why you asked the question?
Karen	No.
Mc	All right. Well . . .
Clare	You were interested in it because, um, *you* wanted to know why she was wondering and thinking at the same time. That – that's what I think you were thinking of.

Comments

Here Clare is trying to help Karen by reconstructing, for Karen, what Karen might have been thinking about (since Karen has forgotten). This is an interesting feature because it shows very clearly how a young child can (and does) put herself in the position of another and try to understand the other's thinking even though it differs from her own. (Young children are not 'egocentric' in Piaget's sense.) Throughout the dialogue, children pay attention to views that differ from their own, sometimes trying to develop those views, sometimes presenting counter-arguments, but nearly always understanding the thinking of others.

Mc	Fern?
Fern	I agree with, I mean I, I don't agree with anybody. I mean I agree with Clare 'cause robots, whatever, can think and talk. Well, they, they can move around and think. And the reason I agree with Clare, robots can think when they're doing something at the same time.
Mc	Chris?
Chris	I agree with Mark because if – 'cause robots do think a little different than humans and I – Mark, I forget what you said. Can you say it again?
Mark	Well, they think a little different from us because they can, they can, they can like – they know a little more than us because they – they're – People make them and whatever people put, whatever people put in their brains for them to know, they know. And like that person might not know it. Like they knew – like a robot that knew everything. Well, yeah, kind of knew everything, could know all the math in the world . . .

Comments

Mark distinguishes between robots and persons. Robots are artefacts and their thinking is not self-originated. Mark describes a feature that distinguishes robots' thinking from human thinking: that once a robot is programmed, it knows. (In a sense, it does not have to learn the way children do.)

Mc	Uh-huh!
Mark	. . . well, not all the math in the world. And lots of other things. Like –
Mc	Well, now, if robots could do that . . .
Mark	But they think slightly, they think slightly different than us.
Kevin	Robots can't do most every . . .
Mark	What?
Brian	Grown-ups can't know most everything in the world!

Kevin   I said robots! Robots!

       GAP IN TAPE

> **Comments**
>
> At a crucial point in the dialogue, the tape runs out.
>
>   Mark suggests that one difference between 'robot knowing' and 'human knowing' is that children forget!
>
>   Then David presents a complex idea about why robots could not recognise human beings as different from them, although humans could recognise robots as different.

David   . . . so robots can't know every, everything. And a robot does not, will not, know – he would know of what a human intelligence was!

> **Comments**
>
> Here David was presenting an argument that robots don't have the kind of intelligence that can put themselves in the place of others.

Mc   A robot wouldn't know what a human intelligence was?

> **Comments**
>
> I highlight David's argument about the kind of knowledge a robot cannot have.

Children Ooh, ooh, ooh.

Joy   But David, can . . .?

David   I agree with Mark because a robot does know things, like he knows what a table's made of or something. [Chuckles.] And he knows, and he knows he's intelligent, but he doesn't know every single thing.

       GAP IN TAPE

> **Comments**
>
> Again, the videotape does not record some astonishing reasoning from David, who argues that a robot does not know it is a robot. He moves towards the idea that a feature of human beings is that they, unlike robots, are self-conscious.

Robert   I disagree with David because a robot does know everything because you can know every single thing for math if you can, if you can put a calculator in it.

Mark	Yeah, that's what I said. To put a . . .
Clare	Well, what – I don't really get that, Robert.
Robert	Well, I – An infant can put the alphabet in it and it, and it could read all the words!

> **Comments**
>
> Robert seems to suggest that a robot can know more than a person. Given the alphabet, the robot could read all the words.

Mark	Well, then I agree with Robert because, and this is what I said before, whatever – if you put a computer in the robot, whatever you program it to do it will do. Like, like probably you don't know something. And you program it into the robot. The robot will do it, and the robot will do anything!

> **Comments**
>
> The robot seems to have unlimited capabilities.

Mc	The robot would do anything?

> **Comments**
>
> I highlight Mark's point that robots do not have free will.

Mark	Well, except – Well, yeah, because the person that made it had it in his com- command. Except if he made the robot and he just let him free and the robot did whatever he wanted to.

> **Comments**
>
> What Mark is saying suggests that people have free will, whereas robots do not. A robot will execute the will of a person (unless it is let free).

SOUND OF SCHOOL INTERCOM INTERRUPTS THE DIALOGUE

Mc	OK.
Mark	. . . a person wouldn't jump off a hundred-foot cliff with a ladder . . .

> **Comments**
>
> Mark's example shows that people have free will whereas robots do not.

GAP IN TAPE

Karen   That's not what I said at all. She's reading something else I said because that's not what I meant at all.

> **Comments**
>
> Karen is referring back to Clare's answer to her (Karen's) question.

Clare   Well, I'm . . .
Mc   Now, Karen, we're talking about a different topic now . . . James?
James   Well, see, I disagree with Mark, robots couldn't know everything. The person who puts the robot − who made the robot couldn't know everything to put into the robot to make it know everything. Because, see, a robot is made out of all sorts of stuff!

> **Comments**
>
> James disagrees with Mark and Robert about the possible extent of a robot's knowledge. He argues that a robot is limited by its program. The program is limited to the knowledge of the programmer. And the programmer could not know everything.

Child   Metal!
James   Oh, yeah, all sorts of metal and wire, so if you put everything in it, no matter how big the robot could be to fit all of it in − and anyway a robot couldn't know everything!

> **Comments**
>
> Here James is saying that it is not size or quantity that sets the limits on a robot's capacity for knowledge.

Mark   Oh! Oh!
Mc   Wait a minute! James, I'm not sure if I quite heard you. Did you say that the person who made the robot knows?

> **Comments**
>
> I did hear James, but the important point which James made − that the people who make the robot don't know everything, so a robot could not know everything − could have been lost at this juncture. If I repeat what James said, he will just say 'yes' without elaborating. So I deliberately 'get it wrong', in order that James will explain again.

James	No, he doesn't know everything, so he couldn't tell the robot everything!
Mc	So you couldn't . . .
Children	Oh! Oh! Oh!
Mc	Wait a minute. Let me see if I understand what James is saying. You couldn't have a robot that knew everything because the person who made the robot couldn't know everything?
James	Yeah!
Mc	So, a robot only knows what the person who made it knows?
Mark	Um! Oh!
Mc	Is that right, James?
James	Yeah.
Sheena	I could know more than that robot knows!
Mark	Well, because I, I . . .
Mc	Well now, Mark, you talked already, so let's give Robert a chance here.
Robert	I, oh, was James the one who was speaking?
Mc	Umm hmm.
Robert	Well, I disagree with James because, because not only one person makes a robot. A lot of people make a robot. A lot of people do different jobs to make the robot. So if they all work together, they could know everything. [James shakes his head.]

Comments

Robert raises a counter-argument: that a robot is not limited to the knowledge of one person. It would be possible for a robot to know everything known by people. James looks frustrated, but does not speak. Having already worked with the children for fifty-six hours, I recognise when James has something different to say.

Mc	You still think it's not possible to know everything, James?
Mark	Oh, please!

GAP IN TAPE

Mc	All right, now, I'm really puzzled. James, do you think it's impossible for people to know everything?

Comments

Every participant in a Community of Philosophical Inquiry is different, and the CoPI Chair learns over time how individuals think and talk. Occasionally, as here, I am sure that James has something important yet to be said.

James   Yes.
Mark   Oh! Ooh! Ooh!
Mc   Mark, we are talking to James for the minute. Why, James?

> **Comments**
>
> Other children are desperate to speak, but (1) James has said little for the first ninety minutes of this dialogue, and (2) he is making an important philosophical point, not yet understood by the other children. So, I persevere with making a space for James to speak.

James   Well, because only – no one knows everything. Because there is no last number!

> **Comments**
>
> Here James makes an important clarification: the limits to what it is possible to know are metaphysical, rather than epistemological. In his example, people can't know the last number, not because of the limits of ignorance, but because there is no last number. It raises an interesting question: in what sense can one have knowledge of what does not exist?

Mc   There's no last number?

> **Comments**
>
> I highlight James's point.

James   There's no last number, so people – and I don't. Most people don't know like names for other numbers after you get outside a thousand billion.
Child   I don't understand.
Sheena   Well, Maggie. I have a question for Maggie. When you said they can ask their parents, what if their parents didn't know everything either? They never – their parents didn't know anything. What if no one in their family knew anything?
Maggie   Well, it would be possible because it would be impossible because – if Sheena, maybe if they went to school or college, they would be smart like my mom.
Mark   Well, I don't, I don't actually know what Maggie's saying, but what was the question again?
Mc   About whether someone could know everything.

Mark   No. Because no one knows what the highest number is, and there is no highest number. No one knows what comes after the . . .

> **Comments**
>
> Mark reiterates James's point that there are limits to what is knowable – as well as limits to what is known. Inquiry into this distinction will have to take place at another time.

Brian   No one knows what comes after . . .

Mark   I'm talking, Brian! No one knows what comes after infinity. So, people can't know everything. I mean people, people don't know where the end of the universe is! And people don't know lots of things. And you just can't learn everything in school!

> **Comments**
>
> Here the film runs out.

There are many remarkable features in this dialogue, including:

- the 5-year-olds' desire and ability to concentrate on dialogue for ninety minutes;
- the logical sophistication of their argumentation;
- the 5-year-olds' performance in analysing abstract concepts;
- their performance in distinguishing whole–part relationships;
- their performance in hypothetical syllogistic reasoning;
- their abilities to empathise and put themselves in the place of other children;
- their active, close listening;
- their abilities in remembering complex arguments put forward by others;
- their willingness to change their minds;
- their disposition to help others and to credit them.

However, the children did not demonstrate these abilities and dispositions when we began Philosophical Inquiry. This was not a class of unusual children – in fact, many of the children were expected to have difficulties in school. For example, David, whose thinking was truly noteworthy, had almost been held back in kindergarten in the previous year because he had not been learning. It is not unusual for Philosophical Inquiry to 'pick up' extremely intelligent children who have been failing in school because they are so bored that they do not learn. Because it is oral, children of all ages (and adults) who cannot read or write flourish in Philosophical Inquiry sessions. They flourish because, in addition to other benefits:

- their imaginations are stretched;
- their reasoning is developed;
- they become equal members of a community in which they can make contributions that are valued by other members of the group who recognise that the different ideas put forward by the non-literate children help the group to think better.

In the early stages of this CoPI group, Mark announced that he did not see the point of discussing and asked why we couldn't just vote on the answer and save time. After four weeks, he was so keen to contribute that he was struggling to refrain from dominating the dialogues.

In the beginning of the CoPI sessions, neither Joy nor Clare spoke at all; they were too shy. By week 5 both were frequent, confident and sophisticated contributors to the dialogues.

Robert had been diagnosed with attention deficit hyperactivity disorder, and because he could not sit still or concentrate at all, he was unable to contribute to the dialogues in the early CoPI sessions. By the time of this dialogue, he still found it difficult to control his physical movements, but his listening, speaking and concentration skills had developed beyond any expectations.

This level of philosophical reasoning by 5-year-old children does not develop by itself; it takes a skilled Chair to elicit and structure the dialogue. As is explained further in Chapter 5, the CoPI Chair's primary responsibility is to create philosophical dialogue with any group of people – whether they are 5-year-old children, 15-year-old teenagers, 45-year-old company directors or 75-year-old senior citizens.[7] To do this, the CoPI Chair must have background knowledge of philosophy and logic, which she or he uses along with the CoPI reasoning structure to intervene and shape the dialogue.

As observed by Karin Murris[8] (with the children's names below changed):

> But looking at the transcript of the actual dialogue (McCall, 1991, p. 7), between [Robert]'s counter-example and [Karen]'s statement, there are crucial interventions by McCall:

> [Robert]: Well I disagree with [David] because of – well he wouldn't – What do you mean he wouldn't like to be able to move any part of his body? Maybe – What if like it was a *robot*?
> McCall: Well, that's an interesting question.

> First intervention: McCall highlights the importance of this contribution, therefore making it more likely that he will continue, or that other children will build on this idea. As it happens [Robert] continues:

> [Robert]: A robot can move every part of his body and a robot isn't real!
> McCall: Now, is a robot a person? (chorus, No! No!)

> Second intervention by the facilitator: McCall – not the children! –

connects [Maggie]'s original question about persons with the present topic of discussion, i.e., whether Elfie is real or not . . .

I agree with McCall that her question may facilitate a further enquiry about the conditions of personhood put forward by the children. However, it is worth bearing in mind that this is the philosopher's 'hidden agenda', i.e., to focus on classical philosophical topics. Knowledge and awareness of the history of philosophical ideas and the attitude and skills to ask the relevant questions is crucial here.[9]

However, it should be noted that in CoPI this agenda is *not* 'hidden'; rather, it is the stated purpose of CoPI to enable groups to engage in philosophical dialogue and reasoning together.[10] And the training for chairing CoPI (at the time of Murris's writing, delivered through the M.Phil. degree in Philosophical Inquiry at Glasgow University) taught postgraduate students logic and philosophy for the *explicit* purpose of enabling them to 'ask the relevant questions', and to give them the background knowledge they needed to use 'the philosopher's "hidden agenda"' so that they would be able to chair a CoPI dialogue in such a way that it *would* 'focus on classical philosophical topics'. These explicit features of CoPI are not shared by other methods of doing philosophy with children, as we will see in Chapter 6.

Part of the difference between CoPI and other methods of philosophy with children (with which Murris was familiar) is a consequence of the history of CoPI. That is, as described in Chapter 2, *CoPI was developed precisely in order to enable children and adults to engage in philosophical dialogue similar to the spoken (rather than written) dialogues of professional philosophers.*

CoPI was not designed to be a forum in which participants ask questions, or muse, or offer opinions, but rather to be a forum in which participants think for themselves about, and then present their own *arguments* about, *philosophical* ideas and theories.

Chapter 5

Creating a Community of Philosophical Inquiry (CoPI) with all ages

Chapter 1 described the development and some of the features of the practice of the CoPI method. However, in order to create a Community of Philosophical Inquiry, one needs to know not only how the CoPI method was developed, but what the Community of Philosophical Inquiry is[1] and what the role of chairing a CoPI involves.

Developing a Community of Philosophical Inquiry among a group of children is a creative, disciplined and skilled activity which requires background knowledge as well as training in the art and craft of chairing CoPI.[2] The Community of Philosophical Inquiry does not come into being immediately or by itself, but is created through sustained practice over time.[3]

In some ways, chairing CoPI is similar to an artistic endeavour. The training in how to chair CoPI is similar in many ways to training in fine art. Just as all fine arts students learn the history of art, learn about applications, learn about colour, learn about different art media, learn how different materials work, practise with different tools, develop skills in line, shade, perspective, etc., all CoPI students learn about background history, applications, how different stimulus materials work, practise with different tools in structuring CoPI dialogues, and develop skills in logic and philosophical understanding. And once the basics are in place, the students' talents can be developed through the guidance of an art teacher or a CoPI trainer.

The first and most important requirement that a person needs to be successful in chairing a CoPI is to be passionate about the activity. Ideally, teachers will be introduced to Philosophical Inquiry through participating in a CoPI themselves. Among its other benefits, participation in CoPI:

- allows teachers to learn about the nature of the practice of CoPI first-hand, through direct experience rather than from hearing or reading about it;
- allows teachers to gain an understanding of the different stages that their pupils will encounter;
- develops both the philosophical understanding and the reasoning skills of teachers, which in turn facilitate their study of philosophy and logic.

There are elements of craft in chairing a CoPI that can and should be learned. There are different tools to use, and the aspiring CoPI student needs to learn how to use all of them. However, in a similar way as one finds in, say, learning to paint, as the CoPI student progresses, he or she will find that while he or she needs to know how to use all the tools, some tools suit his or her individual practice more than others.

There is an art to chairing CoPI which cannot be closely defined. It involves imagination as well as critical analysis; it involves a sense of rhythm and pace like music and poetry; it involves the free flow of wonderment simultaneously with the discipline of a reasoning structure. And finally there is a measure of talent that needs to be present to be successful in chairing PI. Chairing a CoPI is a specialist activity, and, as with all specialist activities, not everybody is suited to the task.

The realist philosophy that underlies the CoPI practice

In order to understand the nature of a CoPI, one needs to understand the philosophy that underlies its practice. Although the early development of CoPI was influenced by a 'Hegelian' model of thought, the practice of CoPI is founded upon a philosophy of external realism.[4] (A CoPI Chair might not subscribe to the philosophy of external realism, but they must understand it.)

According to the philosophy that underlies CoPI, the world is external to our thoughts.[5] And because the world is external to our thoughts, we can be wrong about it. Individually we can make mistakes, and it is also possible that everyone can be wrong about the nature of the world. For example, it is possible for everyone in the world to think that the Earth is flat when in fact it is not. If everyone in the world did think that the Earth was flat, or that the Earth was a turnip on a giant's dinner plate, that would not make these ideas true; they would still be false.

Everyone is fallible

To allow that people are fallible presupposes that there is something to be wrong about. For example, whatever shape it actually is – be it round, oval, egg-shaped, multidimensional or a hitherto inconceivable and unheard-of form – the Earth is and was that shape independently from how or what people think – in the past, the present and the future.[6]

However, while it is possible for everyone to think the same thing (right or wrong), it is very rare that this happens. On almost every question there are people who hold different views about the answer. Some of these views will be closer to accuracy than others. So, in order to come closer to being accurate in our thinking about anything, it can be useful to compare and contrast different views, and to 'test' these views.

External realism[7] holds that the 'world' we live in is external to us and is not dependent upon us for its existence. However, we live in a world composed of ideas and theories and social institutions as well as material objects. We live in a world where there are physical entities such as trees and mountains and birds that human beings did not create, as well as physical objects such as cars and lights and televisions that we did create. But we also live in a world where there is money and political theories and music, which are not physical objects and which were created by human beings. External realism holds that these non-physical entities are also external to us.

The material things in the 'natural' world do not owe their origin to human beings.

The material things made by humans owe their coming into existence as the things they are to human activity. These physical human creations may be 'seen as' different things, 'used as' different things, or given different names according to human inclination. For example, an object made out of wood with a flat surface and four wooden pillars supporting the surface might be seen variously as a stool or a table or a crash barrier, etc. It might be called a 'stool', or a 'table' or a 'crash barrier', and it might be used as a stool or a table or a crash barrier or a weapon or fuel for a fire, or any number of things. But once it has been made, the material thing's continuing existence does not depend upon human perception, understanding or even memory. The object (whether called 'stool', 'table' or 'barrier') is there. Even if it were to be lost in a forest where no human sees it, hears it, smells it, touches it, names it or uses it, the object affects the environment; animals may use it for shelter, plants grow differently around it because it is there.[8] We may not in fact know that it is there, but because it *is* there, we could in principle find out about it. Even when the object deteriorates and loses its shape and chemical constitution, it leaves a trace (in principle, an investigating scientist could discover the evidence of its having been there). Because objects that have existed leave traces, scientists can discover, for example, the evidence of massacres that may be unknown to anyone currently alive. To many people this may seem obvious. But within philosophy there are different theories and understandings of the nature of the existence of both material objects and non-material 'objects'. For example, there is a philosophy in which an object's existence is dependent upon its being perceived. According to this kind of philosophical theory, if no one[9] perceives the buried skeletons, they do not exist. For example, according to Berkeley,[10] 'things' continue to exist while no person perceives them *because* God perceives them – as illustrated in Ronald Knox's famous limerick and the anonymous reply:

> There was a young man who said, 'God
> Must think it exceedingly odd,
> If he finds that this tree
> Continues to be
> When there's no one about in the Quad.'

Dear Sir: Your astonishment's odd.
I am always about in the Quad.
And that's why the tree
Will continue to be
Since observed by Yours faithfully, God.

Most people would probably accept that material objects, such as mountains and stars (not made by humans), exist independently of humans seeing them or thinking about them – that the Earth itself existed prior to human beings. And most would accept that objects made by humans also exist independently of human perception and thought. However, the idea that (immaterial) ideas, symbols and social institutions made by humans also exist independently from our thinking about them is more controversial. The external realist philosophy which underlies CoPI holds that immaterial creations of human beings such as language, concepts, theories, symbols and social institutions, while owing their origin to humans, once made, then exist independently. We can be wrong about them, too!

And the things that are most important to most people are often these immaterial human creations. People can suffer when they make mistakes about the nature of material things in the world, for example when they think mistakenly that a particular bridge is 'safe' – that is, that it has a certain physical configuration which behaves in a certain way – when in fact it is not. But people can also suffer when they make mistakes about the nature of the immaterial things in the world, for example when they do not understand the nature of money, and they think a particular currency is 'safe'. Even though money is a human creation, and even though the value of a particular currency is affected by what people judge it to be, its existence is now independent of the thinking of any one person or group of people. So, for example, when people try to create money by creating coins and notes, they fail. When they try to create money by lying about the capital it is based upon, they also fail.

Understanding all aspects of 'the world' as accurately as possible is important for human thriving. (In fact, in some sense it is vital to any organism's thriving.) To understand material objects, it is useful to be able to test them physically. To understand immaterial ideas – theories, symbols, social institutions – one cannot test them physically, but one can test them conceptually. And this is what Philosophical Inquiry does.

CoPI works by revealing possible error

CoPI works by revealing possible error: it tries to create an environment where it is the norm to 'let your theory die in your stead'. It does not claim to reveal truth, but rather to strip away what cannot be the case.

And it works through the collaborative effort of the participants who engage in this endeavour. The CoPI Chair structures the dialogues in such a way as to elicit the underlying presuppositions of ideas and theories. Most people are not aware of the philosophical assumptions that underlie commonly held ideas. Often people are unaware of the presuppositions that underlie *their own* views, and often they discover that they are holding views that they think are consistent but which are revealed to have contradictory presuppositions – both of which cannot be the case. When this happens, people rethink their theories (the young children invented the phrase 'I now disagree with myself' to indicate this phenomenon).

There is a kind of internal dynamic that works within the practice of a CoPI, in which ideas about a topic are put forward and supported by reasons; these (both the ideas and the reasons) are then 'tested' by the elicitation of conflicting theories, contradictions, counter-examples. This process leads to participants first reviewing their own thinking and the ideas and theories put forward by both themselves and others, and then creating new ideas and theories about the topic, which are in turn 'tested' by the same process.

The CoPI practice of eliciting agreement and disagreement with examples and counter-examples works in a similar way to Popper's theory of hypothesis and falsification in science: that science progresses by theories being falsified.[11] Popper holds that knowledge is generated by the creative imagination in order to solve problems that have arisen in specific historico-cultural settings. Logically, no number of positive outcomes at the level of experimental testing can confirm a scientific theory, but a single counter-example is logically decisive: it shows the theory from which the implication is derived to be false. In a similar way, when the practice of CoPI brings forth an internal contradiction in a theory or idea, then that theory or idea cannot be true.

This process does not show us what is true, only that this theory cannot be true. And the 'event' of showing that an idea or theory cannot be true motivates participants to inquire further, to seek an idea or theory that would not be contradicted by the counter-example or logical contradiction which has been found.

We can see this phenomenon in several parts of the 5-year-olds' CoPI dialogue. The children's reasoning is highly sophisticated! In one part, Clare is reasoning about 'thinking' being a criterion for being a person:

Clare   If you're thinking you must be for real.
Mc   Why?
Clare   Because, because it – when I'm thinking, I'm for real. But you might have brain surgery and you're still for real, but if you're thinking, you must be for real.

. . .

        And robots can think and so – and robots can think and they're for real. So I kind of disagree with that.
David   I, I agree with Clare because I'm thinking what to say and I'm for real right now! And I disagree with Clare is – Well, I agree with Clare on two things. Because if I'm, I'm thinking right now what to say – And

the second thing she said, because robots, robots they're for real. Because they are real. But, but they don't – but they don't think how we do.

Here:

1   Clare presents a hypothetical: *if* you are thinking, *then* you must be a real person.
2   She then emphasises that the implication is one-way; you might be a real person and not be thinking (after brain surgery).
3   Then she discovers a counter-example – that robots think.
4   So either the hypothetical is false because robots think and they are not persons (denial of the consequent), or robots are persons.
5   But it has been established earlier in the dialogue that robots are not persons.
6   So her initial hypothesis cannot be correct!

This CoPI action of 'falsifying' the hypothesis 'If you're thinking, you must be for real' pushes David to inquire further into the topic. And his desire to keep the premise 'If you're thinking, you must be for real' pushes him to the *new* thought that:

7   Robotic thinking is not the same as human thinking.

This new idea, that robotic thinking is different from human thinking, began a new direction in the dialogue as the children then began to inquire into the nature of human versus robotic thinking. This is one of many examples of the action of CoPI in revealing what cannot be the case.[12] The engine of this action is logic, and the CoPI reasoning structure *engenders* logical thinking in the children and adults.

This is why the CoPI Chair must know logic: first, to be able to recognise what is happening within a CoPI session; and second, to be able to intervene to support this action within the CoPI dialogue.

How a unique kind of community is created, and how CoPI changes participants

The collaborative work of participants through CoPI creates a special kind of community among the group. Each Community of Philosophical Inquiry is unique, but all share what can only be described metaphorically as a flavour, which can be recognised. Moreover, for an individual, participating in CoPI creates the conditions in which the individual both changes their mind about the ideas they hold and engages with other participants in the joint creation of new ideas and theories. Although each person has different ideas and theories about the topic under inquiry, those ideas are created in dialogue and are influenced and partly shaped by hearing and understanding ideas that are different from one's own. For example, in the selection from 5-year-olds' dialogue above, it is Clare's reasoning in which she finds a contradiction to her initial hypothesis that stimulates David's creative thinking. Without Clare's prior reasoning, David most probably would not have had his insight to contribute to the inquiry, which in turn stimulated more creative thinking in other children.

The philosophical assumptions that underlie thinking and judgement are fundamental to a particular person's identity – who they are. Experience, life events, psychology, etc. filter how these assumptions play out into character, but do not form them. So when these assumptions are altered through the practice of CoPI, the participants change or recreate themselves – maybe in a very small way; but however small, it is fundamental. And to be involved in this fundamental change of oneself *with* others is to be in a unique kind of relationship with those others.

This unique relationship between participants in CoPI *comprises* the Community of Philosophical Inquiry. For adults, the CoPI community relationship is different from a social or work relationship; CoPI participants know very little or nothing[13] about each other's background, profession or job, or special interests, and come to know each other through their ideas. The CoPI community relationship is different from group relationships in which people share their opinions or experiences; CoPI participants will not know whether the ideas they are sharing are opinions or not, so the intimacy which can result from the fact that one is sharing personal opinions does not happen within CoPI. While people in a CoPI group come to know each other very closely, it is not as a result of such personal sharing, but rather as a result of being jointly involved in creating new ideas and theories. In some ways the CoPI community relationship is similar to a family relationship: CoPI participants are involved in shaping each other's thoughts, as family members can be; and CoPI participants are not required to like each other – they may or may not, but they are united in a community that overarches liking or disliking, just as family relationships can overarch like or dislike. As described by one participant,

> 'At first I couldn't stand X, but then it began to feel like when you have an annoying cousin, you get really annoyed with him, but he is part of your family and you don't let other people disrespect him!'

The aim of CoPI

Within the practice of CoPI the aim is to illuminate the topics, issues, ideas, theories and concepts that arise in dialogue from the questions. One does not aim to come to a conclusion, or to any agreement about the issues in dialogue.

One does not aim to answer the questions, but rather one uses the questions as the starting points for dialogue. The dialogue may take several directions and appear to move quite far from the originating questions. Within the dialogue there may be one, two or three themes running simultaneously. The overall aim of practising the CoPI method is to create a unique kind of community within the group – a community that is formed out of the relationships which develop as a result of joint collaborative reasoning: the Community of Philosophical Inquiry.

The CoPI Chair is responsible for creating the CoPI. And in order to do this, the CoPI Chair uses the CoPI structures to develop philosophical dialogue with the thinking of the participants. When beginning to work with children or adults, the group is not a community, nor do the participants know how to practise Philosophical Inquiry; the development of the CoPI happens over months. The group goes through various stages before becoming a CoPI.

In the first stages, participants need to learn how to use the CoPI structure. Usually children learn quite quickly, while adults have more difficulty with becoming accustomed to the CoPI structure.

In the very first session with a group, the CoPI Chair will not know the participants' individual styles of philosophical thinking – the kind of philosophical approach that underlies most of the participants' contributions. So, for example, when discussing a moral question or issue, one participant may offer contributions to the discussion which assume a moral relativist philosophy, a second participant may be offering contributions which assume a kind of virtue ethics, while a third participant's philosophical assumptions seem to be deontological.[14]

Even when working with a group of people whom the Chair already knows and who know each other, unless the group has already engaged in collaborative philosophical dialogue with each other they will most likely not even know their own philosophical styles of thinking. So, it is necessary for the CoPI Chair to have knowledge of different kinds of philosophy in order to understand the philosophy that underlies the participants' contributions and to call in participants in such a way as to have a possibility of juxtaposing different philosophies.

In the first session the CoPI Chair will be analysing the participants' contributions for the underlying philosophical assumptions and remembering this analysis for use in later sessions.

By the second CoPI session the Chair will begin to use his or her analysis of the participants' philosophical styles of thinking to structure the dialogue by calling in participants to speak in such a way as to juxtapose potentially different underlying philosophies with each other. The participants will not be aware of the philosophical assumptions that underlie their contributions,[15] and they will not necessarily be aware whether their contribution is different in this respect from other contributions; it is the CoPI Chair's job to know this.

Frequently when the group have mastered the structure of agreeing and disagreeing and giving reasons, they are inaccurate in their assignment of agreement or disagreement. So, for example, when participant A says she agrees with participant B, this may not be accurate; the point being made by A might be different from the point made by B (and conversely with disagreement). The CoPI Chair has to make her or his own analysis and decision as to whether the contributions are similar or not.

So the CoPI Chair uses her or his knowledge of both logic and philosophy to:

1   judge the underlying philosophical assumptions of every contribution;
2   analyse the logical relationship between them; and finally
3   use this judgement and analysis to develop the dialogue.

In the early stages, both adults and children often want to defend their views and need time to learn how to listen to others carefully. Gradually, more and more participants begin to enjoy being disagreed with and having ideas and arguments challenged. The impulse to keep at one point and defend or explain their views begins to disappear. In the beginning one often finds several participants who want to dominate the discussion and several who do not volunteer – either because they are too shy or because they are quite happy for others to 'do the work' while they listen. With the Chair's structuring of the dialogue, this tendency diminishes over time. The Chair will make space for the less confident to contribute and call in those who are confident but 'laid-back' and will balance the contributions from the group. There will never be an equal amount of contribution from everyone, but the group will become more balanced.

As the CoPI sessions continue, both children and adults begin to listen more accurately to what is being said, and begin to think more accurately about how their own contribution relates to those of other participants. This often shows in the participants being more specific in their assignment of agreement and disagreement.

If we look at the children's dialogue, we can see the complexity of relationships between different contributions – for example:

Joy   I agree with Fern and Maggie because like sometimes you can think and dream, and sometimes you can't. Because like when you're dreaming – like you can if you're dreaming and then you're thinking in your dream. Sometimes it's hard to think and dream at the same time, especially if you're thinking about something else and you're dreaming about something else. Because then you might get mixed up. When you sleep you can also – when you are asleep you can also think and dream too.

Mc   Mark?

Mark   Well, um, I agree with Fern because, um, you can think and dream sometimes. Because when you're not thinking and you're dreaming,

your imagination is thinking. So your imagination is thinking sometimes but your brain is thinking with it. So I agree with Fern.

Mc David?

David I agree with Mark and I disagree with Mark. Because you control your
imagination. So if you were dreaming – some people say that your
dreams are in your imagination, and some people say you don't – but
if your dreams are in your imagination, then how could you think in
your imagination while you're dreaming in your imagination? But you
could think in your dream while you're in your imagination!

In this example from the children's dialogue, the CoPI Chair has to:

*   attend to the relationships which the children *say* hold between their
    contributions and the contributions from others;
*   remember what Fern, Maggie, Joy, Mark and David said;
*   remember the philosophical assumptions that underlay what Fern, Maggie,
    Joy, Mark and David said;
*   remember and analyse the logical relationships between what Fern, Maggie,
    Joy, Mark and David said;
*   analyse the internal logical relationships within each child's contribution.

CoPI procedure

Ultimately, chairing CoPI is an art. Analyses and judgements have to be made
at every second, and this work is rarely visible to onlookers. Nor is it something
that can be prescribed in advance in any detail.

However, there are some procedures that a learner CoPI Chair follows:

1 **The group of children or adults are seated** in a circle or horseshoe
   shape so that everyone in the group can see and hear each other easily, and
   also in order that the distribution helps to instantiate the equality of all
   participants physically.

2 **The group usually begins by considering** some stimulus material.
   This can be a picture, a video, even some music, but is often a specially
   written text.

3 **The CoPI Chair will ask the group** to look at the picture, watch the
   video, listen to the music or read the text aloud. If the group comprises
   pre-literate children, or others who do not read, a text will be read aloud
   to them.

4 **The CoPI Chair will then ask the group** if there is anything 'interesting or puzzling' about the stimulus, which raises a question for them. *The
   CoPI Chair asks for 'puzzles' rather than asking for what is merely 'interesting',
   because 'puzzles' are more likely to elicit philosophical issues.* 'Interesting' is a
   much wider category and can include questions about plot in a story, artistic
   technique in a painting, etc.

5   **The CoPI Chair then writes those questions** on a board or flip chart, adding the name of the questioner after the question. This is done so that the author of the question can be referred to in the beginning of the dialogue and also to reinforce the understanding of the group that the question(s) they will be discussing are theirs, and not pre-set by the CoPI Chair. The CoPI Chair may also choose to write the questions in a notebook, rather than on a board or flip chart. She or he might choose this because while the questions are the starting point for the dialogue, often participants try to answer the question and resist the dialogue moving into new directions. Keeping the questions visible only to the Chair and not to the participants can help participants to 'move with' the dialogue rather than referring back to the question.

6   **The CoPI Chair finishes writing questions** at an arbitrary point – often when he or she has filled the sheet of paper. This is done so that there is no implicit judgement in the point at which the Chair stops writing.

7   **With a group of adults** or older teenagers, the CoPI Chair explains that:
    a   They are to remain anonymous throughout the duration of the Philosophical Inquiry (which will be a minimum of twenty hours). They should not indicate their work position or special knowledge.
    b   They cannot use 'technical language' or jargon within the dialogues.
    c   They cannot cite authorities or experts or research in their contributions.
    d   They should try to think 'afresh' about the arguments and topics under discussion in the CoPI sessions.

These requirements are not necessary with young children; they are designed to produce a 'level playing field' for teenagers and adults who engage in CoPI, and to help participants to think for themselves about issues about which they may have a lot of secondary knowledge.

8   **The CoPI Chair then chooses one of the questions** to act as the starting point for the dialogue.
    a   The primary criterion for making the choice is: 'Which question holds the most philosophical potential?' This is the only criterion used in the first CoPI session.
    b   In subsequent CoPI sessions, secondary criteria may also be employed in choosing the question.

9   **If there are two or more questions** that would yield equally philosophical domains for discussion, then the CoPI Chair may use other criteria to choose:
    a   She or he would not choose a topic which had been discussed in the previous session.
    b   She or he might choose the question from a quieter member of the group in order to draw them into the dialogue.
    c   She or he might choose the question from a more 'independent' or 'controversial' thinker in order to stimulate different views immediately.

10 **In the early sessions the CoPI Chair explains** to the group that:

  a   He or she will call on people to contribute, but not necessarily in the order in which they have indicated that they wish to speak. People should not feel overlooked, because he or she will use different criteria for the selection order of speakers.

  b   She or he may call on someone to speak who has not raised his or her hand.

  c   The dialogue itself is the focus of CoPI.

  d   Although members of the group may initially feel attached to their own contributions and wish to defend them, this feeling will pass in time during the practice of CoPI.

11 **In the early sessions the CoPI Chair teaches** the children or adults how to use the CoPI reasoning structure to engage in the CoPI form of dialogue.

12 **The CoPI Chair explains that within** the CoPI reasoning structure, people almost always experience that others have misunderstood their point or argument, but the CoPI does not 'move backwards' to allow contributors to explain further.

  a   Over time they will learn to become clearer in their contribution.

  b   Participants will improve in their listening skills.

  c   There will be less misunderstanding.

  d   This awareness of how much others misunderstand what appear to be quite straightforward contributions is an important part of the experience of Philosophical Inquiry. One learns a lot from it.

13 **The CoPI Chair begins by asking the author** of the selected question to speak about what puzzled them in the topic of their question and, if they wish, to suggest a possible response to their own question. The author of the question is given a moment to reflect.

14 **The participants are told that:**

  a   Their own views and opinions are not the topics or focus of CoPI.

  b   Participants *use* their thinking and reasoning to examine the issues in dialogue.

  c   Participants may contribute ideas and arguments that are not their own opinion. These may be:

      i   something about which they have no opinion;

      ii   something they have only just thought of;

      iii something that they think will further the dialogue;

      iv something they disagree with.

15 **Members of the group are asked** to raise their hand if they have a response to the contribution given by the first speaker.

16 **The CoPI Chair selects** who will speak and calls them into the dialogue.

  a   The primary criterion for selection of speakers is 'Which contributions when juxtaposed with each other are most likely to create most conceptual conflict and/or philosophical tension?'

b   The CoPI Chair then uses secondary criteria in his or her selection of speakers. These criteria will vary from group to group, but will be concerned with the balance of contributions within the group, the personalities of the participants, etc.

17 **The CoPI Chair uses the** CoPI reasoning structure to guide the dialogue along philosophical lines. Often, up to three distinct but concurrent philosophical themes will be under investigation at the same time. The CoPI Chair must, among other things:

a   constantly monitor the dialogue;
b   constantly monitor the participants, so that she or he can call in a participant who may have something to contribute, but who has not raised their hand;
c   try to remember everything that has been said in the dialogues;
d   analyse the underlying philosophical assumptions of all the contributions as they are made;
e   use this analysis to structure the dialogue in a dialectical manner;
f   call for examples when these are needed;
g   be aware of the point when the participants have become too tired, and intervene appropriately;
h   be aware of the point at which the dialogue is not moving forward, and intervene appropriately.

18 **The CoPI dialogue continues** over weeks and months, and does not stop at the end of each session. So, when the session time is up, the dialogue stops. There are no conclusions or closure activities.

These eighteen 'steps' do not cover all aspects of chairing CoPI sessions. The art of chairing CoPI depends upon knowledge and skill, which can be developed only through training, but also on sensitivity and a talent that the aspiring CoPI Chair needs. When a CoPI session is chaired well, the role of the CoPI Chair is almost invisible to an untrained onlooker. Just as a novice watching an orchestral conductor may see only a person waving a stick, and does not see the wealth of knowledge, skill and art in the conductor's work, a CoPI novice will not see the background knowledge, art and skill in the work of a CoPI Chair. It can look easy, when in fact it is very difficult and extremely tiring. But the results can be spectacular!

In short, it is impossible to reproduce or show the experience of a CoPI: the experience of the *significance* of different parts of the inquiry is intangible, unheard and unseen, and it includes unspoken thoughts and insights that happen concurrently with those spoken. However, some idea of the richness and complexity of the CoPI can be understood from watching videos or looking at transcripts of CoPI sessions.

Chapter 6

Different methods of group philosophical discussion

Chapter 5 presented some of the basics involved in creating a Community of Philosophical Inquiry. These basics are the same whether one is chairing a CoPI with 5-year-old children, 11-year-old children, 14-year-old teenagers, 21-year-old adults or 65-year-old adults. CoPI is one specific method of working with people of all ages. There are other methods of eliciting philosophical discussions[1] with groups of people, some practised with children and some only with older teenagers and adults,[2] and this chapter will give a very brief sketch of some of the main methods.[3]

Two very influential philosophical methods in Europe and elsewhere which have inspired both those who work with children and those who work with adults are Leonard Nelson's Socratic method and Matthew Lipman's Philosophy for Children (P4C) programme. Both of these methodologies have similarities with the CoPI method, and both have important differences also. This chapter will examine these methods and their underlying philosophies, and compare and contrast them with CoPI. We will see how the different philosophies that underlie the different methods are directly related to the differences in the practices. Leonard Nelson's Socratic method is usually practised with adults, Lipman's Philosophy for Children programme is intended to be used with children and teenagers, and CoPI is practised with both adults and children equally.

We will also look at two classroom methods developed for schools – the SAPERE approach, initially inspired by Lipman's P4C programme, and the Guided Socratic Discussion series, designed to enable school pupils to encounter philosophical reasoning through a series of textbooks – and compare and contrast these methods with the CoPI method.

Some examples of where realism is instantiated in McCall's CoPI practice

Underlying realist philosophy	Instantiated McCall's CoPI practice
1 In the realist philosophy that underlies CoPI, there is a distinction between epistemology and metaphysics.	1 CoPI uses philosophical analysis of the philosophical assumptions and principles that underlie actions, judgement, emotions, etc. – distinguishing between epistemology, metaphysics, ethics, philosophy of mind, philosophy of science, etc.
2 In the realist philosophy that underlies CoPI, the world is held to be distinct from our knowledge of the world.	2 CoPI uses difference and disagreement to elicit contradiction in order to reveal where our knowledge of the world cannot accurately reflect the world as it is.
3 In the realist philosophy that underlies CoPI, the principle of contradiction holds in the world.	3 CoPI uses logic to elicit contradiction and counter-examples that might falsify a theory.
4 In the realist philosophy that underlies CoPI, people are fallible – so *all* of them can be wrong about the world.	4 CoPI uses a group of people because, since everyone and anyone can be wrong, there is more chance of revealing error with more minds.

Nelson's Socratic method

Leonard Nelson was a German philosopher who was concerned with the nature of the discipline of philosophy and the importance of philosophising. As he explains, 'The Socratic method, then, is the art of teaching not philosophy but philosophizing, the art not of teaching about philosophers but of making philosophers of the students.'[4]

Nelson was inspired by his understanding of both Socrates' and Kant's methods of philosophising; that is, the way in which Socrates and Kant came to their conclusions rather than the results of their work. Nelson believed that what he called 'philosophical truth' were to be found at the foundation of experience. These truths have a similar status to Kant's Categories of Understanding and could be arrived at through what Nelson saw as a similar method. This method he called 'regressive abstraction'. As Nelson explains,

> It is the same with all experiential judgments. If we inquire into the conditions of their possibility, we come upon more general propositions that constitute the basis of the particular judgments passed. By analyzing conceded judgments we go back to their presuppositions. We operate regressively from the consequences to the reason. In this regression we eliminate the accidental facts to which the particular judgment relates and by this separation bring into relief the originally obscure assumption that lies at the bottom of the judgment on the concrete instance. The regressive method of abstraction, which serves to disclose philosophical principles, produces no new knowledge either of facts or of laws. It merely utilizes reflection to transform into clear concepts what reposed in our reason as an original possession and made itself obscurely heard in every individual judgment.[5]

For Nelson, everyday actual experiences, like looking for one's coat, should be the subject matter of philosophising *because* it is *in* our understanding of these experiences that philosophical truth is found. As he explains,

> To give a commonplace illustration: If we were here to discuss the meaning of the philosophical concept of substance, we should most probably become involved in a hopeless dispute, in which the skeptics would very likely soon get the best of it. But if, on the conclusion of our debate, one of the skeptics failed to find his overcoat beside the door where he had hung it, he would hardly reconcile himself to the unfortunate loss of his coat on the ground that it simply confirmed his philosophical doubt of the permanence of substance. Like anyone else hunting for a lost object, the skeptic assumes in the judgment that motivates his search the universal truth that no thing can become nothing, and thus, without being conscious of the inconsistency with his doctrine, he employs the metaphysical principle of the permanence of substance.[6]

Philosophical truth is already 'reposed' in our reason (thinking); we just have to use a systematic method to reach it. This means that anyone can uncover philosophical truth, by analysing his or her judgements.

The method which Nelson began with his own students, and which was later developed by his student Gustav Heckmann, operationalised his philosophy; that is to say, the procedures used in Nelson's Socratic method are derived *directly* from his philosophy.

One of the practical problems in using Nelson's idea of regressive abstraction was 'How do you know when you have reached the truth?' Since 'reason' is a faculty that all people have, then the truth that one was seeking would be found within all 'reason'; that is, within everyone's thinking. The truth is therefore the same for everyone. So, a practical way of lending weight to the 'truth' arrived at through regressive abstraction would be to test it – to see if anyone reaches a different conclusion. If even one person did reach a different conclusion after the 'correct' application of regressive abstraction, then neither that person nor the others have reached the truth (because by its nature there is one truth). Of course, it would be impossible to request that everybody in the world sit down and engage in the procedure of regressive abstraction, but if one worked with a group of people and they all came to the same conclusion, then one might be more confident of that conclusion.

Developed out of his philosophy, Nelson's method follows certain procedures. The method involves a group of people who are guided in their practice of regressive abstraction by a Discussion Leader – typically a philosopher who has both understanding of Nelson's philosophy and training in the practice of guiding a Nelsonian Socratic dialogue.

The first step is to find the topic that the group wishes to investigate. This must be a topic that everyone in the group is genuinely interested in, because everyone will need to work on the topic for many hours. Ideally the dialogue will take twenty to thirty hours over the course of a week. Either the topic is chosen through discussion with the group of participants or, where there is limited time, a list of topics will be given prior to the dialogue and participants will choose the topic that interests them most.

The next step is for the group to find an 'overarching' question within the topic. Ideally the group is guided by the Discussion Leader in their choice of this question. Alternatively, where there is limited time, a list of questions will be given prior to the dialogue, and participants will choose the question that interests them most. A typical question might be:

Are there any justified inequalities?

The next stage is crucial and can take a long time. Under the guidance of the Discussion Leader, members of the group generate examples from their own experience which they think answer the question. So, for the example question above, the group might put forward different examples from their own lives that they think show an inequality which was justified, say an example of special consideration being given to a person with disabilities, which might be seen as unequal treatment. The Discussion Leader will choose one of these examples according to several criteria:

- that the example is clearly related to the question;
- that every participant easily understands the example;
- that the example has the possibility of giving an answer of 'yes' or 'no' to the question;

- that the person who gives the example will be able to withstand close questioning about his or her experience.

The first three of these criteria are related to the nature of the example, but the fourth is different. The Discussion Leader needs to be experienced in the Socratic method, and needs to be able to make good judgements about the possible progression of the dialogue because the 'witness' whose example is chosen will be questioned closely about every aspect of their personal experience for many hours. If the example is a close personal experience, and/or if the 'witness' is psychologically vulnerable in any way, the Discussion Leader may not choose it. Usually it is advisable to choose an example from a participant who has already had experience of Nelson's Socratic method and so has at least seen the nature of the close questioning to which he or she will be subjected. There is an argument that the Discussion Leader should not choose a 'witness' who has not previously experienced taking part in Nelson's Socratic method, because a novice participant cannot give 'informed consent' to what can feel like an invasive interrogation. The experience of being questioned within Socratic method dialogue is unique, and so one cannot be informed of the nature of this experience unless one has seen it in practice.

When the example is chosen, the Socratic dialogue usually begins with the Discussion Leader asking the 'witness':

- to explain how the example relates to the question;
- to describe the example in more detail.

The dialogue proceeds by examining the example, rather than examining the question directly. Because Nelson's Socratic method is about finding the truth at the limit of understanding *actual* experience,

- participants may not speculate;
- participants may not hypothesise;
- participants may not use imaginary situations or ideas.

Also, some Discussion Leaders restrict participants' use of abstract ideas or abstract nouns.

The Discussion Leader proceeds to guide the group in examining the central concepts in the question *through* investigating the example. The Discussion Leader does not contribute 'content' to the discussion, but rather acts as an external analyst of what is being said by the participants. So, for example, the Discussion Leader helps participants to understand the presuppositions in their contributions.

At every stage in the discussion the Leader checks that everyone in the group agrees with the articulation of the analyses, and writes down each step as the group reaches consensus. This practical requirement relates directly to Nelson's philosophy – that philosophical truth lies within the foundation of human understanding, so if someone does not agree with the concept or idea being put forward, then it is likely that this is not the 'correct' path to that foundation. The Discussion Leader must make sure that the consensus is 'real'; that is, that people are not agreeing in order to be polite, say, or in order to help the discussion move forward. The progress is very slow and very careful, and the discussion tends to move from a wide range of ideas and concepts to an ever-narrower focus. As one experienced Discussion Leader describes it,

> Participating in a Socratic discussion is very demanding and requires the full integrity, devotion and endurance of the participants. It is easy to overlook important aspects of the matter or run into dead ends. For that reason a Discussion Leader is a precondition. He or she must have an overview of the problem, but does not participate in the discussion. The Discussion Leader steers the discussion by asking if what has been said is clear and convincing for everybody; points back to remarks which have been made earlier, but which have been overlooked, although they could be important; insists on the clarification of a specific point in the discussion; and summarises what has been reached. That is to say, the role of the Discussion Leader is purely procedural.
>
> The Discussion Leader keeps a record of the discussion, preferably on big sheets, which can be seen and read by every participant. This record contains the main steps in the discussion, e.g. the points on which agreement has been reached, or the sub-questions which are esteemed to be of cardinal importance for further progress. If possible, the Discussion Leader makes a more complete record between the sessions, which can then be consulted by the participants.[7]

Another feature of Nelsonian Socratic method is that at any point in the dialogues any participant may call for a 'meta-discussion'. Because the discussion is restricted to examining an actual personal experience of one of the participants, and ideally an experience that is familiar to, though not identical for, the other participants, by definition it is highly personal. This means in practice that the discussion can often raise difficult emotions within the participants. (As philosophical assumptions lie deep within our thinking, *all* methods of bringing them to the surface will have psychological effects as well as cognitive effects upon participants, but this is particularly the case in Nelson's Socratic method.) For this reason it is important that the discussion is as comfortable as possible for participants. If any participant feels that the manner in which the discussion is being held is uncomfortable in any way, they can ask for a meta-discussion to discuss this. Someone other than the Discussion Leader chairs the meta-discussion, as the role of the Discussion Leader may be under question.

Nelson hoped that using his regressive abstraction method would yield results – philosophical truths. However, in practice, groups very rarely come to the end of the process, and the method is used in order to reach insights into the questions under discussion rather than actual answers.

Nelson's Socratic method assumes a philosophical theory of the nature of truth in which philosophical truth is metaphysically objective but internal to human reason. According to this kind of philosophy, it is possible to *find* philosophical truth, as such truths do not depend upon opinion (here he follows Plato); rather, we look inside ourselves to find it. In this, Nelson holds that he is following Kant, and is therefore seen as a neo–Kantian philosopher. But unlike Kant, Nelson distinguishes scientific truth from philosophical truth: scientific truth is external to us and concerns the world and is knowable by induction, starting from factual knowledge by observation, whereas philosophical truth is internal, concerned with the conceptual presuppositions of everyday experience and gained by regressive abstraction from those experiences.[8]

Some examples of where Nelson's neo-Kantian philosophical theory is instantiated in Socratic method practise

Nelson's Neo-Kantian philosophy	Instantiated in Nelson's Socratic method practice
I In Nelson's neo-Kantian philosophy, philosophical truth is found at the limits of human understanding, a 'frame' for understanding – like Kant's Categories.	I In Nelson's Socratic method, only actual lived experience can be investigated.
2 Therefore, in Nelson's neo-Kantian philosophy, philosophical truth is present in *all* human beings.	2 In Nelson's Socratic method, while one cannot engage in regressive method with *all* people, one uses a group of people to come closer to the limits of human understanding.
3 In Nelson's neo-Kantian Philosophy, if one seeks these truths, they should hold for everyone.	3 In Nelson's Socratic method the group continues the undertaking of philosophical analysis of underlying assumptions and principles until no one disagrees.

Similarities between Nelson's Socratic method and McCall's CoPI method

1   Both methods are practised with groups of adults who are volunteers. (CoPI is also practised with children.)
2   Both methods involve group discussion or group dialogue rather than direct teaching.
3   Both methods may start with a question; in fact, Nelson's Socratic method *must* begin with a question.
4   Both methods require knowledge of philosophy on the part of the Discussion Leader/Chair.
5   In both methods, the Discussion Leader/Chair has a responsibility for the philosophical direction of the discussion or dialogue.
6   Both methods aim towards deepening philosophical understanding on the part of the participants.

Some of the differences between Nelson's Socratic method and McCall's CoPI method

1   **Nelson's underlying neo–Kantian philosophy** differs from the external realism that underpins McCall's CoPI method. For example, in Nelson's philosophy the nature of 'equality' is to be found internally within our reason (thinking). By contrast, while making no claims about truth, the philosophy that underlies CoPI holds that knowledge of philosophical domains is of the same kind as knowledge of scientific domains; for both we look at the external world. So, within CoPI when participants are investigating the nature of 'equality', say, it is the investigation of equality as a concept that, while created by human beings, is external to us; it is found in the external world.
2   **In Nelson's Socratic method,** participants strive to come to agreement, whereas within CoPI, participants do not come to a joint conclusion or agreement but rather look for disagreements – because, according to the realist philosophy of CoPI, even if everyone in the world were to agree, they could all be wrong. Unlike in Nelson's method, in CoPI agreement between people is no indication of truth.
3   **Nelson's Socratic method uses only opinion** whereas McCall's CoPI does not. In Nelson's Socratic method, participants must give *only* their real personal opinion because philosophical truth is to be found internally at the foundation of actual experience. By contrast, according to CoPI, since, for example, the nature of 'equality' is external to us, our own personal opinions about it hold no particular weight (and in fact can be distracting in the inquiry), and so CoPI participants are not required to give their own personal opinion and must not assume that contributions from other participants reflect their personal opinions.

4 **'Hypotheticals' are outlawed within Nelson's practice** because only what actually pertained in an actual event is relevant; what might happen or might have happened is never under investigation. By contrast, hypothetical reasoning is frequently used within CoPI as one of the tools of thought to investigate something external to us.

5 **Nelson's Socratic method forbids the use of fictional examples,** whereas McCall's CoPI method frequently uses fictional examples. For Nelson, philosophical truth is to be found at the limits of actual experience, so fictional examples are not allowed. In CoPI, however, participants may use fictional examples as thought experiments to test theoretical ideas.

6 **Nelson's Socratic method forbids the use of abstract concepts,** whereas McCall's CoPI method frequently uses abstract concepts. Within Nelson's philosophy, abstract concepts are taken to be 'abstracted' from actual experience, and therefore are not helpful in investigating the limits of real experience, whereas within the realist philosophy of CoPI, abstract concepts hold the same status as empirical experience in so far as they are open to inquiry and are therefore often the subject of the dialogue.

7 **In Nelson's Socratic method** the Discussion Leader must write up every move within the discussion and make visible the categories and the internal relationships between *all* the ideas and theories. With a CoPI dialogue the Chair will very rarely make such categories and relationships visible.

8 **The movement of the dialogue** within a Nelsonian Socratic discussion tends to be more and more narrowly focused, whereas within CoPI the dialogue tends to expand into several different though interrelated themes, rather like building a spider's web.

9 **A Nelsonian Socratic dialogue moves slowly,** stopping frequently to check that (1) everyone understands and (2) everyone agrees with what is being said. A CoPI dialogue moves quickly, following several themes simultaneously, and does not stop either for checks on understanding or to achieve consensus.

10 **A Nelsonian dialogue** often (but not always) tends to break down ideas into ever-simpler constituents and consider each one separately, whereas a CoPI dialogue becomes more complex as it progresses.

11 **Within a Nelsonian Socratic discussion,** participants may call for a meta-discussion at any point, whereas meta-discussion is not allowed within McCall's CoPI method.

12 **The Nelson Socratic method Discussion Leader is responsible** for the individual people and their comfort as well as for the philosophical direction of the discussion. The CoPI Chair, by contrast, is responsible first to the dialogue (and not to the comfort of the participants; participants often feel uncomfortable within CoPI), and only second to the individual people.

Lipman's P4C programmes

The philosophy that underlies the P4C programmes developed by Matthew Lipman and associates differs from both the external realism of McCall's CoPI and Nelson's neo-Kantian philosophy, and this difference can be seen in the practice of P4C.

The foundation of the P4C programmes is the pragmatic philosophy of John Dewey.[9] Dewey disagreed with the distinction between the mind and the external world and, as a consequence thereof, between philosophical truth and scientific truth. Influenced by Darwin, Dewey developed a kind of evolutionary view of knowledge: that knowledge is an adaptive human response to the environment *aimed at changing the environment.*

For Dewey, the product of finding out about something is not static; we do not find out the truth and then have a piece of knowledge. Rather, we interact with the environment in order to change it. So, when we have changed it the environment is different, but we continue to interact with this new changed environment and in turn change *it.* Thus, there is no stable knowledge; rather, there is an ongoing process.

To distinguish his philosophical approach from others, Dewey named his theory of knowledge a 'theory of inquiry' and outlined 'phases' in the process of inquiry. He thought that where there is a problematic situation in the environment[10] (that is, a situation in which current human behaviour does not succeed in fulfilling human desires and/or needs):[11]

1   People determine the facts or issues of the problem.
2   People make hypotheses about how to solve the problem (these include ideas and concepts and theories).
3   People act upon the hypotheses to solve the problem.

The ideas, concepts and theories developed in phase 3 are 'true' only if they are successful in solving the problem – if they work.

For Dewey, it is important that people act collaboratively in this process. And when they act, people change the environment.

This process is the same whether people are dealing with a scientific problem or a social problem or an ethical problem. Dewey's (epistemological) philosophy can be described as a kind of social construction of knowledge. And as a correlate to his theory of knowledge, Dewey held that democracy was the ideal setting for the advancement of knowledge. As explained by Richard Field,

> The social condition for the flexible adaptation that Dewey believed was crucial for human advancement is a democratic form of life, not instituted merely by democratic forms of governance, but by the inculcation of democratic habits of cooperation and public spiritedness, productive of an

organized, self-conscious community of individuals responding to society's needs by experimental and inventive, rather than dogmatic, means.[12]

Dewey argued that preparation for this democratic community should begin with children's education. Children should be educated to participate in a community by following activities that mirrored his philosophy of knowledge – the process of inquiry.

The central place of democratic community within Dewey's philosophy is carried into the methodology of the Lipman P4C programmes and its derivatives in different countries. P4C and P4C-inspired approaches use activities in which the building of a community and democratic forms of procedure are central.

The P4C programmes are composed of short novels for children accompanied by teacher's manuals which supply a range of exercises, discussion plans and descriptions of 'leading ideas' that explain some of the philosophical ideas within the children's novels. When teachers begin to implement one of the P4C programmes they generally follow a particular procedure.

The group of children are seated in a circle or horseshoe shape so that everyone in the group can see and hear each other easily, and also in order that the distribution helps to instantiate the equality of all participants physically. The children begin by reading aloud from one of Matthew Lipman's novels. When the reading has finished, the teacher asks for questions from the children and writes them on a board or flip chart for everyone to see, and puts the names of the authors of the questions beside the questions.

At this stage the teacher may group questions into themes on the board – often guided by the 'leading ideas' in the teacher's manual that accompanies the novel. So, if there are some questions that relate to one of the ideas in the teacher's manual, those questions will be grouped together. The teacher begins a discussion either with the first question on the board, asking the child who asked the question to talk about his or her question, or by choosing one of the groups of questions. The teacher asks children to raise their hands, or thumbs, to indicate that they wish to speak, or alternatively children may be given 'speaking cards' which they may use to speak. The teacher then calls on each child in turn to say what she or he thinks about the question, and the children talk about either the question or the theme.

At the appropriate time the teacher introduces exercises about the topic from the teacher's manual to help focus the discussion. This is one of the key skills within the P4C programmes: how to choose an exercise and when to introduce the exercise. Teachers learn this skill in specialised training sessions.[13]

When he or she thinks it appropriate, the teacher then moves to the second question on the board and continues.

Some examples of where Dewey's philosophical theory is instantiated in Lipman's P4C practice

Dewey's pragmatic philosophy	Instantiated in Lipman's P4C practice
1 In Dewey's pragmatic philosophy, 'truth' is the product of 'successful, active manipulation' of the world by people, and best encountered within a democratic setting.	1 In Lipman's P4C practice, there is an emphasis on democratic practice in which children are joint creators of meaning.
2 In Dewey's pragmatic philosophy there is no epistemological– metaphysical distinction.	2 In Lipman's P4C practice, the construction of meaning takes priority.
3 In Dewey's pragmatic philosophy, people negotiate and construct truth in relation to their experience of the world.	3 In Lipman's P4C practice, children negotiate the link between ideas and their own experience.
4 In Dewey's pragmatic philosophy, truth is a kind of heuristic relationship between a person and the world.	4 In Lipman's P4C practice, every child's experience and thinking have equal value.

Similarities between Lipman's P4C programmes and McCall's CoPI method

1 **Both methods are practised** with groups of children.
2 **Both methods may begin** with the reading of a Lipman novel (Lipman's P4C programmes always begin with the reading of a Lipman novel; CoPI may begin with a number of other stimuli).
3 **Both methods involve discussion** or dialogue with children.
4 **Both methods emphasise** the primacy of the children's thinking.
5 **Both methods develop a community** within the classroom.
6 **Both methods eschew** the direct teaching of children.

7   **Both methods require teachers** to undergo substantial university-based training prior to implementing the method in the classroom.[14]

Some of the differences between Lipman's P4C programmes and McCall's CoPI method

1   **Lipman's P4C programmes are based upon Dewey's** pragmatic philosophy whereas McCall's CoPI method is based upon a realist philosophy.

2   **The concept of 'democracy' is central** within the Lipman P4C programmes and is instantiated in the practice by, among other things, the teacher's encouragement that every child should speak and have an equal chance to contribute to the discussion. In some implementations of P4C children will be given 'speaking cards' that allow them one turn at speaking for each card. This is done in order to ensure that every child has an equal amount of time to contribute to the discussion. This kind of conception of 'democracy' (equal time or equal turns at speaking) is not a central feature of McCall's CoPI method, because the focus of the CoPI dialogue is not the children, but rather the philosophical dialogue itself. There is an aim within the CoPI practice that every participant should contribute *philosophically* as equally as possible, but this does not mean equal time to speak or an equal amount of turns at speaking. So, for example, some children speak for only a short time but the weight of their contribution in philosophical terms is larger than that of other children who spend more time speaking and speak more often.

3   **Within the P4C programmes** the discussion is concerned with the views and opinions of the participants. This differs from CoPI, where participants are told they may contribute any idea, whether it is their opinion or not.

4   **In P4C the questions to be discussed** are not selected on any evaluative criteria; either the teacher goes through the list of questions in the order they are asked or a theme is chosen from a group of questions. Within McCall's CoPI method, by contrast, it is the CoPI Chair's job to make a judgement as to which question will be most philosophically fruitful and use that judgement as the main criterion for choosing the question.

5   **Within the general P4C approach** the teacher's responsibility is to the children and to the building of a community, whereas within McCall's CoPI method the Chair's responsibility is to *the dialogue*, and this is the Chair's service to the group: to provide an external expertise that the group of adults or children do not have.

6   **Within P4C** participants may ask questions at any point in the discussion, whereas within CoPI participants may not ask questions as part of the dialogue. This is because within CoPI questions do not have an argument structure of premises and conclusions. The aim of CoPI cannot be achieved with questions.

7 **Within P4C** participants have to think how to articulate their point of view in the discussion, whereas within CoPI participants must think at several different levels simultaneously in order to make *explicit* the relationships (as they see them) between the different parts of their current contribution and arguments that have been made previously in the dialogue. This extra cognitive task requires CoPI participants to think on several levels simultaneously: they have to think about the content of their contribution, they have to think of the supporting premises, but they also have to think at a meta-level about the logical structure of the whole dialogue and how their contribution fits within it, so that they can make this explicit.

8 **In P4C the discussion is open,** whereas in CoPI the dialogue is conducted within a strict reasoning structure.

9 **According to Lipman,** P4C does not aim to 'turn children into philosophers',[15] but rather to take elements of the discipline of philosophy to develop critical, creative and caring thinking in a community of inquiry within the classroom. Thus, there is no requirement within P4C that discussions are directly philosophical, whereas the CoPI method is designed to develop explicitly philosophical reasoning and not other kinds of discussion.

10 **In Lipman's P4C programmes** the philosophy is provided through (1) the Lipman novels and (2) the discussion plans, exercises and leading ideas in the teacher's manuals, which the teacher is trained to use to focus the discussion in a philosophical direction. In McCall's CoPI method there are no manuals; rather, it is the responsibility of the Chair to use his or her knowledge of philosophy and logic to structure the dialogue so that it is philosophical.

11 **In Lipman's P4C programmes** teachers are not required to study philosophy and logic prior to implementing the programmes (although it is of great benefit to them and their children if they do so). A CoPI Chair *is* required to study philosophy and logic prior to learning the CoPI method itself.

The SAPERE approach to P4C

Inspired by the BBC documentary *Socrates for Six-Year-Olds*,[16] SAPERE (the Society for the Advancement of Philosophical Enquiry and Reflection in Education) developed a general approach for schools that emphasises the importance of the 'critical, creative and caring' teaching developed by Matthew Lipman. While not explicitly based in Deweyan philosophy, the practice that SAPERE advocates follows a Deweyan line. The SAPERE approach advises teachers to follow these ten steps:[17]

1 **Preparation.**
  a   Arrange the chairs in a circle so that all the members of the 'community' can see each other and hear each other clearly.

    b   Conduct guidelines, to enable the community of philosophical inquiry to be a respectful, caring and collaborative environment:

       i   listen to the speaker;

      ii   respond to the discussion (think about what is being said);

     iii treat everyone's contributions with respect;

     iv contribute such that you support the community.

    c   Warm up/cool down games. Depending on the group, teachers use warm up or cool down games to prepare the group to concentrate, listen and talk.

2 **Presentation (stimulus).** The stimulus could be a story read or told to the group, a picture book, a work of art, a poem, a piece of music or a video clip.

3 **Thinking time:** for each child to reflect upon the stimulus. Children can be asked to think:

    a   about their feelings regarding the stimulus;

    b   about things that interested them or confused them;

    c   about things that provoked a reaction within them.

Children may record this reflection in the form of a cartoon, a speech bubble, a mind map, a concept map or simply by listing some key words.

4 **Conversation.** Children share their private reflections with the whole group or within smaller groups by:

    a   a timed activity where each child is given the opportunity to speak for one minute while the rest of the group listens;

    b   passing around their recorded reflection without discussion;

    c   presenting their recorded reflection to the large group and talking the others through their thinking;

    d   presenting their recorded reflection to a small group and talking the others through their thinking.

5 **Formulation: generating questions.** Children are given time to think about the stimulus as individuals, pairs or groups in order to raise questions, issues, problems or ideas. The teacher asks the children whether they have any questions. Each question is written up with the name of the author(s) next to it.

6 **Airing of questions.** The questions may be reflected upon, discussed or critiqued before selection begins. Each group, pair or author is invited to explain or clarify their question for a minute or so, followed by an opportunity for the rest of the group to ask any queries they may have about the question.

7 **Selection: voting.** The children vote for the question they would like to go forward to the discussion. This helps to give the 'community' a sense of democracy as well as allowing all contributions to be considered in a fair way. There are different kinds of voting:

    a   first past the post – everyone has one vote to cast;

    b   multiple votes – for example, everyone has three votes to cast;

    c   'omnivote' – everyone can vote for as many questions as they like;

    d   'secret vote' – everyone closes their eyes when they vote, or a secret ballot is taken.

8 **First words.** The child or children who formulated the question voted for is or are invited to:

    a   say how they feel about the question;

    b   explain why they asked the question;

    c   give a preliminary answer to their question.

9 **Building.** After the first words, the teacher asks for responses from the group.

10 **Last Words:**

    a   At the end of the discussion everyone reflects silently upon:

        i   what has been said;

        ii   what they have heard;

        iii   their own thoughts, views and opinions about the question or issue that has been discussed.

    b   After a period of reflection, each child shares his or her final thoughts about the question (possibly writing a sentence to compare to that which they may have written in response to the question before the inquiry).

Similarities between the SAPERE approach and McCall's CoPI method

1 Both methods are practised with groups of children.
2 Both methods may begin with a text, an image, music, etc.
3 Both methods involve discussion or dialogue with children.
4 Both methods emphasise the primacy of the children's thinking (but in different ways and for different purposes).
5 Both methods develop a community within the classroom.
6 Both methods eschew the direct teaching of children.

Some differences between the SAPERE approach and McCall's CoPI method

1 **Although not explicitly, the SAPERE approach** follows Lipman in its underpinning Deweyan philosophy, whereas CoPI is based upon a realist philosophy.
2 **The concept of 'democracy'** present in Lipman's P4C programmes is even more explicit in SAPERE's approach, for example in the practice of having the children vote for the question to be discussed. This concept of democracy is not dominant in CoPI because, as was explained earlier, the aim within the CoPI practice is that every participant should contribute *philosophically* as equally as possible, but it is the Chair's responsibility to ensure that this occurs, not the children's.

3   **The SAPERE approach emphasises democratic** procedures by having
    the children vote for the questions to be discussed. In McCall's CoPI it is
    the responsibility of the Chair to select the question that holds the most
    philosophical potential to begin the dialogue.

4   **In the SAPERE approach** the teacher does not need to learn philosophy
    or logic prior to implementing p4c[18] in the classroom. The CoPI Chair must
    learn both philosophy and logic prior to learning the CoPI method, and
    must practise and be assessed in her or his use of their knowledge of philo-
    sophy and logic in chairing CoPI prior to implementing it in the classroom.

5   **In the SAPERE approach the opinions** of participants are important,
    whereas in McCall's CoPI, whether a contribution is or is not the opinion
    of the participant is irrelevant.

6   **In the SAPERE approach** teachers introduce games and exercises as well
    as discussion, whereas in McCall's CoPI there are no games or exercises.

7   **Meta-discussion may happen at any point** within a SAPERE p4c
    session, and is also built into the ten steps, whereas meta-discussion is not
    allowed within a CoPI session.

8   **In the SAPERE approach** the session always ends with 'Final words', in
    which the participants reflect on, and may summarise, the session, whereas
    in McCall's CoPI there is no conclusion or closure, nor any summarising;
    the session just stops when the time is finished.

9   **In the SAPERE approach,** participants work together jointly to address
    a question, whereas in McCall's CoPI the Chair elicits disagreement
    between the participants in order to reveal the complexity of the theory or
    topic under dialogue.

10 **In the SAPERE approach** there is no restriction upon the kind of
    contribution that participants may make; contributions might be questions,
    musings, ideas, etc. By contrast, within CoPI, participants are restricted to
    presenting arguments in statements; participants are not allowed to
    contribute questions or musings or wonderings, only statements with
    which others can agree or disagree.

11 **The SAPERE teacher does not control the discussion,** whereas the
    CoPI Chair is 'in charge' of the dialogue.

12 **After twelve hours of a SAPERE introduction** a teacher may begin
    to practise in the classroom. By contrast, teachers who wish to implement
    CoPI in a classroom must take a minimum of eighty hours of training,
    which includes logic and philosophy, delivered by a trainer who has a Ph.D.
    in philosophy as well as experience in implementing CoPI with children
    and adults, assured by a university.

Guided Socratic Discussion programmes

The Guided Socratic Discussion (GSD) series comprises eight textbooks for
schoolchildren and accompanying teacher's guides.[19] Each textbook has ten

lessons, and pupils progress through the Guided Socratic Discussion course following the textbooks, which introduce pupils to philosophical concepts and to the reasoning and cooperation skills that are required to become competent in philosophical thinking and dialogue. The 'core' of each textbook is a story in which philosophical concepts, ideas and puzzles are embedded in an ordinary, everyday setting that children and teenagers recognise. Each lesson is composed of a combination of the following of six elements:

1 skills exercises,
2 meta-cognitive exercises;
3 shared reading aloud;
4 discussion questions;
5 guided group discussion;
6 group review.

The different elements are designed to work together in progressive stages to build:

- critical thinking skills;
- creative reasoning skills;
- moral reasoning skills;
- listening skills;
- talking skills;
- communications skills;
- comprehension skills;
- concept-forming skills;
- meta-cognitive skills.

The teacher's guides that accompany the textbooks provide a step-by-step guide for the teacher in how to help the pupils use the textbooks.

Similarities between the Guided Socratic Discussion programmes and McCall's CoPI method

1 Both involve groups of children engaging in collaborative work.
2 Both introduce children to different and contradictory philosophical theories.
3 Both include discussion with groups of children. In the GSD method this is one element of the lesson; in CoPI it is most of the session.
4 In both methods the teacher or CoPI Chair, as the case may be, does not input any content.
5 Both methods explicitly develop children's logical reasoning skills.
6 Both methods explicitly develop children's understanding of philosophical concepts.
7 Both methods place a primacy on the thinking of the children.

Some differences between the Guided Socratic Discussion programmes and McCall's CoPI method

1 **GSD uses teacher's guides** that give teachers step-by-step instruction as to what to do, whereas in CoPI the knowledge and skill are entirely 'in the mind' of the Chair.

2 **GSD uses textbooks for children** that tell the children exactly what to do, whereas CoPI uses a stimulus to start but thereafter the direction is unforeseeable.

3 **In GSD** philosophical questions for discussion are set in the textbook, whereas in CoPI the children ask the questions and the Chair chooses the question that has the most philosophical potential.

4 **GSD uses exercises and activities** to develop children's listening, talking and thinking skills, etc., whereas CoPI does not use any exercises.

5 **GSD uses a 'talking stick'** to ensure that every child has a turn and has practice in the exercises and also, at the beginning of each course, in the discussion. In CoPI there is no 'taking turns'.

6 **GSD instructs the children** to use the skills they have practised in the exercises during the discussions, and these skills become more complex and build throughout each course. In CoPI the complex reasoning structure is used from the beginning.

7 **In GSD the children practise explicit meta-cognitive** thinking, self-evaluation and reflection through exercises in each lesson, whereas in CoPI the children are thinking meta-cognitively continuously as an integral part of the dialogues.

8 **In GSD every lesson finishes with a reflection** about the whole session, which involves meta-talk, whereas in CoPI meta-talk is not allowed.

9 **In GSD the teacher** does not need to know any philosophy or logic; the philosophy and logic are provided for the children in the textbooks. In CoPI the Chair must know philosophy and logic.

10 **In GSD the children engage in taking turns** to say what they think in the discussion, or in open discussion. In CoPI, on the other hand, the Chair uses the CoPI reasoning structure and calls in children in the order that is most likely to create a philosophical tension in the dialogue.

11 **In GSD teachers require only short introductory** 'in-services' to become familiar with the way the textbooks work before beginning to implement the GSD courses. A CoPI Chair, by contrast, requires a minimum of eighty hours' postgraduate-level training in philosophy, logic and the CoPI method before being ready to implement the method with children.

The descriptions given above are not intended to be complete, but rather serve as outlines that show some of the main similarities and differences between different methods of engaging children and adults in discussion. One of the differences involves how the philosophy is 'delivered' to children and adults. This can be illustrated as a dimension that ranges from those methods in which the philosophy and logic are 'located' in the mind of the discussion director to those methods in which the philosophy and logic are 'located' in materials (usually books).

As one can see in Figure 6.1, in CoPI the responsibility for the philosophy and logic belongs entirely to the Chair, and is located initially 'in the mind' of the Chair. In Nelson's Socratic method the responsibility is largely with the Discussion Director, who needs to know philosophy in order to help the participants. In Lipman's P4C programmes the philosophy and logic are largely in the novels and teacher's manuals, though some knowledge of philosophy helps the teacher to know when and how to use the exercises and discussion plans from the teacher's manuals. In GSD the philosophy and logic are located entirely in the pupil textbooks, and the teacher does not need to know any philosophy or logic, but rather is guided step-by-step in how to help the children as they follow the textbooks.

Note: it is hard to place SAPERE's approach in this dimension because different teachers (and different SAPERE trainers) will use very different materials in their implementation. Some use books that are very directive, while others begin with a picture or a piece of music.

The next chapter will look in more detail at the background knowledge and skills that are required to implement CoPI.

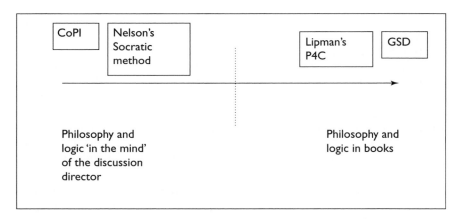

Figure 6.1

Chapter 7

What you need to know to chair a CoPI with 6–16-year-olds

Chapter 5 gave a 'rough guide' picture of chairing a CoPI, but it must be stressed that specialist training is required for a teacher (or any person) to learn how to implement CoPI. This chapter will explain how training in basic logic and philosophy is a necessary but not a sufficient foundation for being able to chair a CoPI.

At the first level the CoPI Chair needs to develop skills in analysing ordinary, everyday language to identify the philosophical assumptions that underlie what is being said by participants in a CoPI, and he or she also needs to develop the ability to make a logical analysis of the relations of different contributions, both 'internally' – that is, identifying the logical structure within a participant's contribution – and 'externally' – that is, identifying the logical relationships between different contributions. It is not enough simply to know philosophy and logic; philosophy graduates know these disciplines, but do not necessarily have the skills to apply them in live analysis.

At the second level the CoPI Chair needs to develop the skills that will enable him or her actively to shape the dialogue using the analysis described above.

At the third level there are social or group aspects of developing the community for which the CoPI Chair is responsible. The CoPI Chair needs to be able to make a space for less talkative participants to enter the dialogue by restricting the verbal dominance of some confident participants and ensuring that they also listen.

And at a fourth level the CoPI Chair needs to be able to make continuous meta-judgements about which of the second- and third-level criteria are paramount at every juncture of the dialogue.

These are all demanding intellectual tasks, and they have to be done live within a dialogue which is constantly changing and moving, and which may throw up totally unforeseen ideas and theories at any juncture.

For this reason, as we have seen, the Chair is largely invisible to the spectator. Even an experienced schools inspector will not be able to see the intellectual work being undertaken by a trained CoPI Chair. He or she might be able to analyse the results of this intellectual work, given the luxury of time to study a video or a transcript, but will fail to see it 'live'; it happens too fast.

Logic

The CoPI Chair needs to know only some very basic logic but she or he needs to know it very well.[1] Furthermore, it must become almost second nature to the Chair to be aware of the fundamental logical structure in everyday speech, and thus to be able to apply that skill during live dialogues. Knowledge of the following would give the aspiring CoPI Chair a good foundation:

1 'speech act theory' and the different functions of language;
2 the similarities and differences between formal and informal argumentation;
3 the identification of premises and conclusions in argumentation;
4 the nature of logical fallacies and informal fallacies in argumentation;
5 the nature of propositions and their role in logic;
6 Aristotelian syllogisms;
7 hypothetical syllogisms;
8 basic set theory;
9 the difference between valid and invalid arguments in logic;
10 the difference between sound and unsound arguments in logic;
11 the role of truth and falsity in logic;
12 the role of hidden or suppressed premises in argumentation.[2]

Philosophy

The CoPI Chair needs to know some basic philosophy,[3] and, as with logic, he or she needs to know it very well. The aspiring CoPI Chair has to learn and practise the skill of recognising the different kinds of philosophical theories and assumptions that underlie everyday speech, and then needs to practise using this skill while implementing CoPI, under the guidance of a specialist trainer. Knowledge of the following different areas within philosophy would give the aspiring CoPI Chair a good foundation:

1 **Metaphysics** – What is real? What exists? Including:
  a realism;
  b idealism;
  c phenomenalism;
  d the problem of universals.
2 **Epistemology** – What can be known? In what ways can it be known? Including:
  a the difference between a priori knowledge and a posteriori knowledge;
  b the difference(s) between belief, truth and opinion;
  c different theories of scepticism;
  d rationalism;
  e empiricism.

3 **Ethics** – What is good/bad? What is right/wrong? Including:
   a virtue ethics;
   b deontology;
   c utilitarianism;
   d egoistic ethics;
   e moral relativism.
4 **The philosophy of mind** – If there is a mind, what is it? Including:
   a monism;
   b materialism;
   c idealism;
   d dualism;
   e epiphenomenonalism.
5 **Aesthetics** – What is art? Including:
   a idealist theory;
   b significant form theory;
   c institutional theory;
   d intentional theory.
6 **The philosophy of politics** – How should people live together?
   Including:
   a Plato, *The Republic*;
   b Hobbes, *Leviathan*;
   c Locke, *Two Treatises*;
   d Rousseau, *The Social Contract*;
   e Mill, *On Liberty*.
7 **The philosophy of science** – What is and is not science? Including:
   a induction;
   b deduction;
   c Popper's falsification theory;
   d Kuhn and Feyerabend – paradigms;
   e foundationalism
   f coherentism;
   g externalism.

Studying and reading logic and philosophy are therefore requirements for an aspiring CoPI Chair, and while it is possible to undertake such reading and studying by oneself, most people need guidance in their study and under-standing of both philosophy and logic from qualified philosophers. This is even more relevant in the modern age of Internet access to philosophy texts and courses, because the quality (and one might even say the legitimacy) of courses and advice available on the Internet varies enormously and the novice student has no means of discriminating between legitimate philosophy courses and others that may call themselves 'philosophy' but are not suitable background training for a CoPI Chair.

However, while this background knowledge is a necessary foundation, in itself it is insufficient. The specific way in which the CoPI Chair uses such knowledge to undertake instant analysis of live and often very rapid dialogue is not taught in even the best philosophy and logic courses. This is why, having gained the background knowledge, the aspiring CoPI Chair needs to undertake 'apprentice model' training with a specialist trainer.

There is no standard formula for training to implement CoPI, just as in fine art there is no one formula for every learner painter. Every art student should learn the basics of the craft and the skills with drawing, shade, line, perspective, colour, composition, etc. and learn how to use the different tools and media. Once these are learned, the art teacher will teach each student individually, according to that student's needs and strengths. In a similar way, once the necessary background knowledge has been learned,[4] the specialist COPI trainer will observe each student's implementation and give one-to-one advice that suits the student's particular skills and strengths.

The guidance given to one student might not be suitable for others. For example, there are different ways of helping children to become familiar with the CoPI method. When the Chair is beginning to implement CoPI with a group of children, the children will tend to look at the Chair because they are accustomed to looking at the teacher. Over time the aim is to have the children look at the speaker and not at the Chair. One 'strategy' that can be used to help with the process of encouraging the children to look at the child who is speaking is for the CoPI Chair to walk behind the group of children (who are sitting in a circle) and to stand behind the child who is speaking. This strategy works in two ways: first, the child who is speaking cannot look at the Chair when she or he is standing behind them, and so will be led to address the group of children rather than the Chair; second, by using the children's tendency to look at the 'teacher', the Chair directs the eyes of the children who are listening towards the child who is speaking. This strategy works quite quickly. However, it cannot be used by every CoPI Chair. For example, if the aspiring CoPI Chair is a rugby player who is over 6 feet tall and 2 feet wide, walking behind a group of small children and standing behind one of them will intimidate them! The best 'strategy' for the rugby player Chair is to sit on the floor with the children, making himself appear as near to their size as he can.

Similarly, for *some* CoPI Chairs it can be a good 'strategy' to smile at the children and nod encouragement. The practice of CoPI is very different from other forms of activity to which children are accustomed, and they may be nervous about whether they are 'doing it right'. However, if the aspiring CoPI Chair is not a natural 'smiler', then the trainer will not advise him or her to put on an unnatural fixed grin. That would just scare the children.

The trainer will model how to implement a CoPI for the students, initially with all the students in the class of students and later also (preferably) with each student's own children (where the student is a classroom teacher), or with community groups (if the student is not a classroom teacher). However, the students do not 'blindly' copy *everything* the trainer does. The trainer will guide each individual student in how best he or she can implement a CoPI.

Chairing CoPI is not for everybody. There are people who, while they can learn the necessary philosophy and logic, nevertheless lack the kind of social understanding and awareness needed by a CoPI Chair to 'read' a group of children. The CoPI Chair has to be able to recognise when a child has a thought; when a child has something to say but is not assertive enough to enter the dialogue; when a child wishes to speak only to have his or her voice heard; when a child wishes to speak only to impress the teacher or his or her her peers; and so on.

The ability to read emotions in other people accurately cannot be learned. If a person has this ability, then it can be enhanced and sharpened; he or she can become more skilled in its use. But not everyone does. For example, many great teachers who are inspirational to listen to, who are experts in their fields and who can engage an audience do not have this ability. There are many ways of teaching and many ways of interacting with people, and one can be a successful teacher and a popular leader without having the specific ability to be aware of the thinking of every child in a group.

The CoPI reasoning structure is not enough by itself

Simply using the CoPI reasoning structure will not by itself ensure that philosophical dialogue is happening.

First, the CoPI reasoning structure should be used by a trained CoPI Chair who can use the skills she or he has learned while being trained in order to balance the dialogue and intervene when necessary to make the space for the possibility of emerging philosophical ideas and theories (with all the invisible analyses that this involves). The CoPI reasoning structure is a powerful tool, and becaust it is powerful, its *misuse* can damage children, as we shall see.

Even when used by an experienced CoPI Chair, the CoPI reasoning structure does not always ensure philosophical dialogue.

1   Within *any* CoPI session there may be periods when the discussion looks like a dialogue but is not.
2   Within *any* CoPI session there may be periods when the children (or adults) are using the CoPI structure, but there is no philosophical movement. What is happening is a kind of 'ersatz dialogue'.

When these periods of 'ersatz dialogue' occur, the CoPI Chair might:

•   Allow the 'ersatz dialogue' to continue because the group needs a rest from the intense intellectual tasks that CoPI dialogue involves.
•   Allow the 'ersatz dialogue' to continue in order to make a space for some

participants who are normally quiet and need encouragement to contribute to the dialogue.

- Move to a new question in order to 'refresh' the dialogue philosophically.
- Intervene by asking for an example or asking a question so as to move the discussion towards a more philosophical reflection on the topic. A typical example might be when children begin to recount the content of their dreams one after another. At some point the Chair might intervene by asking how the children know that these *are* dreams. This question might open the space for a philosophical consideration of the nature of reality or the nature of consciousness and more. However, the question might not have the desired effect; each child might be so determined to tell their dream that they will continue to do so. The CoPI Chair then has to decide whether to let it run or move to another question. This decision will depend on many factors.
- Finish the session. Usually the CoPI Chair will decide to do this when the session has been running for some time, and because the participants are just too tired. In such circumstances, moving to another question may not work, as the reason that the group has 'retreated' into discussion mode is simply that they have worked so hard during the CoPI session that they cannot sustain the CoPI dialogue any longer.

For example, during the CoPI session transcribed in Chapter 4, there is a period in the middle where, although the children are using the reasoning structure, there is no philosophical dialogue:

David Yeah. When I, when I pinch myself – when I pinch myself and when I don't wake up when I pinch myself in my dream. And then when I, when I pinch myself and I, and I'm waking – and I woke up when I pinched myself, that's how I know if I was pinching in my dreams or if I wasn't pinching in my dreams.

> *Comments*
>
> When he 'dream-pinches' himself he does not wake up. When he pinches himself from outside his dream, then he wakes up. This is how he knows whether the pinch was within the dream or not.

Mc Right! Clare?

> *Comments*
>
> At this point in the discussion, the class became suddenly tired. We had been talking for about an hour. No one could follow David's

explanation of the difference between 'dream-pinching' within his
dreams and deliberately pinching himself to make himself wake up.

Clare   I have a question for you, David. How can you do that? How can you
         like, if you're on the middle of the bed, how can you just fall off and –
         pinch yourself in your dreams?
David   What I do, what I do to do that is: when I pinch myself I – Sometimes
         my sis- my sister pinches me or something and that's what, and that's
         what I do to – And that's what it feels like. So, and then what I do to
         – to not – for her to not pinch me, is I roll, is I roll, is I roll to my mom
         and dad sometimes. It happened to me. I thought I was downstairs in
         my den and, then when I pinched myself, I fell – I rolled and I fell off
         the bed.
Mc   OK, let's look at this question here. 'Why did she touch her eyes?'
         Mark, why did she touch her eyes, Mark?

> *Comments*
>
> As everyone is tired and needs a break, the next question provides
> an interlude before returning to a more philosophical question.

Mark   To see if she was awake. But if she touched her eyes, she could've hurt
         her eye or something. Because if she didn't cut her fingernails, but
         maybe she didn't – then if they were very sharp, they, they could've like
         – she could've pinched – she couldn't – she could've hurt her eye. And
         why I was interested in that question is because she could have – that,
         that's a weird thing to do, to pinch your eyes to see if you're awake.

> *Comments*
>
> The next phase of discussion is not philosophical dialogue. Even
> though some of the children use the 'agree and disagree . . . because'
> structure, this is *not* Philosophical Inquiry.

Mc   Aha, what's weird about it?
Mark   Well, see like when you're awake you usually like, like try and, like try
         and move around and go and turn on the light or something so you
         can really see if you're awake. And then, and then, and if you, and if you
         didn't have a light, if, if, if they were – if you couldn't find them in the
         dark, you, you could at least just, just like, go like to do something.
         I don't know.
Mc   You could go and do something?
Mark   Yeah, like get off. . .

Child   Go off the bed!

Mark   . . . get off the bed and go downstairs and if you, and if your mind already had, already knew where the bathroom was already, you could go in the bathroom and get a drink of water, or pour it on yourself.

Mc   Karen?

Karen   I, I disagree with Mark because – about touching your eyes. I think what they mean by touching your eyes is when they close their eyes and they just wipe theirs or like do this [Demonstrates.] but not really touch the eye. But they just mean something like that or something like. [Demonstrates.]

Mc   So why do you – why did she do that in the story, Karen?

Karen   Maybe because they say in the story like 'Are you awake?' So she did it just to see if she was awake or not.

Mc   And do you think that's a good way to tell if you're awake?

> ### Comments
>
> This intervening question might have opened a space for a more philosophical direction to emerge, but did not – see below.

Karen   Kind of.

Mc   James?

James   Well, Karen, because see I think what they meant by touching their eyes was not poking their eyes with your fingernail. That's poking. [Demonstrates.] But like doing this, touching the, the inside of my finger, like touch like that.

Mc   Would you do that? All right, let's – we've had a demonstration already. James, would you do that to see if you were awake? David?

David   I'm adding on to Mark's question and I'm agreeing with him and I'm disagreeing with him. Why couldn't she pinch herself like I did?

Mc   Do you think that would be the same kind of thing?

Mark   Yeah, 'cause then you would, then you would struggle. [Demonstrates waking up with pinching.] You'd go 'Aaagh!'

David   And the reason I disagree with Mark is, is – and I'm agreeing with James about that one part of the – like you went like this or you went like that. [Demonstrates.] But, and that's why I disagree with him is that I don't think she took her fingernail and just put it in her eye. And the reason I agree with Mark is because if, if she like poured the water – I – mean and why I still disagree with Mark is because if sh- If she didn't know if she was asleep or awake, how would she be able to wake, wake up if she was asleep, get out of bed, then go pour water on herself?

Comments

Again, even though David makes the structure of his argument and the relations between his contribution and the contributions of other children very clear, and even though he uses the words 'agree', 'disagree' and 'because', this is not Philosophical Inquiry.

Mc	If she didn't know?
David	Yeah.
Mc	OK.
David	How could she know? And how could she know if she was awake or if she wasn't?
Mc	How would she know if she was doing it or she wasn't, if she didn't know if she was awake or asleep?
David	She could've sleepwalked.

Comments

David seems to think that pouring water on oneself is not an adequate test for discovering whether one is asleep or awake, because one could be sleepwalking. He wonders how Elfie would know whether she was sleepwalking or really awake.

Mc	She could've sleepwalked?
David	Yeah.
Mc	Fern?
Fern	I agree with Mark. Well, when you like poke your eye and you haven't cut your nails, that would really hurt. And the reason why I agree with Mark if you like poke your eyes, it will really hurt. And, and when you like touch your eye, that, if you touch like your eyelash, that will, will not hurt.

Comments

'Health and safety' requires the CoPI Chair to move on from this topic, now – before eyes are poked or scratched, as children are about to try touching their eyes and/or eyelashes.

Mc	OK, let's look at the next question here. [Indicates.] Karen, why did she say to herself, 'Dummy, if you can wonder, you must be thinking'? Let's go back a bit. What was it she was wondering about? Does anyone remember what she was wondering about? You can look at it if you don't remember. What was it she was wondering about? [Children look at the text.]

> *Comments*
>
> After an interlude of discussion with no philosophical dialogical movement, it is time to go back to more difficult philosophical topics. So, I intervene to move to a more philosophical question.

Although the CoPI practice is not (yet) common, because of the spectacular results for children and their families, there has been great media interest in Philosophical Inquiry over many years. Beginning in 1985, when a journalist happened to overhear a 5-year-old child reasoning with her parents over breakfast in a New Jersey diner and proceeded to investigate and write an article for a New Jersey broadsheet, there have been many documentaries, news items and features on television, on radio and in newspapers. This media attention has served to make the public aware that it is possible to 'do' philosophy with children in general, but even an hour-long documentary could not explain how to implement the specific methods featured.

The most influential of the television programmes is the 1990 BBC documentary feature film *Socrates for Six-Year-Olds*, which featured two heavily edited clips of a class of 6-year-old children in CoPI sessions, filmed five months apart. *Socrates for Six-Year-Olds* also showed edited clips of a class of teenagers using Lipman's P4C programme. The distinctions between the two methods were deliberately blurred to make the programme attractive to the general public. The creators of this film never intended it to be taken as a description of the philosophy with children methodologies it featured; it was intended to be a film for the general public which gave a flavour of the field. It was not a documentary, but rather a *documentary feature film* that, in the words of the producer and director, showed 'the poetic truth rather than the literal truth'.[5] However, *Socrates for Six-Year-Olds* was such a good film, and so powerful, that it has been used in teacher training colleges and universities all over the world since 1990, and continues to be used in training courses to this day.

Lacking any adequate explanation, many people have copied what they saw in documentaries and read in newspapers without knowing about either the nature of CoPI or the background knowledge in philosophy and logic needed to implement CoPI. Practices that attempted to copy Philosophical Inquiry were then passed to teachers through training.

For example, the practice of copying the CoPI reasoning structure by asking children to preface their contributions with 'I agree with . . . because . . .' or 'I disagree with . . . because . . .'

- without knowing what the CoPI reasoning structure is;
- without knowing how the CoPI reasoning structure was developed;

- without knowing the purposes for which the CoPI reasoning structure was developed;
- without knowing how to use the CoPI reasoning structure; and
- without specialised training in how to implement CoPI

has had devastating results upon children.

Unfortunately, some teachers and others have thought that simply encouraging children to say, 'I agree with . . . because . . .' or 'I disagree with . . . because . . .' before their contribution will make the children's discussion 'philosophical', or at least encourage reasoning – because children are giving reasons. But this is not true! It is *the way* in which the structure is used by the CoPI Chair that shapes a discussion into a philosophical dialogue.

For example, the following transcript shows a discussion in which children had previously been taught to say, 'I agree with . . . because . . .' or, 'I disagree with . . . because . . .' by someone who did not know what the structure is for, nor how it should be used. The children have not been introduced to CoPI, but rather are discussing a question from one of the Guided Socratic Discussion series of books. In a normal Guided Socratic Discussion session, the children will pass a 'talking stick' around the circle and follow the exercise in the textbook; and the teacher would not intervene at all but rather help the children to follow the instructions in the textbook.[6] But in this session I had to intervene because the children were engaging in a subtle form of bullying.

I had never met these children before, so they were not used to my guiding their discussion. The set question is 'Can you be nowhere?' Following the textbook, children should say, 'I think . . .' and then pass the talking stick to the next child.

In the following transcript the children's names have been changed. Jo is a little girl with physical disabilities.

Speaker *Discussion*
Mc The first thing we're going to do is talk about Question 1 using the talking stick. And we'll look at the rules . . .
  [The children take turns to speak, going around the circle. The group have already been discussing a different question for ten minutes when this part of the discussion begins.]
. . .
Mc Looking at the next page. Again we are going to start with the talking stick and we are going to think about this question [reading Question 2 from the textbook]: 'Can you be nowhere?' . . . OK, we'll start here, Peter, and then go around.
Peter I say 'no' because you always have to be somewhere.

> *Comments*
>
> Peter's contribution is typical of a Guided Socratic Discussion class.

Joy   I say 'yes' because . . . like say if you're somewhere that you don't know what it's called. Like you might say, 'I'm in the middle of nowhere' if you don't know what it's called.

> *Comments*
>
> Joy's contribution is also typical of a Guided Socratic Discussion class.

Charlie   Em. No. Because you always have to be somewhere because say you were having a dream? Then you are still somewhere because you are in your head! Like say you were in Asda – you can't say you are nowhere because you are at Asda.

> *Comments*
>
> Charlie's contribution is also typical of a Guided Socratic Discussion class, and adds a new idea.

Tommy   I think yes, because – say you're at Asda, you have to be somewhere, you're never nowhere!

> *Comments*
>
> Tommy's contribution is also typical of a Guided Socratic Discussion class.

Jo   I think you have to be somewhere because see if someone comes up to you and says . . .
[At this point Jo is drowned out by a loud noise made by Tommy, who is sitting next to her, pulling the Velcro on and off his shoes.]

> *Comments*
>
> Tommy is timing the noise so that it prevents anyone from hearing Jo speak. It is obviously deliberate. I was surprised, but I did not know the class. In retrospect, this is where the bullying begins. But at the time it seemed like just one child being deliberately unkind.

Mc   Right! Stop! If you can't help yourself with playing with your shoes, I'll ask you to take them off and put them over there! And that way you won't be disrupting and distracting Jo. OK? [Silence.] OK? Do you think you can mange to do this without playing with your shoes?

> **Comments**
>
> The children are surprised that I have stopped the discussion 'just' for Tommy playing with the Velcro on his shoes. It seems as though they do not see anything wrong with Tommy's behaviour.

Tommy   Mmm.
Mc   No?
Tommy   Yeah.
Mc   Yeah? OK, Jo. Start again.
Jo   I think you have to be somewhere. Because suppose someone is asking about where you live because they want to take you back to your home, and you say 'nowhere', that can't be possible – because you have to be somewhere.

> **Comments**
>
> Jo gives an example to illustrate that using the word 'nowhere' can't really make sense. She uses an example from her experience. Being disabled, she has to be driven to and from school in a taxi, so she is used to people asking her where she lives.

John   I think you have to be somewhere because there's no such thing as nowhere. Because if you are nowhere, you'd be in a time warp or something, and there's no such thing as a time warp.

> **Comments**
>
> John's contribution is typical of these discussions, where children are asked to begin their contribution with the words 'I think' and then say what they think. So, it looks as though we are 'back on track' with the exercise.

Al   I **disagree with Jo** [Giggles and looks around at the other children for approval.] because . . .

Comments

Here, Al is using the form of words 'I disagree with Jo' as a deliberate attack on Jo. This class is *not* a CoPI class, but the children have learned this from someone. It is not a natural form of words that would arise from children spontaneously! Someone who has not been trained in CoPI has copied the CoPI structure and taught the children.

[Laughter in response from five other children.]

Comments

The response from the other children demonstrates that they know what is being done to Jo. And also that this is not the first time they have used the form of words, in effect, to bully an already disadvantaged little girl.

Al   Because she said that your house would be nowhere!

Comments

Jo did not say this. Al is using the 'disagree' form of words to twist what Jo actually said.

[More laughter from seven other children. Jo hangs her head and looks at the floor.]

Comments

It is obvious from Jo's reaction that this bullying under the guise of discussion is upsetting her.

Al   [Giggles.]
Mc   [To the group of laughing children] No! [To Al – before it is his turn to speak] We want to know what you think, Al. You begin by saying, 'I think'.

Comments

I immediately intervene to tell the children that they cannot laugh. I then indicate to Al that he should be talking about what *he* thinks and following the textbook where it says to begin with 'I think'.

Al   I think you can't be nowhere because you have to be . . .

> *Comments*
>
> My intervention has appeared to work as Al 'starts over' and says
> only what he thinks. At this point, while I was concerned about the
> way the children were using the 'disagree' form of words, I expected
> that since the children (1) had been told to stop and (2) told to say
> the words 'I think' and follow them with their own thought, the
> bullying would stop and the lesson would then proceed 'normally'.

Ann   I think the same as Al because you say that you're in the middle of
          nowhere if you don't know where you are, and **I disagree with Jo**
          because you wouldn't say . . . someone just comes up to you and you
          say where you live, you wouldn't just tell them where you live if you
          don't know them.

> *Comments*
>
> However, Ann gets round the injunction to follow the exercise in
> the book by beginning with 'I think' but then immediately using the
> form of words 'I disagree with Jo' to attack Jo. Her point about not
> telling people where you live completely misconstrues Jo's example.
> It adds another dimension for children to 'disagree' with Jo.

[More laughter from other children. Jo looks at the floor.]

> *Comments*
>
> Now it appears that the children do not know that it is wrong to do
> this.

Mc   [To the giggling children] The rules are: one person talks – they say
          what they think, and everyone else listens! Right!

> *Comments*
>
> I intervene again. Now it is obvious from my tone of voice and
> expression that I am cross with what is going on. But many of the
> children are perplexed by this. They do not seem to know that what
> they are doing is wrong.

Danielle I think you have to be somewhere like school or Asda and **I disagree**
           with Jo [Looks around at other children and giggles.] because . . .

> **Comments**
>
> Danielle also appears to think that if she follows the rules to say 'I think' in the beginning, then everything is fine. I begin to suspect that the children have done this before and also that they have been told that it is a good thing to do.

[More laughter from other children. Jo looks as though she is about to cry.]

Danielle . . . because if you said that, you would have to live in the street.

> **Comments**
>
> This is not what Jo was saying at all!

Mc　　Tell everyone what you mean by that.

> **Comments**
>
> I give Danielle the benefit of the doubt and intervene to emphasise a new meaning.

Danielle Because if you said 'nowhere', you live in the street.
Mc　　It means you don't have a house?
Danielle Uh–huh.
Clara　I think you have to be somewhere because . . . **and I disagree with Jo** because if you don't know where you live . . . [Looks around at other children.]

> **Comments**
>
> Like Danielle, Clara appears to think she is doing something right! And again this misconstrues what Jo had said.

Clara　[Giggles behind hands from other children. Jo now has her hand hiding her face.] . . . then you don't live anywhere.
Mc　　OK, Stuart, we are going to hear what *you* think!

> **Comments**
>
> This is my last attempt to steer the children away from using 'I disagree with Jo' as a means to humiliate and bully Jo.

Stuart   I agree with [Ann] about **disagreeing with Jo** because . . . if someone asked you where you live and you say 'nowhere' then you'd be a homeless person . . .

Mc   OK. We are going to stop this discussion now because when we're doing our 'Wondering' discussion we do not say . . .

> **Comments**
>
> I stop the discussion. Jo looks very grateful that someone has recognised that this is wrong, and stopped it.

During the discussion, most of the children were puzzled that I clearly disapproved of the way they were using 'I disagree with Jo'. When they managed to work this form of words into the discussion while still following the instructions of saying 'I think' in the textbook, most of them were even more puzzled that I did not approve. A few of them were not puzzled because they were aware that they were bullying. But from their reactions it seemed as though the children had not been reprimanded or questioned about it before.

Very worryingly this group of children not only did not see that it was wrong to use the form of words in this way; they seemed to think it was right. Their behaviour indicated that someone had taught them that this was good! When I asked them where they had learned to say 'I agree' and 'I disagree', the children explained that a visiting teacher had taught them that, when they did not *like the behaviour* of another child, they were to *say to the teacher* 'I disagree with . . . because' and give a reason. We do not know whether the visiting teacher told the children to do this, or whether the children misunderstood. However, it is clear that this was not the first time they had practised using this form of words in this way.

The CoPI reasoning structure of saying 'I agree with . . . because . . .'

- is *not* designed for children to indicate what they like or do not like – CoPI has nothing to do with individual preferences, likes and dislikes;
- is *not* designed for children to discuss the behaviour of other children – CoPI does not discuss the behaviour or personality of any particular person in the group;
- is *not* designed for children to tell the teacher anything at all – it is designed for children to place their arguments in a logical relation with the arguments of other children.

The CoPI reasoning structure should not be used as a form of behaviour control. It is designed to structure arguments about philosophical topics: to place philosophical ideas into a structure that makes the premises and conclusions explicit. And it is designed to provide the dynamic of a dialogue through which the CoPI Chair can build a complex, interleaving set of logically structured arguments.

This example of abuse of the CoPI reasoning structure is serious because it gave the children much more powerful tools than they would otherwise have had, and they used them to humiliate and bully an already disadvantaged little girl.

Not all 'non-educated' misuse of the CoPI reasoning structure leads to this kind of subtle but powerful bullying, but it can. It is a powerful tool and should not be used by those who are not educated and trained in how to use it.

Chapter 8

Implementing CoPI in primary and secondary schools

Chapter 7 described the kind of background knowledge and skills required for a CoPI Chair to work with all ages of participants. This chapter will look at some of the features one can often, but not always, expect to find when beginning to implement CoPI in primary and secondary classrooms. Note that the features I shall outline below concern some of the conditions that a CoPI Chair is likely to meet when beginning to implement CoPI in primary and secondary classrooms. However, the practice of CoPI *changes* many of these conditions.

Many of the features typically encountered when beginning to implement CoPI in primary and secondary classrooms are illustrated two transcripts below: a transcript of the first CoPI session with a class of 8-year-old children; and a transcript of the second CoPI session with a class of 13-year-olds. Comparing these transcripts with the transcript in Chapter 4 also illustrates the difference between classes that are just beginning with the CoPI method and a class that had been practising CoPI for fifty-six hours. While it is necessary to have an example of a class in which a CoPI has been established and in which the children are reasoning philosophically in order to show how a CoPI should 'look', it is also useful to see how classes look at the very beginning, when they are being introduced to the CoPI method.

Primary and secondary classrooms

1   **In both primary and secondary classrooms,** the more frequently one can hold CoPI sessions, the better. For example, the children featured in the transcript in Chapter 4 had CoPI sessions every day. This may not be possible in some schools. However, twice a week is better than once a week, especially since CoPI is so different in nature from other school subjects and activities. The more often one can hold the CoPI sessions, the less is 'lost' in the intervening time.

2   **In both primary and secondary classrooms,** one needs to have a minimum of twenty hours with a class to allow the development of the group to the stage where they are practising CoPI. Ideally a teacher will

work with one class throughout the whole school year. There is no way of foretelling how long this process will take with any particular group. Some classes develop very quickly and some take twenty hours before they are past the stage of wishing to defend their own views and ready to move forward with the dialogue.

For example, the 8-year-old children, whose first CoPI dialogue is transcribed later in the chapter (pp. 136–154), developed very quickly.[1] In their first session, although they mastered the CoPI reasoning structure *immediately*, a lot of time was spent 'teaching' them to wait and to listen. This is typical with primary children; with many primary classes the CoPI Chair will spend weeks 'reminding' the children to raise their hands, speak when called upon and listen. Some primary children will master the reasoning structure very quickly, as this class did, but others will take longer.[2] On the other hand, with the 13-year-olds, whose second CoPI dialogue is also transcribed later in the chapter (pp. 158–170), it took much longer for most of the class to master the CoPI reasoning structure. The length of time any group takes to master the CoPI reasoning structure varies enormously.

3   **In both primary and secondary classrooms,** the ideal number of children to have in a CoPI group is fifteen. One can work with groups of ten to twenty, but it is not possible to have a discussion of any kind in which thirty people *of any age* can have an opportunity to contribute meaningfully. If one has a class of thirty or more children, then one has to split the class into two groups. It can take longer for a CoPI to develop when there are more people involved. On the other hand, if one has a group of fewer than ten, the possibility of eliciting different and contrasting ideas and arguments diminishes – and the CoPI Chair depends upon being able to elicit difference for CoPI to emerge.

For example, there were twenty-three 5-year-olds in the class whose CoPI session is transcribed in Chapter 4.[3] This was a very large number for a CoPI group, especially with 5-year-olds, and not recommended unless unavoidable. One of the results of having such a large group was that the CoPI sessions ran for an hour or more each time to give everyone a chance to speak. A second consequence of the large size of the group was that it took many more weeks for all the children to master the CoPI reasoning structure.

While the core nature of CoPI does not differ depending on the ages of the participants, every group is different and so the way in which each group develops is unique to that particular group. That being said, there are some general features that one initially finds more often in primary school classrooms and some that one initially finds more often in secondary school classrooms.[4]

Primary school classrooms

1   **One feature which one often finds in primary school** classrooms is that (almost always) the younger children find the CoPI reasoning structure of prefacing their contributions with 'I agree with (name of the person) because (reason)' or 'I disagree with (name of the person) because (reason)' much easier to use than do either adults or teenagers. Everything is new for younger children, and so for them CoPI is just another new and interesting thing to do, with some new rules to follow. For example, in the first transcript below, all the children mastered the CoPI reasoning structure quite easily.

2   **The young children tend to internalise the actual *reasoning*** that lies behind the form of words more quickly than teenagers or adults. However, in the early CoPI sessions they often forget to say 'I agree with (name of the person) because (reason)' or 'I disagree with (name of the person) because (reason)', so the teacher should write up the structure on a board, flip chart or screen in large letters, and use it to remind the children to say 'I agree with (name of the person) because (reason)' or 'I disagree with (name of the person) because (reason)' when they are speaking.

   One can see the difference between the young children who have internalised the reasoning but forget to say the words, and teenagers and adults who forget the words. When the young children are reminded to use the words, they have little difficulty in doing so because their thinking is often already logically structured by the reasoning structure (even if they forget to say the words). When teenagers and adults forget to use the words, they often have real difficulty in *rephrasing* their contributions into the reasoning structure because they are not (yet) *thinking* logically. When a participant is thinking logically, it is easy to phrase his or her contribution within the CoPI reasoning structure, but this can be very difficult to do if the participant is not thinking logically. Conversely, the use of the CoPI reasoning structure by a trained Chair induces logical thinking in participants – over time.

3   **Another feature that one often finds in primary school** classrooms is that in classes of younger children, lots of children wish to speak at once. They can become so excited by the ideas that they cannot restrain themselves. So, in the early CoPI sessions, a teacher may find him- or herself spending a lot of time getting the children to speak one at a time and to wait. This can be seen quite clearly in the transcript of the session with 8-year-olds below.

4   **One often finds that young children** have a multitude of questions. A teacher may find that he or she needs to limit the questions to just one from each child who has raised their hand, otherwise much of the allotted time is taken just in writing down the questions. Moreover, the chosen question is intended to be merely the starting point of the dialogue; the

CoPI dialogue is not designed to answer the question, but rather to use it as the beginning of a forward-moving dialogue. When the CoPI is established, the dialogue will quickly move beyond the initial question into new directions and new philosophical territories.

5 **A further feature** commonly found with CoPI groups of young children is that there is very little or no silence. The children nearly always have something more to say, and often do not wish to finish the session. When beginning to implement CoPI with primary schoolchildren, the CoPI Chair has to be very patient. A lot of time will be spent reminding them of the structure, getting them to listen and wait to speak, etc.

6 **Young children often become excited** by the ideas and possibilities that are opening up before them, and their excitement at the ideas manifests itself in physical squirming, wriggling and moving. The CoPI Chair needs to be able to see the difference between physical movement that is caused by the fact that children are excited by ideas and their own thinking, and what would normally be seen as disruptive physical movement. It can be hard for teachers who are accustomed to 'keeping order' to allow the wriggling, squirming and general movement – but one has to try to overlook it *as long as the children are still engaged*, as too much intervention about behaviour can stop the dialogue.

7 **In primary school classes** one almost always finds one or more children who interrupt, either intentionally or not, at least at the beginning. As with the physical wriggling and squirming, the CoPI Chair will try to limit the number of occasions she or he must intervene to manage this behaviour. If the behaviour is distracting other children, she or he will need to intervene, but if the rest of the class can ignore the behaviour and continue with their thinking and their dialogue, then the CoPI Chair should avoid stopping the dialogue for the behaviour of one child. It takes experience to recognise when a child's interruption is distracting the group and when it is not.

For example, in the 5-year-old class featured in Chapter 4, Robert had attention deficit hyperactivity disorder (ADHD). At the beginning of the year he could not control either his physical movements or his speaking. By week 16, when the class was filmed, he could control his speaking and no longer interrupted constantly, although he still had difficulty controlling his physical movements. Like many children with ADHD, he blossomed in CoPI (where the emphasis is on thinking and speaking and not on reading and writing), and became one of the participants with the most original insights and arguments. Similarly, one can see in the transcript that follows that Steven, while extremely engaged in the topics and ideas in the dialogue, has difficulty concentrating and controlling his behaviour in the first session of CoPI. However, even within that first session the other children developed the ability to ignore his interruptions, and he rapidly improved his own control in subsequent CoPI sessions, becoming, like Robert before him, one of the most original contributors to the dialogue.

8 **With groups of primary schoolchildren,** one will usually find laughter from the very first session. This is a feature of CoPI: one finds laughter in *all* established CoPI groups. In some schools and some settings the sound of laughter can be perceived as something contrary to the 'work' that ought to be happening in the classroom. However, laughter in CoPI is the consequence of, first, the joy that children experience in taking part in CoPI, and, second and more importantly, the conceptual conflict that the Chair aims to engineer by the use of the CoPI reasoning structure to juxtapose different philosophies. Note – many jokes also work by inducing conceptual conflict!

The features described above are often found with primary school classes but by no means always, and every class is different. But after time, if not from the first class, one main feature is always present: joy in the eyes of the children! Although there are always exceptions, since 1984 almost every primary school-child who has engaged in CoPI that was implemented by a specially trained CoPI Chair over an extended period of time has loved the experience.

Example of beginning to implement CoPI in primary school

The following is a transcript of the first CoPI session with a group of 8-year-old children. Although new to CoPI, these children had experience with Guided Socratic Discussion (GSD) and Community of Enquiry,[5] both of which use exercises and activities with children as well as discussion. Immediately prior to beginning the CoPI dialogue transcribed here, the children had undertaken two exercises from the GSD series in which they had been using the 'talking stick' to take turns around the circle answering the set questions in the set format from the GSD textbook. While under the discipline of the GSD 'talking stick', the children had no trouble listening and waiting for their turn to speak. But when we moved to the more 'open' dialogue of CoPI, the children found it very difficult in their first session to discipline themselves into waiting and listening.[6] However, they had no difficulties whatsoever in talking and contributing, wishing to do so all the time, and easily mastered the CoPI reasoning structure.

When working with groups of any age, a CoPI Chair will often find a lot of time in the first session taken up with reminding the participants to agree, disagree and give reasons.

Before we look at the dialogue, it is worth noting the kinds of question the children ask (the children's names have been changed to preserve anonymity). Words emphasised by the children are in bold type.

1   Can you go nowhere? (Robyn)
2   Do you **think** that you can go nowhere? (Rick)

3 How do you **know** you are nowhere? (Michael)
4 Can you **forget** where you are? (Polly)
5 Why do people **say** that you are in the middle of nowhere? (Jane)
6 Why is Laura so forgetful? (Steven)
7 Why do grown-ups always change the subject? (Maggie)
8 Have you ever **been** nowhere? (Dave)
9 How do you **know** you are lost? (Tom)
10 Why do grown-ups never understand? (Dan)
11 How do you know if you are dead? (Al)
12 How do you know if you are **dreaming** or you are **not dreaming**? (Chrissie)
13 When you are lost, are you **actually** lost? (Jack)
14 Why do you daydream? (Ellen)

Note:

- Only one child asks a question about a character in the book.
- There are six questions about mental actions or states.
- The sequence of the first three questions indicates that the children are making philosophical distinctions right from the beginning – even as they formulate their questions.

Speaker Dialogue
Mc   Now . . . We are going to do our reading, everyone.

> *Comments*
>
> Most of the children are talking excitedly.

Mc   Sh, sh, sh! Reading one sentence each, remember.
Steven It can only be one word.
Mc   It could, quite right, Steven; you remembered that from last time [reading from the GSD textbook]. It might only be one word. All right? So, Michael, you start and then we'll go to . . .
Child   Dan, Judith, Rick.
Mc   Yes. Dan, can you come in a wee bit, so that you're not behind everyone? And the other thing we have to remember is? Sh! When one person is talking, everyone else is listening.

> *Comments*
>
> Dan is sitting back, outside of the circle. The children are all talking.

Child   Reading strategies!

> *Comments*
>
> 'Reading strategies' comes from other schoolwork.

'*Mum, did you ever not know where you are?*'

    Mum laughed. 'Yes dear. Last week I got the wrong bus and when I got off I didn't know what street I was on. I was lost.'

    Laura screwed up her face. She was thinking, 'It's so hard to say what you mean. Lots of times you say something, and then the grown-ups talk to you like you said something else.'

    '*I don't mean if you're lost, I mean, I mean if you're, um, no-where!*'

    '*That's where I'm going these days, nowhere! Maybe I'll meet you there,*' *Dad said, with a humph sound.*

    Laura thought, 'Sometimes grown-ups are so silly! Dad pretends he's talking to me, but he's looking at Mum.'

    '*Funny child,' Mum said, smiling. 'You can't be nowhere, you've got to be somewhere. If you don't know where you are, you are lost. And what do you do when you're lost? . . .*'

    Laura could hear her Mum's voice but it sounded far away. Sometimes Mum's voice sounded just like the teacher's, and it sort of faded away.

    '*If you can't be nowhere, how can Dad say he's going nowhere?' Laura wondered. 'Mum didn't tell Dad that you can't go nowhere. It doesn't make sense. You can go to school, and when you get there you can be at school. You can go to the shops and when you get there you would be at the shops. You can go somewhere, and Mum says you have to be somewhere.*'

> *Comments*
>
> Children read from Chapter 2 of *Laura and Paul*.[7]

Steven   You can go to the toilet.

> *Comments*
>
> Steven interrupts the reading.

Mc   [To Steven] Wait a minute!

> *Comments*
>
> Children resume reading.

Mc   '*So how is it you can go nowhere, but you can't be nowhere!*'[8]

Mc   Very good! Now everyone hand the sheets back to me.

> **Comments**
>
> The books are collected so that children do not refer back to the book during questions or discussion.

Child   You can't always go to the toilet! [Many children start to move.]

> **Comments**
>
> Many of the children think we have finished because I collected the books.

Mc   No. We're not finished. You're just giving the sheets back. Then sit down. Steven, go back and sit down!

> **Comments**
>
> Lots of children are talking and moving. Steven has moved into the centre of the circle and is starting to push another child.

Child   [To Steven] This is just the end of part one!

> **Comments**
>
> Lots of children are talking with each other in pairs and threes.

Mc   Now, Robyn, I want you and Steven to change places.

> **Comments**
>
> Steven is easily distracted and also distracts others, especially when he is sitting next to his friends. He has to move to sit between two girls, which he does not want to do.

Steven No!

> **Comments**
>
> Robyn gets up and walks across the circle to change places.

Mc   [To Stephen] Yes. Off you go! Off you go! [To the class] OK, now think about that wee story.

> *Comments*
>
> Steven moves to his place across the circle between two girls, but does not sit.

Mc   Sit down there, Steven! [To the class] Now, was there anything . . .

> *Comments*
>
> Steven has sat down, but back outside the circle and all the children laugh. I point to where he should sit – in the circle.

Mc   Steven, in the circle, please.

> *Comments*
>
> Steven is still not sitting in the circle, so this 'request' is said in a stronger, deeper voice. Steven pays attention and moves into the circle.

Child   He won't do *that* any more!

> *Comments*
>
> The children seem surprised at Steven's (eventual) compliance and begin to talk.

Steven   I won't do that any more!
Mc   Now . . . [to the class] Sh! – Was there anything interesting or puzzling in that story that you read, that would make you want to ask a question? And I'm going to write the questions down. Michael?
Michael   About the 'nowhere' part.

> *Comments*
>
> At this point other children try to 'help' Michael to put his idea into a question by suggesting questions for him.

Mc   Can you say that again?

> *Comments*
>
> Michael cannot be heard over the 'helping' of other children.

Michael The nowhere part, 'cause . . .

> *Comments*
>
> Michael is still drowned out by 'help' from other children.

Mc What's your question? [Other children begin to ask questions.] Let's hear your question.

> *Comments*
>
> It is important to write down exactly what each child says in their own words and not in the words of another child or those of the teacher.

Michael You can't be nowhere.
Mc Is that a question?
Children [Other children still offer questions.]
Mc [To Michael] What's your question?
Steven I've got one!

> *Comments*
>
> Six children have their hands raised to ask questions:

Mc [To Michael] OK, I'll come back when you've put it into a question. Robyn?

> *Comments*
>
> Michael has become confused by the 'help' from the other children.

Robyn Can you go nowhere?
Mc [Speaking the words aloud slowly while writing them down] Can you go nowhere?
Children Yes, you can!
No, you can't . . .
If you were . . .

Comments

The whole class begins to discuss Robyn's question in pairs and threes.

Mc   OK, now let's wait until we have our discussion. Next question? Rick?

Rick   Do you **think** that you can go nowhere?

Comments

Rick has made an important philosophical distinction – in distinguishing *what one can think about X* from *whether X is possible*!

Steven   Ooh!

Mc   [Speaking the words aloud slowly while writing them down] Do you **think** that you can go nowhere? From Rick. And OK, Michael?

Comments

Repeating the question serves several purposes: to check that I have the exact words from the child; to give the class a second chance to hear and think about the question; to give the children a focus during the time it takes to write; and to help prevent the talking that erupts after each question.

Michael   How do you **know** you are nowhere?

Comments

Michael has made the second important philosophical distinction with his question. He distinguishes between 'thinking' and 'knowing'.

Mc   [Speaking the words aloud slowly while writing them down] How do you know you are nowhere?

Children   Because you know that . . .

Comments

The children are so interested in the questions that they cannot restrain themselves from talking about them immediately.

Mc   Right. Polly?

Polly   Can you, um, **forget** where you are?

> ### Comments
>
> Polly's question also raises a philosophical topic – about the nature of memory.

Mc   [Speaking the words aloud slowly while writing them down] Can you forget where you are? Uh–huh. Now, sit back a bit, Jane, I can't see the people behind you. Steven?

> ### Comments
>
> Jane is so keen to ask a question, she has come forward in front of other children.

Steven   Em. [Pause.] I know it. [Pause.] Em.
Mc   [To Steven] It's OK; I can come back to you when you are ready. Jane?

> ### Comments
>
> Steven is possibly the most excited child in the class. He has talked about every child's question as soon as it is said, but now forgets his own question.

Jane   I wonder why – why do people **say** that you are in the middle of nowhere?

> ### Comments
>
> Jane's question opens another line of inquiry – about figures of speech versus literal meaning.

Mc   [Speaking the words aloud slowly while writing them down] Why do people say that you are in the middle of nowhere?
Children I've got one.
        I've got one.

> ### Comments
>
> Lots of children have their hands raised with questions to ask.

Steven   Please – I've got one!

Child	Everyone's got one!
Mc	Steven?
Steven	Why is Laura so forgetful? 'Cause last week she couldn't figure out where she was and now she's, she is, um . . .

> **Comments**
>
> Steven is the first child to ask a question about a character in the story.

Child	Nowhere.

> **Comments**
>
> The children wish to help Steven.

Steven	Nowhere!
Mc	OK. [Speaking the words aloud slowly while writing them down] Why is Laura so forgetful? Maggie?
Maggie	Why do grown-ups always change the subject?
Mc	[Speaking the words aloud slowly while writing them down] Why do grown-ups always change the subject?
Steven	I know, I know – because one time I was trying to tell my dad about the five [unclear sound] and . . . 'you know you go . . . downstairs'.

> **Comments**
>
> Steven moves into the centre of the circle and imitates his father's voice, actions and face. The children all laugh. Without saying anything, I gesture to Steven to move back into the circle, and he does so right away.

Mc	I'm writing this so fast; I hope I can read my writing! Now, Dave?
Dave	Have you ever **been** nowhere?
Children	[The children are all answering the question and discussing it with each other in pairs.]
Mc	[Speaking the words aloud slowly while writing them down] Have you ever been nowhere? Sh, sh! Tom?

> **Comments**
>
> Children reduce their talking to whispering.

Tom	How do you **know** you are lost?

Mc   [Speaking the words aloud slowly while writing them down] How do you know you are lost? Dan?

Dan   Why do grown-ups never understand?

Child Ow!

> *Comments*
>
> As Dan talks, three boys begin to push each other.

Mc   Boys!

> *Comments*
>
> The boys stop pushing each other and go back into the circle.

Mc   Steven, get back! Steven! Now I could hardly hear Dan's question.

> *Comments*
>
> As the three boys move back into the circle, Steven comes across the circle to join in. Steven moves back again.

Dan   Why do grown-ups never understand?

Mc   [Speaking the words aloud slowly while writing them down] Why do grown-ups never understand?

Steven That's a good question because my dad never understands bouncing
         . . .

> *Comments*
>
> Steven begins to tell a story about his father, to illustrate how grown-ups never understand. His story is drowned out by other children who begin to copy him – all talking at the same time, beginning to tell their stories about parents who do not understand.

Mc   Sh, sh!

> *Comments*
>
> Within CoPI, one should limit the revelation of personal home lives to only those 'generic' examples that could apply to everyone. CoPI does not discuss specific people.

Mc   OK. [Lots of hands raised.] Just someone who hasn't asked a question already? Al?

Al   How do you know if you are dead?

> **Comments**
>
> Al's question suggests an interesting 'reading' of being nowhere!

Mc   [Speaking the words aloud slowly while writing them down] How do you know if you are dead?
Children [All start laughing and talking at once, loudly, about Al's question.]
Mc   Sh, sh, sh! Chrissie?
Chrissie How do you know if you are **dreaming** or you are **not dreaming**?
Mc   Did everyone hear Chrissie's question?

> **Comments**
>
> Children are still talking, quietly, about Al's question.

Children Yes!
Mc   Steven – did you hear Chrissie's question?

> **Comments**
>
> Steven is lying on the floor in the middle of the circle (possibly playing 'dead').

Steven   How do you know how to bounce a ball?
Mc   No! How do you know if . . .
Steven   You are dreaming?

> **Comments**
>
> In his own way, Steven is trying to concentrate. It is harder for him than for other children.

Mc   . . . or you are not dreaming? [To Chrissie] Is that the question?
Chrissie Yes.
Children [All begin to talk about Chrissie's question in loud voices.]
Mc   [Speaking the words aloud slowly while writing them down] How do you know if you are dreaming or you are not dreaming?
Mc   OK. Sh! Jackie, what is your question?
Jackie   When you are lost, are you **actually** lost?
Child   I don't know, because . . . [Children begin to talk about Maggie's question in loud voices.]

Mc	[Speaking the words aloud slowly while writing them down] When you are lost, are you actually lost?
Tom	If you know you're lost, you're lost because . . .
Child	No, no, because . . .
Mc	OK, Ellen?
Steven	Because if you're in Hawaii . . .

> *Comments*
>
> Steven stands up and mimics a hula dance.

Mc	OK, sh! Back in the circle, Jane! Did you hear Ellen's question? All right, now everyone quiet!

> *Comments*
>
> Jane has moved towards the middle of the circle. Some children begin to copy Steven.

Ellen	Why do you daydream?
Mc	[Speaking the words aloud slowly while writing them down] Why do you daydream?
Steven	Yeah, yeah, because you're thinking about something and then it goes weeee . . .

> *Comments*
>
> Steven demonstrates, with sound effects, how thinking can become daydreaming.

Mc	Sh, everyone! Right. Now, I'm sorry I've run out of room, but I know you'll have lots and lots of questions next time as well. So I'm going to choose one of your questions and we're going to talk about it. But this time, when we're talking, look at the board here. See where it says, 'I agree with . . . because . . .'

> *Comments*
>
> The children's questions were written in a notebook, not on a flip chart.
>
> The CoPI reasoning structure – *'I agree with (name of the person) because (reason)' or 'I disagree with (name of the person) because (reason)'* – is written in large letters on the whiteboard screen for all the children to see throughout the session.

Mc	Steven, you are going to have to leave the class if you don't stop! Stay quiet. Speak when it's your turn. And don't speak otherwise. [To the class] Now, pay attention. Look at the screen. In our discussion we are going to say, 'I agree with . . . (Michael) because . . .' (and give a reason).

Comments

Steven is back in the middle of the circle trying to play with the boys on the other side of the circle. He moves back to his place and stops talking.

Children	'I agree with . . . because'.

Comments

The whole class reads aloud from the screen.

Mc	Or 'I disagree with . . .'
Child	Tom!

Comments

Children 'practise' inserting names.

Mc	'Tom . . . because . . .' and give a reason.
Steven	I agree with myself because Laura *is* forgetful!

Comments

Steven is very keen, so it is good to have an opportunity to praise him, rather than focus on his disruptive behaviour.

Mc	Well, that's very good! That's what we'll do in the discussion, just like that! So you're going to listen to what everyone says.

Maggie, you have to listen! You have to remember what everyone says, so you can think if you agree or disagree, and you have to give a reason. All right? So, you have to listen too! And raise your hand when you have something to say, and I will call on you and everyone else has to listen.

OK, there's so many brilliant questions I'm just going to pick one of them. All right – Michael, this is Michael's question – 'How do you know you are nowhere?' Raise your hand when you have something to say.

> *Comments*
>
> Maggie is talking to her neighbour.

Child   When you have something to say then . . .

Mc   Raise your hand.

Children [All talking] Quite a lot are really interesting! Yes, I know like . . .

Mc   All right – Michael. This is Michael's question – 'How do you know you are nowhere? . . . How do you know you are nowhere?'

Steven   Because you know what that means!

Mc   [To Steven] Now wait a minute – raise your hand when you have something to say. All right? [To everyone] Raise your hand when you have something to say.

Children [All talking together.]

> *Comments*
>
> Children begin to talk about what it means.

Mc   [To everyone] When you have something to say – raise your hand. Right, Jane?

Jane   I don't really think that you *can* know if you're nowhere, 'cause if . . . You're not really nowhere, nowhere *is* somewhere!

> *Comments*
>
> Jane's contribution echoes a classic philosophical argument.

Children [Lots of children begin to talk.]

Child   I know because if you are nowhere . . .

Mc   Wait! Hands up and I'll call on you. Michael, do you agree or disagree with Jane?

> *Comments*
>
> Lots of children begin to talk about Jane's contribution.

[Children with hands up.]

Mc   You say, 'I agree with Jane because . . .' or 'I disagree with Jane . . . because . . .'

Steven   I agree with . . .

Mc   [To Steven] Wait, wait. Give Michael a chance to speak first, because it
           was his question!

Michael   Um . . . [Pause.]

Mc   I'll come back to you, then, if you don't want to say now. Steven?

Steven   I agree with Jane because, em, yeah, because what if you were an
           astronaut and you go to Mars and you say, 'I'm in the middle of
           nowhere.' But you're somewhere! You're on a planet!

Mc   Chrissie?

Chrissie Well, I agree with Jane and Steven because you wouldn't be nowhere.
           Because if you were like an astronaut and you were in space, then you
           are *in* space. And if you're like just in a room and it's dark, then it's just
           dark.

Mc   Tom?

Tom   I agree with Steven . . .

Steven   Yes!

Maggie   [To Steven] Sh!

Tom   . . . because you can't be nowhere, because if you're nowhere – you
           can't be, because you have to at least be somewhere! Because say I was
           in a street I didn't know, I'd still be somewhere! I'd probably be on
           Irvine Street or something.

Mc   Polly?

Polly   I'm getting a bit confused because everyone's saying you're really somewhere, and it's a bit confusing!

Mc   Well, do you agree or disagree with anyone, Polly?

> **Comments**
>
> Unusually for a first CoPI session, this is the first time I have to remind a child to use the reasoning structure.

Polly   Well, I think I agree with everyone because if you are in space, then you are somewhere.

Mc   OK.

Children [Children all talking at the same time.] It'd be like when you go . . .

Mc   Dan?

Dan   I agree – if you were somewhere, that doesn't mean that you *have to be* somewhere, because it could be somewhere undiscovered.

Mc   Did everyone hear what Dan said?

> **Comments**
>
> Rather than ask for quiet before Dan speaks, which can stop the dialogue, I ask the children afterwards if they have heard.

Children Yeah, it could be somewhere . . .

Mc   Say it again, Dan!

Dan   You don't have to be somewhere because it could be somewhere that's not discovered yet.

Children [Children all talking at the same time.]

> **Comments**
>
> Lots of children begin to talk to their neighbour about Dan's contribution.

Steven But it would be . . .

> **Comments**
>
> Steven's voice is louder than everyone else's, and he shouts to the whole group – over all the other children.

Mc   [To Steven] Wait, wait, Steven, put your hand up. Rick?

Rick   I agree with Steven because if you're – and Dan, because he said you're somewhere that's not discovered yet, you still would be somewhere!

Steven   But how would you get there?

> **Comments**
>
> Steven is still desperate to say what he thinks.

Mc   Hand up, Steven, when you have something to say. Dave?
Dave   I agree with Dan, because if it was undiscovered it doesn't *have a name*, so you couldn't – call it something, and – I forgot.

> **Comments**
>
> Dave links the idea of 'place' with having a name.

Children [Lots of children laughing and talking.]
Mc   [To Dave] That's lots already! Jane, do you agree or disagree with someone? Otherwise you're listening, aren't you? OK, Jane?

> **Comments**
>
> Jane is talking to her neighbour.

Jane   I disagree with Dan because if you're somewhere undiscovered it might not have a name but you're still somewhere! And even if you're in a dream, then you're still somewhere – you are *in a dream*! So you can't be nowhere!
Mc   Tom?
Tom   I disagree with Dan because even if it's somewhere undiscovered and it's – you don't know what it's name is, it could be a big red block or something, but it's still somewhere!
Child   But what if it has a . . .
Mc   Hands up. Hands up when you have something. Maggie?
Maggie   You may not think you're somewhere . . .
Mc   You agree or . . .

> **Comments**
>
> The second reminder to agree or disagree.

Maggie   I agree with Tom and Jane; you may not think you're somewhere but you actually are somewhere. Like even if you're daydreaming that you're somewhere, you're thinking and you're in a memory!
Rick   Oh, yes!
Mc   Al? Do you agree or disagree with anybody?

Al   I disagree with Dan because if you were . . . [He stops speaking.]

> *Comments*
>
> Dan darts forward towards Al, then quickly moves back again.

Mc   [To Al] OK, carry on.
Al   . . . because if you were like, even if it wasn't discovered, you'd still be somewhere – you'd be anywhere!
Mc   Anywhere? Rick?
Rick   Well, I agree with . . .
Steven   You disagree with . . .

> *Comments*
>
> Steven tries to interrupt.

Mc   [To Rick] You agree with . . . ?

> *Comments*
>
> Most of the children are no longer being distracted by Steven. So instead of stopping the dialogue to speak to Steven, I encourage the children to ignore his interruptions and continue.

Rick   I agree with Maggie in some ways because you could be somewhere, but it's *called* 'Nowhere'!
Mc   OK.
Steven   I agree with Michael and you!

> *Comments*
>
> Steven jumps in here, but is no longer distracting other children from the dialogue.

Mc   Robyn?
Robyn   I agree with Jane because of, em, when you're sleeping in your room you are in your room! And when you are outside you're outside. And like if you went on holiday that would mean you're on holiday.
Steven   And if you're holding a pen, you're holding a pen.
Children   [Children laugh at Steven holding a pen.]

Mc	Dan? Agree or disagree?
Dan	I agree with Polly. [Pause.]
Mc	Because?
Dan	Because if 'kandera' actually means 'I don't know' in another language, it could be somewhere called something that actually means 'I don't know'.
Mc	Dave?
Dave	I disagree with Dan because he disagreed with himself!
Mc	And how did he disagree with himself?
Dave	Because he was arguing with Steven about Steven disagreeing with himself.
Mc	OK. You can disagree with yourself any time you like! Maggie?
Maggie	I think I agree with Dan this time, now, because what he said there, I actually suddenly started to think to myself, 'That's actually quite true!'
Mc	[To Maggie] Tell me again what Dan said?
Steven	He said something about kangaroos!
Children	[Children laugh.]
Maggie	He said that sometimes words mean something in another language!
Mc	So you could be in a place and the name of that place is 'Nowhere'?

Children	Yes, because . . .
Dan	You could ask someone, 'What's that?', and he said, 'I don't know', but he said, 'kangaroo' because that's what it is in his language.
Child	It could be.
Dan	It could be called 'I don't know' in another language.
Child	It could be called 'I don't know' because that's the name of it!
Children	[Children all talk about places called 'I don't know'.]
Mc	OK, one at a time! Maggie?
Maggie	Well, I'm still agreeing with Dan because I remember that there are some strange names in the world – like take for example New Zealand. It's not exactly new; it was discovered quite a time ago!
Child	That's where the rugby captain's from!
Children	[All the children are talking so it is impossible to hear the rest of Maggie's contribution.]

Mc   Now, did everybody hear what Maggie said?

Steven   Ooh!

Children No.

Mc   Did everyone hear what she said? Did you hear, Tom?

Tom   Yes.

Mc   You're good at listening. Steven, did you hear?

Steven   Um.

Mc   I don't think you hear everything she said. You can sit back a little bit.

> **Comments**
>
> Steven is moving in towards the middle of the circle (again).

Child   I can't remember.

Mc   [To the class] Yes, it's hard to remember. [To Maggie] Because you said so much. But try to say it all again.

Maggie Well, sometimes places in the world have strange names. Like 'New Zealand' isn't actually new; it was discovered quite a time ago. But you can't really just change the name of something, unless it's like that's what you personally call it. Like I personally sometimes give countries nicknames.

Mc   OK, Dan?

Dan   I don't know if I agree or disagree.

Mc   Try to say. If it's different, you just say, 'I disagree'. OK?

Dan   I disagree with Steven because 'America' could mean something different in a different language.

Mc   So actually you are agreeing with Maggie? Rick?

> **Comments**
>
> Lots of older children begin to come to the classroom at this point.

Rick   I agree with Maggie because if you're in America, you could be in New Orleans ... [Too much noise from older children entering the classroom.]

Mc   OK, everybody. We just finish when the time's up. So we're finished when that's the end of our lesson time. So − I think this is the end of our lesson time for today.

       That was absolutely brilliant!

> **Comments**
>
> This is an 'open-plan' classroom where different classes work in the same space.

Secondary school classrooms

Young teenagers

While the Chair has the same aims in implementing CoPI with every group and follows the same procedures with every group irrespective of age, one age range poses special challenges: young teenagers of between roughly 13 and 15 years old. It is useful to know that one *may* meet these challenges; however, not every class of teenagers will present all of the challenges, and some will not present any particular challenge.

It is also good to keep in mind that, while it may take longer to establish a CoPI with young teenagers, it is extremely beneficial to them when one succeeds.

1 **Young teenagers** who have been through the school system[9] have learned which kinds of answer are desired by teachers and encouraged by the curriculum. They have become used to asking 'comprehension' questions about texts, and are also accustomed to giving comprehension answers. For example, the questions raised by the 13-year-olds, whose second CoPI dialogue is transcribed on pp. 158–170, are mainly 'comprehension' questions.

2 **Young teenagers are often struggling** with the changes brought about by hormones that affect their moods and their behaviour. For example, in the session transcribed below, the 13-year-olds are virtually silent at the beginning of the session. Initially their mood is sullen, and it takes a long time before this mood begins to change.

3 **Young teenagers are more easily embarrassed** than either younger children or older teenagers and adults. They are also much more self-conscious than other age groups, and they are more susceptible to peer group pressure at this age. When beginning to engage in CoPI, young teenagers will rarely disagree with anyone, but most especially they will avoid disagreeing with the popular pupils.

4 **Within the UK school system,** 13–15-year-olds are even further affected by the school institutions. Most children move to secondary or high school after seven years of primary school. The children are suddenly faced with a completely different environment:

   a They are no longer 'in the care of' one teacher who knows them well. At the age of 11 or 12 they now have lots of different teachers who do not know their names, or anything about them.

   b Instead of being taught most of their lessons in one room, they have to move around the school to go to different classrooms and many of them get (physically) lost.

5 **While they have been taught** different subjects in primary school, those different subjects were mainly taught by one teacher who would make connections between the different lessons. In secondary school they

suddenly have discrete subjects that can appear to have no connections between them.

6 **After being used to one small building** they are suddenly attending an institution housed in a large building or even a series of buildings.

7 **Many children were accustomed to small primary schools** that hold 80 to 200 pupils, but suddenly they are in a school that will have over 1,000 pupils.

8 **They suddenly find themselves faced with** intimidating older teenagers who may be over 6 feet tall, while they are often barely 5 feet tall.

9 **They are faced with new discipline codes,** often designed for older teenagers, which are strange for them after the gentler rules of primary school.

10 **In primary school they encounter only a small group** of new pupils each year, and (apart from their first year) those pupils are always younger and smaller than they are, so they are not frightened of, or intimated by, them. They have a possibility of getting to know the new pupils in primary school. In secondary school, however, they are suddenly faced with 1,000 new people, all of them older and larger than themselves, and whom they will have little chance to get to know.

Despite the care that staff wish to give, many children are virtually traumatised by the changes in their school life in their first year of secondary school, especially boys. However, the problems, particularly in behaviour, tend to show in their second year of secondary school – and this time often coincides with the hormonal changes that they must cope with.

So, in their second year, at age 12 or 13, pupils *can* be extremely sensitive, difficult, withdrawn and resentful. This is not always the case, but often enough it is.

While both younger children and older teenagers will usually be delighted to talk and to explain their ideas, young teenagers can be the opposite: reluctant to talk or to participate; too embarrassed to say what they think; too conscious of their peer group to venture an original idea – wishing to appear to be the same as everyone else; and too wary of stepping into yet another new activity where they are not sure what is expected of them.

When beginning to implement a CoPI with younger children, the Chair expects to have to encourage the participants to listen and be patient when another child is talking, to take turns, etc. But with young teenagers the Chair might expect that only a few will be willing to talk: many will stare at the ground in silence and be unwilling to be seen to volunteer an idea or argument.

One of the most important aspects of chairing a CoPI with this age group is to refrain from intervening – to allow silence for as long as it takes before one of the pupils volunteers. This can take three minutes or longer with some groups. Eventually the teenagers will understand that the Chair is not going to tell them an answer, or give them a hint, and slowly they will begin to talk.

The features outlined above do not appear in all groups of young teenagers, and vary between different individual pupils and between different classes. Many factors affect how a class of pupils can be transformed into a CoPI, and one of the reasons a teacher will persevere is that the practice of CoPI does overcome many of the features that pose a challenge at first: the young teenagers do begin to lose their self-consciousness as they practise CoPI over time, they begin to talk more, they become less embarrassed, they develop some resistance to peer group pressure and they begin to show enjoyment.

Usually the change comes when they realise that it really *is* their own thinking which is the focus of the dialogues. In the beginning they are often sceptical that this is true; they suspect that there must be answers that the teacher wishes to hear, if only they could figure out what they are. Some of them think it is a 'trick', designed to show them up. But after some time they realise that there is no 'trick', and then they begin to contribute more and more.

Example of beginning to implement CoPI in a secondary school

The following transcript is from the second session of CoPI with a group of 13–14-year-old pupils nearing the end of their second year at secondary school.

Before we look at the dialogue, it is worth noting the kind of questions the young teenagers ask:

1   Why is Michael not a police officer any more? (Peter)
2   What is Michael's problem? (Mike)
3   What happened when Michael was under cover? (John)
4   Why won't he tell the kids? (Rosie)
5   Is the problem to do with the people in the story last week? (Pat)
6   Why did Michael quit the police? (Mike)
7   Is there a problem with drugs in the school? (Kate)

Note:

• In contrast with the younger children, all the questions except one are about a character in the book.
• The questions asked by the young teenagers are very similar to the 'comprehension' questions they are accustomed to asking in other school lessons.
• In contrast with the younger children, there are no overtly 'philosophical' questions.

The following dialogue began extremely slowly. There were long pauses and silence at the beginning of the session. The beginnings of Philosophical Inquiry began to emerge only towards the end of the session. This group of younger teenagers began to become a Community of Philosophical Inquiry only after many weeks of practice.

Speaker *Dialogue*

Mc Now, remember when we're doing this — this is called CoPI, Community of Philosophical Inquiry — and we start with reading, reading aloud. And then I'll ask you if you have any questions — which could be anything. Anything that is either from the story or something it just makes you think about — an idea or a puzzle. Anything at all that comes into your mind. I'll write the questions up on this piece of flip chart paper. And then I'll choose one or two of the questions which we'll discuss. And I'll remind you about the structure we use when we are discussing when we come to that part.

So it's entirely up to you! It's *your* thinking and *your* ideas — that's what the whole process is about. OK?

So, this week, Fergus, could you start reading? One sentence each and we'll go that way round, OK?

Michael Ross was sitting in the pub drinking orange juice. He didn't usually go to the pub on a weekday, and he didn't usually drink orange juice in a pub. But he needed somewhere quiet to think, and the pub was usually empty at 5.00 p.m.

He was just starting a new career as a teacher. He never expected to have such a big problem so soon.

'Michael! Hey — how are you?' He heard a familiar voice call out across the pub. 'I didn't expect to see you in here so soon.' It was the barmaid, Joan.

'So, what's up?' Joan said as she sat down at Michael's table.

'What do you mean?' Michael asked.

'I don't think you would be in here, drinking orange juice in an empty pub, unless something was troubling you,' Joan explained.

Michael sighed. 'I've got a problem and I'm not sure what to do,' he said.

'Well a problem shared is a problem halved,' Joan said.

'I'm not sure if I can even tell you,' Michael said.

'Give it a try,' Joan said. 'Sometimes when you talk about something, you know — put it into words, it helps you understand what it's about.'

Michael smiled ruefully. 'No, you don't understand . . .' He stopped speaking. 'Sorry, I mean I was not clear. I know what the problem is. I just don't know if it would be ethical to tell you.'

Joan gave him a questioning look. 'You know I can keep a confidence,' she said after a pause. 'I mean — remember how we come to know each other!'

'Yes,' Michael replied. 'But that was different. I was under cover, and the rules were written down. With this situation I think I know what the rules are, but that is actually part of the problem.'

Joan glanced around the bar. There was no one else in; the lunchtime patrons had gone. Though soon people would start coming in after work. She thought for a minute. 'Do they know, at the school, that you used to be a police officer?' she asked.

'The Head Teacher knows, of course, and the senior staff. But I don't tell the kids. A lot of these kids think of the police as the enemy. They don't understand that we are here to . . .' Michael stopped and laughed. 'I mean the police,' he said. 'They don't understand that the police are there to protect them. Some of them even see drug dealers as kind of heroes: making money, being tough, et cetera. They don't see the dealers as the parasites they are – actually slowly killing their victims.'

Joan wiped her hands on the cloth she was holding.

> **Comments**
>
> Pupils read in turn, aloud. Some pupils read very slowly. Some appear to have difficulties reading. Because some of the pupils are very slow readers, the reading takes almost fifteen minutes. When the reading is finished, I read over the text to the pupils.

Mc	OK. Anyone got any questions? Anything that's puzzling or interesting? Just anything that comes into your mind. Raise your hand and I'll write the questions up. Peter?
Peter	Why is Michael not a police officer any more?

> **Comments**
>
> The first question is raised quite quickly.

Mc	[Writes Peter's question on the flip chart.] Mike?
Mike	What is Michael's problem?

> **Comments**
>
> The second question is raised immediately after the first.

Mc	[Writes Mike's question on the flip chart.]

> **Comments**
>
> After the second question, there are *two minutes* of silence while pupils look at the floor.

Mc	Cara, do you have a question?

> **Comments**
>
> Cara is whispering to Paul. Cara has no question. Thirty seconds of silence follow.

Mc OK, let me collect the books.

> **Comments**
>
> Collecting all the books takes thirty seconds. Note: I should have collected the books or asked the pupils to put them on the floor before they began to ask questions. Now the pupils are all looking down at the books (not reading).

Mc [To a boy] What's your name?
Andrew Andrew.
Mc Andrew, could you put your badge on? Thank you.

> **Comments**
>
> Everyone should wear his or her name badge during CoPI sessions. Wearing a name badge is important in CoPI because it can be hard to remember a person's name when participants are thinking about how to articulate their ideas.

Mc Any other questions? Anything – it doesn't have to be directly from the story, it could be just something it makes you think about – an idea or a topic.

> **Comments**
>
> *Three minutes* of silence follow this request for questions. Pupils do not move or speak. I sit back out of the circle and wait in silence. Then a hand is raised.

Mc OK?
John What happened when Michael was under cover?
Mc [Writes John's question on the flip chart.] Rosie?
Rosie Why won't he tell the kids?

> **Comments**
>
> Rosie's question comes immediately after John's question.

Mc	[Writes Rosie's question on the flip chart.] Pat?
Pat	Is the problem to do with the people in the [inaudible] last week?

> **Comments**
>
> Pat's question comes immediately after Rosie's question.

Mc	Did you say 'with the people in the school last week'?
Pat	With the people in the story last week.[10]
Mc	With the people in the story last week. [Writes Pat's question on the flip chart.] Mike?
Mike	Why did Michael quit the police?
Mc	[Writes Mike's second question on the flip chart.] Kate?
Kate	Is there a problem with drugs in the school?

> **Comments**
>
> Some pupils begin to talk quietly to each other about Kate's question.

Mc	[Writes Kate's question on the flip chart.] OK. [Reading from flip chart] Why is Michael not a police officer any more? From Peter.

What is Michael's problem? From Mike.

What happened when Michael was under cover? From John.

Why won't he tell the kids? From Rosie.

Is the problem to do with the people in the story last week? From Pat.

Why did Michael quit the police? From Mike.

Is there a problem with drugs in the school? From Kate.

Now, remember when we're having our discussion you're going to say, 'I agree with so and so because . . .' and give a reason, or 'I disagree with so and so because . . .' and give a reason.

When we're doing this CoPI kind of discussion, if you have something which is just different from what someone else has said, that's when you say, 'I disagree with so and so'. It doesn't mean you don't like them or anything, it's just a shorthand way of saying, 'I've got something to say that's different'. OK?

Yes, Paul?

Paul	I've got to go to the toilet.
Mc	OK – two minutes!

> **Comments**
>
> Paul leaves the room.

Mc	So – you're going to say, 'I agree with so and so because . . .' and give a reason. And when you've something different to say, you're going to say, 'I disagree with so and so because . . .'
	So, let's look at question four: Why won't he tell the kids? From Rosie . . . Peter?
Peter	I think it's because like, the kids think the police is the enemy and all that.

> **Comments**
>
> Peter has deduced this from the text; he is talking about the character.

Mc	Rosie, do you agree or disagree with Peter?
Rosie	I think I disagree because it's not about being a policeman but about being a teacher, and he wants them to like him – 'cause it's harder to teach them if they don't like him.

> **Comments**
>
> Rosie's voice is very quiet. Her contribution moves further away from the text than Peter's: attributing motivation to the character, which is not stated in the text.

Mc	It's harder for him to teach them if they don't like him?

> **Comments**
>
> Repeating her point to make sure it is heard correctly.

Rosie	Uh-huh.
Mc	Anyone agree or disagree with that?
Pat	I agree with Rosie because if they don't like him, they won't tell him things because they might not trust him!

> **Comments**
>
> Pat's voice is very quiet. She develops the explanation given by Rosie by attributing emotions to characters in the story.

Mc	They might not trust him? Because?

> **Comments**
>
> Checking that this is what Pat said.

Pat	Because he was a policeman.
Mc	Anyone agree or disagree with that? Or with what Rosie said – that it would be difficult to teach if the pupils didn't like him? Jane – you agree with that?
Jane	[Too soft to hear]

> **Comments**
>
> Paul comes back into the room.

Mc	Now I'm going to ask everyone to speak as loud as you can . . . It's important that everyone hears what you say. Can you say that again?
Jane	. . . won't behave well for him.
Mc	[To Jane] If they don't like the teacher they won't behave well for him?

> **Comments**
>
> Checking that this is what Jane said.

Jane	Yes.
Mc	Paul?
Paul	I agree with that.
Mc	Because?
Paul	They'll no learn anything!
Mc	The reason for behaving badly is because they don't like the teacher?

> **Comments**
>
> I intervene to clarify the reasoning.

Paul	Not always.
Mc	Cara, what do you think? Do you think that's a good reason for behaving badly – whether you like or don't like the teacher? [Silence for thirty seconds.]

> **Comments**
>
> Cara is whispering to Mike. I ask her to contribute (1) to remind her to listen, and (2) to encourage her to state her view aloud to everyone, not just to her neighbour.

Mc	Martine – what do you think?

Martine I agree with Rosie because some people just act up if they don't like the teacher.

> **Comments**
>
> Martine's contribution is moving the discussion away from the story to a more general point about school behaviour.

Mc So you agree that that's the reason that they misbehave?
Martine Uh-huh.
Mc Do you think that's a good reason?

> **Comments**
>
> I intervene to encourage the pupils to think at a meta-level.

Martine No.
Mc Because?
Martine Because it's not good for the other kids that are in that class.

> **Comments**
>
> Martine gives an ethical argument – harming other people in the class by misbehaving 'outweighs' the justification of 'not liking the teacher'.

Mc Anyone agree or disagree with that?
Cara I agree with Martine, 'cause if they're acting like that and then . . . the teacher doesn't like them. And then . . .

> **Comments**
>
> Cara's voice is so quiet that her point cannot be heard.

Mc And what happens if the teacher doesn't like them?
Cara Well, that's when you make them not like you, and then . . .

> **Comments**
>
> Cara cannot be heard.

Mc And then? Does it matter if they don't like you?
Cara It just makes it harder in the class.
Mc Peter? You agree or disagree with anything that's been said?

Peter   I agree with Martine that they're basically just a troublemaker when they don't like the teachers.

> *Comments*
>
> Peter appears to agree with Martine that 'acting up' in class is not excused by 'not liking the teacher'.

Mc   [To the whole class] So, if they don't like the teacher, then they behave badly; and if they behave badly, then the teacher doesn't like them; and if the teacher doesn't like them, then they don't like the teacher; and if they don't like the teacher, then they behave badly; and so it keeps going. Is that it?

> *Comments*
>
> This summary produces laughter from the class, who begin to look at each other and not the floor for the first time.

Andrew   Yeah! If you shut down mentally, then you can't learn! Like if a teacher gives you in trouble for no reason, and thinks you're doing something when you aren't actually, then . . . [Andrew is interrupted by the classroom door opening.]

> *Comments*
>
> Here, Andrew's contribution supplies a different perspective on Peter's point that not liking the teacher is equivalent to being a troublemaker.

Paul   I don't know if I'm agreeing or disagreeing, but it's like if you misbehave – like I'm not perfect, I'm not perfect, right? [Pupils laugh at Paul saying he is not perfect.] Well, I'm not! But if I get into trouble and then she sends me out, then really it's kind of her own fault because if she sends me out, then I miss my work.
    And then another one, if I get in trouble with some . . . then one day I might get sent out of what I want to do! Then some other people might miss out because of me.

Mc   So, do you agree . . .

Paul   Some of them just don't like me because of my bad reputation!

Mc   You know what, Paul, we are not talking about *you* here. We're talking about anybody, anybody. OK? Andrew?

Comments

This intervention is intended to move the dialogue away from discussing any particular person to the general issue.

Andrew I agree with Paul because it could be about anybody. Because she doesn't know anyone's name! Like if something that happened last week, which was actually the person on the other side of the classroom and she didn't even know your name, and she expects you to answer, to answer to it, when she can't even say your name!

Comments

Andrew has taken my explanation (that our discussion is about 'anybody') to mean that teachers don't distinguish between pupils – that is, for the teacher, a pupil could be 'anybody'. His contribution also introduces the philosophical domain of 'personhood'.

Paul Well, it would . . .

Mc Wait a minute, Paul, put your hand up when you've got something to say. Let's look at that question, just in general. We're not talking about anyone in particular, just the general question: 'Is it important for a teacher to know everyone's names?' Ann?

Comments

This is the second intervention intended to move the dialogue away from discussing any particular person to the general issue, using the pupils' ideas to make a space for 'personhood' to emerge.

Ann It is important because if they don't know your name, you shouldn't be in their class. If you are in their class, they should know you!

John I agree with Ann.

Mc If you're in their class, they should know your name?

John Uh-huh.

Mc Jane?

Jane I agree with everyone that they should know your name, but at the start they can't. We know their name but they can't know ours!

Mc You'll have to explain to me, as I don't know. How many classes does a teacher teach in school?

Peter A teacher teaches everybody.

Mc So that would be?

Pupil Loads!

Mc	How many names would they have to learn?
John	Thousands!
Mc	Mike?
Mike	If they don't know your name, you can get really frustrated. If they don't know your name, then they can't know if you're the same as anyone else in your class.

> **Comments**
>
> Mike makes the same point (in different words) as Andrew did earlier: that if the teacher does not know the pupils' names, he or she cannot differentiate between them.

Paul	It's kind of ignorant if you don't call someone by their real name!
Mc	Can you explain what you mean by 'ignorant'?

> **Comments**
>
> 'Ignorant' has two different meanings: (1) the standard meaning, 'lacking in knowledge'; and (2) the local meaning, 'rude'.

Paul	If they call you something else . . . it's offensive!
Andrew	If they've had you for almost a year, they should at least remember the first letter of your name. Instead you often go in their class and they ask you about something, but they ask another person, then you think that it was you that they asked but it wasn't.

> **Comments**
>
> Andrew reiterates his argument about differentiation.

Mc	What's the connection between learning and the teacher knowing you, knowing your name? Ann?

> **Comments**
>
> The third intervention, using the pupils' ideas, intended to make a space for a philosophical topic that underlies much of the discussion: 'personhood'.

Ann	Well, if they're going to get you into trouble and then they don't know that it's not you – you're not doing it.

> *Comments*
>
> Ann explains that lack of differentiation can have unethical results.

Mc   Joanne?

Joanne Like if you were in the supermarket and they put the wrong label on something. It could . . .

Mc   It could . . .? [Thirty seconds of silence as pupils think about the wrong label.] Supposing you just gave everyone numbers? Everyone has their own number and everyone knows the numbers and it would be absolutely clear who was to do what! [All the pupils laugh.] Mike?

> *Comments*
>
> I intervene to give a kind of 'counter-example' of differentiation that does not involve using names, because the pupils' contributions suggest that more than differentiation is at issue here.
>
> The pupils' laughter may be connected to the conceptual conflict that this counter-example is intended to produce.

Mike   [Laughing] That would be OK, as long as you weren't number ten.

Mc   Amanda?

Amanda It's easier to get mixed up with numbers.

Mc   It's easier to get mixed up with numbers? Jane?

Jane   I agree – it's easier to remember a name than remembering a number.

Mc   Andrew?

Andrew If *you* can remember all your teachers from primary school, and then you can remember them all up to high school, then *they* should at least remember *your* name for one year!

> *Comments*
>
> Andrew is still angry about teachers not knowing his name. He sits slumped in his chair, looking down (making himself literally as small and metaphorically as invisible as possible). He does not usually speak.

Mc   Jane?

Jane   See, if you had a number instead of your name, then it would just be the same. The number would be your name!

Comments

Jane makes an important philosophical point: that it is not the word or symbol itself, but the use or function of the word or symbol that determines its status as a name.

Mc   Martine?

Martine I disagree with Jane because the number is not the same as your name. Because you were given your name for a reason, and it's taking away your identity if you're just called a number!

Comments

Martine's argument is actually consistent with Jane's. However, she also makes a further important philosophical point (in the domain of 'personhood'): that a person's name is part of their identity.

Mc   Rosie?

Rosie   I agree with Martine.

Mc   Can you say why, in your own words?

Rosie   Because your parents gave you your name for a reason! Like if it's your auntie's name.

Comments

Rosie's argument, like Martine's, shows that the issue of teachers knowing pupils' names is not just about differentiation. Personal identity concerns more than differentiation.

Paul   It's not . . .

Mc   Paul, can you put it into 'agree and disagree'? If it's different from what Martine or Rosie said, you say, 'I disagree'; if it's similar, you say, 'I agree'.

Paul   I disagree because there's people with the same names, like there's two Pauls and three Peters, so it would be easier if everyone had a different number.

Comments

Paul is arguing about differentiation rather than disagreeing with Martine's point about identity.

Amanda I disagree with Paul because then we would be like sheep with numbers!

> *Comments*
>
> Amanda brings the dialogue back to the philosophy of naming persons.

Paul   Oh yeah! Sheep have got numbers on them!

> *Comments*
>
> From his intonation and the expression on his face, Paul (suddenly) appears to realise that the issue is not differentiation, but something else.

Pat   Is that the bell?
Mc   OK, we just stop when the time is up. Well done, everybody . . .

> *Comments*
>
> The dialogue has only just begun to become philosophical when the time is up. (However, these topics are not lost; they will come back in later dialogues.)

Older teenagers

As was said earlier, many of the difficulties that one can face when implementing CoPI with younger teenagers result from a combination of the effects of the onset of hormonal changes and the effects of the institution in which they find themselves. When the teenagers become more settled, both biologically and sociologically, many of these difficulties dissipate.

Groups of older teenagers, from approximately 15 to 18 years old, are more similar to groups of adults than to groups of younger teenagers.

1   **They are still very aware** of how they appear to others and concerned about their image, but less acutely embarrassed. They are more likely to talk than younger teenagers and they are likely to be more 'long-winded' in their contributions.

2   **Many (but not all) older teenagers** have developed some resistance to the intense peer group pressure that affects younger teenagers. This is seen particularly in boys, who are more likely to volunteer contributions than the younger teenage boys.

3   **Some older teenagers find** the CoPI reasoning structure quite difficult, as they have had many years of schooling in different forms of discussion

and the CoPI form can seem alien to them. However, once they become used to this new form of dialogue, they are usually as interested in the philosophical topics as the younger primary schoolchildren.

4   **Most, though not all, older teenagers** are more self-disciplined than young children, and have learned how to listen and to wait.

5   **Unlike primary schoolchildren,** older teenagers quite often ask only a small number of questions – though this does vary and also changes over time.

6   **For reasons concerning curriculum** and timetabling, older teenagers are more likely to be 'volunteers', which has a positive effect upon the ease with which a teacher can implement CoPI.

The good news

The longer a primary or secondary class practises CoPI, the more balanced the groups become. In primary classes:

- Children become skilled listeners.
- They learn patience.
- They improve their concentration.
- They improve their memory.
- They become more articulate.
- The children who initially talk more begin to listen more.
- The children who initially do not talk start to contribute.

In scondary classes:

- Teenagers become braver.
- They develop a disposition to seek the truth.
- They contribute their own ideas.
- They develop respect for others.
- They learn how to relate to people they do not like.
- They laugh more.
- They develop a real community in which everyone is equal.

Further benefits that engaging in CoPI brings to both primary and secondary pupils will be described in the next chapter.

Chapter 9

CoPI, citizenship, moral virtue and academic performance with primary and secondary schoolchildren

Why invest the time and money required for training to implement CoPI in the primary and secondary classroom? This is a question often asked by education administrators and by individual teachers. There are two main types of answer:

1   for the benefit of each and every child;
2   for the benefit of society.

For the benefit of each and every child

Engaging in CoPI transforms the life chances of every child. When one shows films of children aged 5 or 6 philosophising in a CoPI,[1] the audience cannot see the work being done by the CoPI Chair. The initial reactions of most people include:

•   amazement that such young children will sit for such a long time and talk;
•   delight at the patience of most of the children waiting to speak;
•   smiles at the evident joy of the children, seen in their eyes and their faces.

Many adults do not initially recognise or understand the children's philosophical reasoning, and regard the children's contributions as 'sweet' but not examples of serious thinking. For example, when I first showed the video of the children's CoPI transcribed in Chapter 4, one of the teachers watching commented, 'That little boy is just being silly!' The teacher's comment referred to David's contributions in the following part of the dialogue. The text (*Elfie*, referred to in earlier chapters), which the children had read forty-five minutes earlier, says, '"I think all the time. I even think when I sleep. I don't have fancy dreams. I just think when I'm asleep about the same things I think about when I'm awake."' The text *suggests* that the character, Elfie, does not dream but rather just thinks in her sleep. But David asked the question: 'How could she have dreams and think at the same time?' When he is asked to explain his question, David makes the correct logical analysis that saying, 'I don't have fancy dreams' is not the same as saying, 'I don't have dreams'. The property of 'fancy' being applied to dreams logically limits the subject of the sentence to 'fancy dreams' and not 'dreams'. David correctly deduces that the combination of these three sentences:

1   I even think when I sleep
2   I don't have fancy dreams
3   I just think when I'm asleep about the same things I think about when I'm awake

does *not* exclude the possibility of both thinking and dreaming while one is asleep – as long as the dreams are not 'fancy' dreams, but some other kinds of dream. David is interested in that possibility: that one can think and dream at the same time when one is asleep.

David   Well, what I think was interesting about it is, um, even though it didn't say that, oh, she, um, Elfie thought and dreamed at the same   time – it's just that she said, 'I don't have fancy dreams', but she never said that she didn't have dreams. But she also said that she thought. So that's why I said that.

Joy proposes a solution to the puzzle of how one can think and dream at the same time: that it might be possible if one was thinking within a dream – a kind of 'dream-thinking':

Joy   I agree with Fern and Maggie because like sometimes you can think and dream, and sometimes you can't. Because like when you're dreaming – like you can if you're dreaming and then you're thinking in your dream. Sometimes it's hard to think and dream at the same time, especially if you're thinking about something else and you're dreaming about something else. Because then you might get mixed up. When you sleep you can also – when you are asleep you can also think and dream too.

Mark has a different solution – that dreaming is one's imagination thinking:

Mark   Well, um, I agree with Fern because, um, you can think and dream sometimes. Because when you're not thinking and you're dreaming, your imagination is thinking. So your imagination is thinking some-times but your brain is thinking with it. So I agree with Fern.

Amazingly, David, then a 5-year-old child, correctly recognises that the solution put forward by Mark is not logically consistent with the solutions put forward by other children. Moreover, his intention is also remarkable. He recognises what were in fact philosophical and logical problems with the contributions from Joy, Mark and the other children, and he wanted to 'rescue' the substance of their contributions.

David: I agree with Mark and I disagree with Mark. Because you control your imagination. So, if you were dreaming – some people say that your dreams are in your imagination, and some people say you don't – But if your dreams are in your imagination, then how could you think in your imagination while you're dreaming in your imagination? But you could think in your dream while you're in your imagination!

Far from being silly, David's contributions here constitute an example of truly stunning logical and philosophical analysis. But they also demonstrate several other features that are remarkable in a 5-year-old. David's action is an example of *empathetic thinking*: caring about others and about the thinking of others. It also demonstrates his desire to credit other children – a *selflessness* that is unusual in 5-year-olds. Within the dialogue many children demonstrate this consideration for others and the selfless crediting of other children's contributions – even to the extent of crediting other children with a better formulation of their contributions than was given by the original authors.[2]

Watching the video, most adults think that the role of the 'teacher' (the CoPI Chair) is easy. The audience often thinks that the CoPI Chair in the video just lets the children speak in turn and that is all there is to it! When the audience begins to learn what is actually involved in chairing a CoPI, many audience members are dismayed. They love what they see, they would like to have CoPI for their own children, but when they discover what is involved in chairing a CoPI,[3] they wish for an easier way.[4] Sometimes teachers will try to copy what they *think* they see in the films. However, they cannot see what the CoPI Chair is actually doing. To return to an analogy used earlier in the book, it is rather like watching a conductor conducting an orchestra: to someone who does not know what the conductor is doing, it can look as though she or he is just 'keeping time' for the players. But, unlike in a CoPI session, the orchestra is playing a score that an observer or listener could read, whereas in the CoPI session there is no 'score': the CoPI 'players' under the guidance of the CoPI Chair make 'philosophical music', following a structure but improvising on the themes. There is no way to know ahead of time what those themes will be.

The background knowledge of philosophy and logic and the use of this knowledge in chairing the CoPI[5] are not visible to an audience that is unaware of the nature of CoPI. The criteria that are being used by the CoPI Chair to select the children to speak in a specific order are not visible at all. The instant philosophical analysis that underlies the choices and interventions made by the CoPI Chair is not visible. And finally, because there is so much to observe in the children's behaviour and thinking, most people cannot see all the different aspects of these in one viewing, or even in one reading of the transcript. So, a lot of explanation is required to make visible what is actually happening; and even more is required to demonstrate the *results* of what is actually happening.

Why, then, go to all the trouble of learning philosophy and logic in order to learn how to implement CoPI, and then take the specialist training in the CoPI method?

First, because engaging in a CoPI over an extended period of time *transforms individual participants* and improves their life chances. It is not that the participants learn skills that they can use in other settings; rather, they themselves are changed, and everything they then do is different from what it would have been had they not been part of a CoPI. This is why children behave differently in the playground, at home and in the community – not just in the classroom.[6]

For example, in 1994–1995 a CoPI community project called 'Philosophy Is Fun' ran in a deprived area of Glasgow. The aim of the funders of the project, an organisation called 'Safe Castlemilk', was to reduce aggression and violence in Castlemilk. Other initiatives had failed, and so (almost as a last resort, with nothing to lose) the funders and the community took the 'risk' of trying a project that would develop a Community of Philosophical Inquiry across the Catholic–Protestant divide – a major source of conflict. Four groups of children and three groups of adults were created.[7] In these groups, children and adults from the two sectarian and gang sectors in the community were brought together to engage in a CoPI. For most of the adult and children participants this was the first time they had talked to members of the opposite sectarian grouping. The results were spectacular! So spectacular that they put philosophy into a main news programme for the first time in the United Kingdom[8] – moreover, as an item about the reduction in violence rather than an education item.[9] As the children and adults developed their philosophical reasoning skills and became members of a community with people from 'the other side', their behaviour changed. Violence decreased and, equally important, the hold that the respective gang leaders had over the communities was weakened.

The results of the 'Philosophy Is Fun' project demonstrated the benefits both for individual children and for the community or society.[10] Individual children improved their performance in school, their behaviour changed, and they gained the opportunity to get to know a whole segment of their community they would not otherwise have known. Society benefited directly from the reduction in violence and the lessening of the gang leaders' power, as well as from the presence in the community of people who now had the skills and disposition to become active citizens and make further changes in their community.

There were many other effects from this and other community and school projects, resulting from the way in which engaging in CoPI transforms individuals (both children and adults).[11] For example:

1   CoPI enables participants to examine:
     a   their own thinking;
     b   their own philosophical assumptions;
     c   the philosophical assumptions that underlie the thinking of others.

Thus, CoPI empowers them to understand themselves and other people, and makes it easier for participants to change their minds about ideas, theories and opinions – both their own and those of other people.

2   CoPI enables participants to examine:
   a   the philosophical assumptions that underlie science;
   b   the philosophical assumptions that underlie art;
   c   the philosophical assumptions that underlie maths;
   d   the philosophical assumptions that underlie the social sciences;
   e   the philosophical assumptions that underlie language.

Thus, CoPI improves their performance in science, art, maths, languages and the social sciences. It allows children to understand these academic subjects, and to make connections between them.

3   CoPI enables participants to examine:
   a   the philosophical assumptions that underlie politics;
   b   the philosophical assumptions that underlie politicians' speech;
   c   the philosophical assumptions that underlie advertisements.

Thus, CoPI gives children a defence against manipulation by politicians and advertisers, and helps them to understand the nature of politics and political systems.

4   Guiding participants in their use of CoPI reasoning structure develops *cognitive* skills by:
   a   developing their ability to recognise inconsistency and contradiction;
   b   developing their abilities in analogical reasoning;
   c   developing their abilities in hypothetical reasoning;
   d   developing their understanding of set theory;
   e   developing their understanding of whole–part distinctions;
   f   developing their ability to recognise fallacious arguments.

And finally:

5   Guiding participants in their use of CoPI reasoning structure develops *moral virtues* in participants by:
   a   developing the participants' tolerance for people who have different views from their own;
   b   leading participants to enjoy difference instead of feeling threatened by difference and by people who are different;
   c   developing the participants' desire to search for truth and to reject falsehood;

d   developing a disposition in participants to be honest – as participants increasingly wish to find the truth, they also recognise the advantages in truth-telling to this end;

e   developing a disposition in participants to be brave – as participants increasingly wish to hear different and contradictory arguments that make the dialogue more interesting and more enjoyable, they develop the courage to put forward potentially contentious arguments.

Why do CoPI with children? Because these things, when combined through the practice of CoPI, transform the life chances of individual children.

For the benefit of society

CoPI develops citizens who are both active and reasonable.[12] In order for a democracy to work, it is not enough merely to allow a vote for everyone. An effective democracy requires effective citizens, people who are active in the organisation of their own lives and in their society. But to be active and effective as a citizen, a person must be able to think critically, to weigh different alternatives, to evaluate reasons given for particular decisions or policies that affect the community.

To be an active and effective citizen requires both the disposition to reason and the skills required for effective reasoning. So, for example, the person who wishes to be effective in the workplace needs to be able to evaluate written instructions, manifests or reports, some of which may be ambiguous or unclear. To be an effective citizen, a person needs to be able to make reasoned judgements concerning the views of others, and to modify his or her own view if necessary. This requires comprehension skills, which in turn require skills in reasoning such as:

• recognising and evaluating analogies;
• identifying assumptions;
• recognising fallacies;
• being careful about jumping to conclusions;
• recognising part–whole relationships;
• always being aware of alternatives;
• seeking out consistencies and inconsistencies in every sphere of life.

Within a CoPI, children demonstrate both the disposition to reason and skills in reasoning – exactly the kind of disposition and skills that are required for a person to be an effective citizen.

Proficiency in reasoning, as in any skill, requires practice. Yet not many people actually learn or practise reasoning. There may be many factors that impede the development of reasoning skills, but one of the biggest obstacles to encouraging the development of such skills is the belief that not everyone is capable of reasoning or higher-order thinking. In particular, it is assumed by many that children are not capable of abstract thought.

Our notion of childhood has many roots, but a recurrent feature in the literature of childhood involves a notion of children as non-rational or pre-rational beings. This feature traditionally relies on two strong lines of support. One line, described more fully in Chapter 3, stems from developmental cognitive psychology, particularly stage in maturation theories which claim that the cognitive capacity for rationality is not present until a person has matured to a certain age, usually around 10 or 11. Hence, it is claimed, young children can think neither abstractly (i.e. using abstract concepts) nor logically. The other, often found in philosophical accounts, is a definition of rationality that relies on criteria drawn from formal logic. This definition, if broadly applied, would also exclude many adults from the category of 'rational being'.[13]

Since theories of childhood affect and sometimes even determine the activities in which children engage, the result has been that very few children ever have the chance to practise and become proficient in abstract reasoning using formal operations.

Reasoning must develop in situations and circumstances that are 'natural' environments for reasoning, in the way in which water is the natural environment for swimming. A situation in which reasoning is called for – rather than, for example, obeying orders, or making arbitrary decisions, or memorising information – would be such a 'natural' environment. Such a 'natural environment' for reasoning would be one that *calls for* reasoning, in the sense that swimming is called for when one is in deep water – one in which other forms of thought and behaviour would not be successful. And this is what the CoPI does: it *requires* participants to engage in philosophical reasoning, because other forms of participation are not successful within a CoPI.

While other environments are appropriate places for reasoned argumentation, one important feature of CoPI is that kinds of thinking and behaviour that are not reasonable cannot succeed within a CoPI dialogue. The CoPI dialogue requires members of the community to listen to the ideas and arguments of others, to make explicit the relationships between viewpoints or arguments being presented, to present arguments and counter-arguments, to give reasons and to evaluate the reasons given.

It is through engaging in the CoPI dialogue that participants come to discover for themselves that certain kinds of thinking and interaction do not further the dialogue. So, for example, the group comes to know by experience that aggressive argumentation in forensic style does not and cannot succeed. It does not take long for the group and its individual members to realise that the inquiry has 'gone cold': what was an interesting and even enthralling dialogue has died. It just does not work, so it gets dropped. Similarly, in the initial stages, members of a group who are uncomfortable with disagreement often try to nullify differences by redescribing the issues so as to present a consensus. Again the group's experience of what happens to the inquiry leads to this style of interaction being dropped. Without different ideas and theories there is no CoPI; the dialogue diminishes into a discussion or an exchange of similar opinions – enjoyable in some social circumstances, but not the intellectually fascinating, challenging and liberating[14] dialogue that participants have experienced, and wish to continue.

Because issues about which there are no definitive answers comprise the content of philosophical discussion or argumentation, there is no other successful way to proceed to engage in CoPI. There are no authorities on philosophical questions. While there are famous philosophers (alive and dead) whose views are influential, the jury is never in on philosophical questions. This is why other ways of proceeding – such as obeying orders, making arbitrary decisions, memorising information, following algorithms, etc. – cannot be successful.

There are other kinds of environment that require this kind of reasoning. For example, a theoretical physicist at the forefront of the field is likely to be in an environment in which obeying orders, making arbitrary decisions, etc. would be entirely unsuccessful procedures. The answers are not known; there are no authorities or precedents. I would note here that a great deal of the work undertaken by scientific researchers and investigators does not require such procedures; but theorists at the conceptual edge need to be able to generate and reason about theories. Their environment requires innovative, rational thinking and inquiry.

However, the conceptual inquiry in theoretical physics requires knowledge of a specialised kind, whereas very little knowledge is needed in order to engage in Philosophical Inquiry – for example, into the nature of reality, or truth, or justice, or beauty. These are basic human issues and anyone, no matter how little experience they may have, can think about them, reason about them and engage in dialogue on them. Experience and knowledge about the world can provide the inquirer with illuminating examples to bolster his or her arguments, and to enrich the inquirer's investigations, but the basic questions are the same for a 6-year-old child as they are for a 60-year-old philosopher. Moreover, within a CoPI, the way in which the reasoning structure uses logic to build the dialogue and the way in which the contributions from different participants are 'placed' next to each other by the CoPI Chair lead to new ideas and theories being generated within the dialogue.

New knowledge or insights can be made possible by the combination of different people. To illustrate this point, imagine the following scenario:

> The Bishop and the Duke are at a party. First the Bishop and then the Duke confide in the Hostess. The Bishop tells the Hostess that the very first confession he heard as a young priest was from a man who confessed to a murder. Later the Duke tells the Hostess that thirty years ago the late Prince had been very troubled and did not wish to go to his regular

confessor. So, the Prince's confessor had advised him to make his confession instead to a young priest who was new in the diocese – and this was the young priest's first confession. That young priest is now the Bishop! So, the Prince had been the very first person to make a confession to the Bishop!

Syllogistic reasoning now provides *new knowledge* that the late Prince was a murderer. But two different people, each unaware of the other's knowledge, have provided the premises of the syllogism. Without the conjunction of these people with their limited knowledge, the conjunction of the premises is not possible. Since the only person who formerly knew both premises, the Prince, is now dead, the knowledge could not exist without the Bishop and the Duke being brought together.

As in the fictional story above, the knowledge of any one person is limited. So, joint inquiry provides a larger pool of experience. And the role of the CoPI Chair in deliberately conjoining different premises from different people generates new conclusions that would not have been possible without the conjunction of the people together with the role of the Chair in using the CoPI structure to elicit premises and conclusions from participants, rather than questions, musings or opinions.[15]

This function, of creating new and alternative ideas, is necessary for any society that wishes to thrive and grow, and it is a function to which democratic forms of society aspire.

Another feature of CoPI that is vital for a functioning democracy is that within a CoPI *everything is open to question*.[16] Citizens in a democracy must be able to hold their governments and other institutions to account – not least to prevent the rise of tyranny – and to do this successfully they must be able to recognise the assumptions that underlie the decisions and proclamations of their 'leaders'. Now it may be that every case of deliberation, reasoning or inquiry must start with assumed premises, or unjustified assertions, but – and this is a crucial point – questions concerning

• the truth of assumed premises;
• ethics;
• the consequences and implications of solutions that go beyond any set problem

are all crucial within a CoPI.

So, for example, during an inquiry about the nature of moral action the community may raise an initial question as to whether an action should be judged good or bad by considering three different aspects:

- the intention of the actor;
- the action itself;
- the consequences of the action.

Within a CoPI session, this is the temporary starting point of the inquiry, and a dialogue may ensue with different views concerning the implications of weighting these different factors.

However, in a CoPI the very assumption that *action can be divided into these three components* can be challenged! Inquiry would arise into the nature of 'action' itself:

- What is meant by 'action'?
- Is there such a thing as unintentional action?
- Is it possible to judge the intention of another person at all?

In short, the assumptions that lie behind the initial question are themselves open to inquiry, as are the possible implications of theories or statements about the question. Note that the participants are also required to show the relevance of this questioning of assumptions to the issue under investigation, as it is always possible to question every assumption as a matter of course, in what could be considered a trivial way.

While children and adults who are taught logical or analytical thinking (e.g. in Critical Thinking courses) can gain mastery of problem-solving and decision-making procedures, these, although similar in the reasoning skills involved in a CoPI, are limited in their subject area.[17] They take an isolated area of experience and define the boundary of experience to be considered. And the difference between the use of reasoning skills (logical and analytical thinking) in closed problem-solving or decision-making and the emergence of reasoning skills within a CoPI is important.

Let me illustrate with an extreme, but *real*, example. The group of doctors who worked with human subjects in Nazi concentration camps used logical procedures to further their inquiry. They discovered more about the subject matter under investigation. (The information gained is still used by the scientific community today.) They communicated with each other. No doubt they even agreed and disagreed with each other, gave reasons for their assertions, looked at counter-examples, etc. So, in what way did that group differ from a CoPI?

The primary way was that certain kinds of assumption – for example, that Jews, Gypsies and others were subhuman – were *not open to question*. Neither their truth nor their ethical implications were debated. The considerations that arose out of the children's inquiry into the nature of personhood in Chapter 4 *could not arise for the group of doctors in the concentration camps.*

When the children are considering how one could find out the nature of an entity, they consider and *reject* a scientific test, not dissimilar in kind to the experimental tests undertaken by the concentration camp doctors:

Mark   Because if, if it looks just like a person, then you wouldn't be able to. Because you can't, you can't rip off – you can't like do something to it because what if it's a real person? . . .Yeah.You can't like rip stuff off of it. Because then, because then, because if it was a real person, you'll hurt it.You'll hurt the person then.

And when later in the children's dialogue Robert suggests that one could test to see whether an entity was a real person by throwing a needle at it, Karen clarifies the distinction between what is *possible* and what is *morally* permissible:

Karen   Well I, I think that that's not really a good idea to find out how it works, because if it was a real person, it would hurt very badly and the person could get hurt. I think that you could, that it's pretty good, but you shouldn't do it.You should pick a different way to disc- . . . to, to find out.

In the case of the concentration camp doctors, the assumption has been made that subjects were in effect not real people, and therefore any moral prohibition against harming people would be irrelevant.

While the example of the Nazi doctors is extreme, it is real. This book cannot hope to address the systems of thought, moral systems and socio-political systems that created the conditions in which the horrors of the death camps occurred; there are too many factors involved. All I would suggest is that, although one can find similarities between the operation of analytical thinking in such instances and the kinds of reasoning skills evidenced in a CoPI, there are important differences.[18]

Another major feature of CoPI, which it is important that citizens in a democracy *fully* understand,[19] is the importance of human fallibility.[20] Premises and assumptions are open to question because anyone and everyone, even the most knowledgeable authority on a subject, can make mistakes. Citizens in a democracy, no matter how wonderful they may think their leaders are, must be confident and skilled enough to recognise the mistakes government makes, and where possible prevent governments from taking actions that would have bad consequences.Within a CoPI, children (and adults) become accustomed to the idea that everyone is fallible. Because of this, the community provides both a way to check on mistakes, and a desire to do so.

There are many procedures which, recognising human fallibility, operate as checks on mistakes. For example, a mathematician may ask another to check his calculations; or when writing this I may use a spell checker. In both of these examples, however, there is an assumption that there is a correct answer. The CoPI operates differently. In allowing for the recognition of human fallibility, it allows individual participants, through following the dialogue, to inquire into a subject unfettered by the need to defend the correctness of their own views. Over a hundred years ago, Charles Sanders Peirce wrote:

Only once, as far as I remember, in all my lifetime have I experienced the pleasure of praise . . . and the praise that conferred it was meant for blame. It was that a critic said of me that I did not seem to be absolutely sure of my own conclusions.[21]

In the children's dialogue in Chapter 4, we find Clare changing her mind about a theory she is proposing as she takes into account a counter-instance given earlier by another child:

Clare   If you're thinking, you must be for real.
Mc   Why?
Clare   Because, because it – when I'm thinking I'm for real. But you might have brain surgery and you're still for real, but if you're thinking, you must be for real. And . . .

. . .

And robots can think and so – and robots can think and they're for real! So, now, I kind of disagree with that.

Like Peirce, 5-year-old Clare is prepared to revise her conclusion. People who are sure of their own conclusions are not curious; people who are not curious have no desire to inquire. The disposition that drives inquiry, either in a CoPI or in Peirce's community of scientists, arises from curiosity.

If there were infallible human beings, there would be no need to engage in philosophical dialogue in order to inquire. But again, if there were infallible human beings, any form of democracy would be an inefficient way to organise society; and effective membership of such a non-democratic society would require very different forms of behaviour as compared with the kinds required for effective citizenship within a democracy.

It is not a coincidence that in requiring certain kinds of behaviour from its members, CoPI simultaneously induces reasoning skills. The disposition to reason with others, which involves behavioural skills of listening, relating one's thoughts to those of others, taking into account other points of view and alternatives, etc., cannot be effectively actualised *without* such skills. For example, take an episode from the children's dialogue in Chapter 4. At the beginning of the session Karen asks, 'Why did he say to himself, "Dummy, if you can wonder, you must be thinking"?' Other children find this interesting too, but by the time the group comes to consider the question, Karen has forgotten why she was interested in it. This piece of dialogue occurs:

Karen   I don't [understand] what I said!
Mc   OK, Karen. You don't understand what you said?
Karen   I don't know why I even said it!
Mc   You don't remember why you asked the question?
Karen   No.

Mc   All right. Well . . .

Clare   You were interested in it because, um, you wanted to know why she was wondering and thinking at the same time. That — that's what I think you were thinking of.

Here Clare wants to help Karen. She has listened to what Karen originally said, and she has noted how Karen's question came after a question from David, both of which raise questions about the relationships between classes of mental events. At the beginning of the session a sequence of questions was asked:

David   How could she have dreams and think at the same time? . . .

Mark   Why did she touch her eyes? . . .

Sheena   Why did [she] say, 'maybe I don't talk that much'? . . .

Karen   Why did he say to himself, 'Dummy, if you can wonder, you must be thinking'?

Clare infers that Karen had been prompted by David's question about the relationship between thinking and dreaming to ask a question about the relationship between thinking and wondering. So, Clare's *desire to help* Karen remember her original interest *is actualised* by her (Clare's) use of analogical reasoning to infer an analogy between David's question and Karen's question.

Clare makes it clear that this reconstruction is what *Clare* thinks *Karen might* have been thinking. But this is different from what Clare herself wishes to say about the topic. She can only do this and therefore be of help to Karen if:

- first, she has listened to both David's and Karen's questions;
- second, she now remembers both David's and Karen's questions;
- third, she uses analogical reasoning to draw on a possible relationship between the two that will help explain the genesis of Karen's question.

It is important to note that Clare is not simply attributing to Karen similar thought processes to her own. She makes clear that her own thinking on the question is different. This example shows Clare's ability to put herself in the place of another and reconstruct the other's possible thought processes! In her own thinking about the question, Clare continues by using hypothetical reasoning, and again incorporates points made by another (this time David):

Mc   And so why did she say if you can wonder you must be thinking?

David   I don't know why she said that. I don't know why she said that. But maybe she — maybe she said that because even though dreaming and thinking are not the same thing — But it could and it couldn't. Like if you're wondering, like what's in that — what's over that fence, and you're thinking, and then you could think, 'What's over that fence?'

. . .

Clare   . . . when I'm thinking I'm for real. But you might have brain surgery
         and you're still for real, but if you're thinking, you must be for real.

. . .

         And robots can think and so – and robots can think and they're for real!
         So, now, I kind of disagree with that.

Being reasonable – in this case agreeing and disagreeing and giving reasons
for the points of view being put forward – is not just being polite and kind,
although it does involve being polite and being kind. The making explicit of
agreement requires listening and trying to understand others' thinking; and the
giving of reasons for the agreement or disagreement involves making the
relationships between the points of view clear. These relationships are usually
logical relationships. So, the requirement of being reasonable in one's behaviour
towards others in the group in this context requires reasoning skills.

Although for most people it is a given that the kind of reasoning portrayed
in the CoPI is a good thing, this is an assumption. And, as with all assumptions
within a CoPI, it is open to question. Why is it desirable to reason?

One answer derives from what might be taken to be an implication of
Aristotle's 'Man is a rational animal.' It can be argued that if one accepts (and
there are those who do not) that rationality, or the ability to reason, is a property
that distinguishes human beings from animals, then to be fully human, one
should engage in reasoning. The very fact that the ability to reason is one of the
features of personhood might be taken to imply that human well-being must
include the exercise of this ability. Wolves are social animals that range over
hundreds of square miles, and therefore life in isolation in a cage is detrimental
to a wolf. Similarly, so the argument goes, the capacity to reason is part of human
nature, and therefore a life without the exercise of reason is detrimental to a
person.

But why should a life without the exercise of reason be detrimental?
The answer would seem to be that human beings, while they may be rational,
are also by nature fallible (a feature that, according to the children, distinguishes them from programmed robots). The attraction of ratiocination as
a form of thought lies in its promise of avoiding error. This is not to say that
rational procedures alone will guarantee the desired answers or results: for
example, the correct use of certain logical forms cannot guard against the
use of mistaken or untrue premises; but structural forms limit certain kinds of
error.

In the 'Western model' of rationality, rational action exhibits certain features:

* *Universality*. Any rational agent will arrive at the same decision and act in
  the same way in a given set of circumstances. Whatever is the rational thing
  to do is rational for everyone and anyone to do.
* *Necessity*. It is not enough that all rational thinkers arrive at the same
  conclusion; this might occur through massive coincidence. A rationally

acceptable conclusion must follow with necessity from the information given.

- *Recognition of necessity.* Moreover, to be rational, a person must arrive at a necessary conclusion through a process of reasoning that recognises the existence of a necessary connection between information and a conclusion. It might be possible to guess at the conclusion that necessarily follows, but guessing is not in itself a rational activity.

From all this, there emerges a fourth feature of the traditional concept of rationality:

- *Rules.* The rationality of a conclusion is determined by whether it was arrived at by following appropriate rules.

According to this model of rationality, a lone mathematician is exhibiting rational behaviour when she or he makes calculations. And although it is certainly possible that the mathematician may ask a colleague to ensure there are no mistakes, asking a colleague to check is not itself part of calculation.

Moreover, the checking procedure assumes that there is a correct answer. Western models of rationality seldom make allowance for another feature of human nature that is crucial in reasoning: that people are *creative*. Although others may have made it in the past, the first time an individual puts forward an argument, he or she must innovate. The person has to meet objections, interpret evidence and make connections between elements in the situation, which for him or her had not previously been coordinated. Any person who wishes to reason well also wishes to consider new connections. And others provide new connections unforeseen by the reasoner. (Note that to say that it is a feature of human nature that human beings are creative is to say that everyone is capable of generating original ideas. This does not mean that every person does in fact originate new ideas, but that by virtue of the fact that an individual is a human being, any individual has creative potential.)

Rationality and reasonableness are therefore not synonymous. If one understands rationality in the way in which the dominant Western model portrays the concept, it is possible to be rational while not being reasonable. For example, it allows the actions of the doctors in Nazi concentration camps to be described as rational. But is it possible to be reasonable while *not* being rational? Could there be a case of reasonableness that was irrational? I argue here that if it is the case that human beings are fallible and creative, then being reasonable *is* rational. But not only is it rational to be reasonable; I would argue further that being reasonable involves reasoning with others, and reasoning with others develops reasoning skills – the very same skills that are required to be proficient in logic or analysis.

The importance of the connection between human nature and the *social* aspect of reasoning can be seen when considering what sometimes appears to be a dichotomy between the kind of analytical thinking skills that can be used privately, and the ability to reason with others. How do we describe the person who has tremendous analytical abilities – for example, someone who can program computers at a high level – and yet either will not or cannot tolerate anyone else's point of view, to the extent, perhaps, of bringing harm to him- or herself, or to others? Such a person is usually described as unreasonable, despite his or her mental abilities.

There is, in short, an *ethical* dimension to reasonableness. It requires a measure of tolerance and respect for others as autonomous, creative (though fallible) agents, capable of original thought, whose potential views or arguments merit consideration. To be reasonable is to be prepared to listen to whoever may have differing opinions or new insights to suggest. Being reasonable, in a strong sense, means that in principle no person's views are excluded from consideration.

Considering all people as potential contributors to one's reasoning has very strong egalitarian implications. As was mentioned earlier, taking into account the fallibility of all people does not mean that any person is at any instant incorrect or wrong in what they claim, but rather that by virtue of being human it is possible. Similarly, taking into account the creativity of all people does not involve considering every contribution creative, but rather means that everyone has the potential to be creative. CoPI assumes that at any one instant any person – child or adult – might have an insight of great value to contribute. At any one instant anyone, even a leading expert in some field, might be wrong. This is an assumption of the equality of people, in a strong sense.

When politicians and others use the terms 'citizen' and 'citizenship' rhetorically, it becomes particularly important to examine what the concept actually entails.[22] An appeal is being made, but what is being appealed to? One aid in understanding the concept is to look at its origins. The concept of citizenship evolved, as it were, in conjunction with the concept of democracy.

Not all meanings of 'citizenship' necessarily involve being a citizen in a democracy. One can be a consumer-citizen without being a member of a democracy; one can be a member of a republic that is not a democracy; and one can have a certain nationality without being a member of a democracy. The understanding of 'being a good citizen' may also sometimes seem to involve only a character description – that a person is kind, respectful, etc. But all these fail to take into account the *role* aspect of citizenship; and this was historically, and I would argue still is today, determined by democracy. By 'determined', I mean that a role (as such) cannot exist, or at least cannot be actualised, without a context: so, for example, the role of a teacher requires the context of having students. The role aspect of citizenship requires the context of democracy.

Although there is much disagreement about exactly which specific forms of organisation count as 'democratic', democracy or democratic government is usually held to mean government by the people, and is thus distinguished from other forms of government, such as despotism, theocracy, etc. The paradigm of a people governing itself is the direct democracy of Athens, where citizens participated personally in policy decisions, by discussion and voting directly on issues. Every citizen had an equal opportunity to state a case and influence decisions (although citizenship itself was a hereditary privilege, excluding slaves, women, etc.). This paradigm of democracy involves relatively small groups. When the numbers of citizens – the size of the *polis*, as it were – becomes large, the mechanics of direct participation in policy- and decision-making become difficult. So, modern equivalents to the Athenian paradigm tend to be found in organisations where relatively small numbers of people participate in the deliberation of policy, etc.

The historic connection between citizenship, democracy and reasoning highlights the role aspect of citizenship. Citizenship is not concerned solely with character. Although we have no verb for it, 'citizening' was taking part in deliberation.[23] To be an effective citizen one must have both the disposition to reason with others, and the skills to reason well. But as was said earlier, reasoning with others assumes an ethical stance: that of treating other individuals as autonomous agents, capable of original thought, whose potential views or arguments merit consideration.

Thus, to be a good citizen commits a person to regard others as equals (so one cannot be a good citizen and, for example, simultaneously regard women as being unequal to men). In a democracy, all citizens have an equal right to participate in deliberation and policy-making.

The egalitarianism assumed by democratic forms of organisation, including a CoPI, does not imply that every person is the same. Having the *potential* to put forward views and arguments or to offer insights or to reason does not mean that a person does any of these things. But to use arguments from the fact that a group of people do not show proficiency at some activity as justification for denying them the opportunity to engage in such an activity is to make a kind of category mistake, as well as, I would claim, to misunderstand some important features of human nature.

In Chapter 3 it was stated that although children do not do well on tests of reasoning, that does not mean that they are incapable of it. One would not expect any person to be proficient at an activity of which they have no experience. Anti-democratic arguments frequently fall into this class of justification – for example, assertions that claim the mass of people do not deliberate (are illiterate, uneducated, etc.) and are therefore incapable of self-government. People are *capable* of reasoning by virtue of being human beings, but to be proficient takes practice; and creating conditions that allow for the emergence of both the disposition to inquire and the skills to reason empowers people, in a way that simple enfranchisement does not.

So, for example, the development of reasoning skills enables young people to recognise the logical mistake of racism as well as the moral dubiety of racist views, while simultaneously making them sensitive to occurrences of racism. It helps them to protect themselves from sliding into stereotypical views of other people, and it gives them the tools to counter such views when they see them.

Recognising inconsistencies and demanding 'good reasons', such as the recognition of relevancy – 'Is this reason relevant to the issue in hand?' – can help protect them from being manipulated by others. Practice in recognising analogies and metaphors, in questioning them (for example, 'Is this a good analogy? Why? Why not? Which part of the relationship is being highlighted? In which ways does it not work?'), not only develops skills in analogical thinking but simultaneously gives people powerful tools for thinking for themselves and not being swayed by persuasive but fallacious rhetoric in advertising or politics, by racist groups, etc.

Developing a CoPI with children maintains their natural desire to find the truth, while at the same time giving them the skills to handle the truth, however unpleasant it may be. They develop the ability and the means to judge for themselves. They are not left 'hanging on their own', defenceless in a cruel world. So, for example, when there is (as there often is) a class or school bully who rules by fear, children are enabled to recognise how the rule by fear operates. They can discuss it. The bully exerts power over others through their fear of being physically hurt, or of being psychologically hurt or shamed within the peer group. But much of the power that a bully holds can be dissolved once children understand it. And the kind of influence with which a bully usually operates is not effective within a CoPI.

CoPI is not cosy in the sense of hiding the truth about the world and the evil therein, in a nice but inauthentic 'let's all like each other' sort of sense. Children, especially young children, just won't buy that. They know it is inauthentic to pretend to like someone when they simply do not like them. They may play along with the teacher, and even fool the teacher that they all love each other under those conditions, but it will not carry over into their lives – because it is pretend.

Children are not citizens in the sense of having the right to influence policy-making, being self-governing, etc. But creating conditions for them to develop the disposition to inquire and the reasoning skills to be proficient in inquiry prepares them for it; and this empowerment of children who have been involved in a CoPI is fundamental to the creation of future active and reasonable citizens.

Chapter 10

Afterword

The past, the present and the future?

In the previous chapter I argued that in order to be active and effective citizens in a democracy, people need to have the kinds of skills and dispositions that are developed through the practice of CoPI. In fact, there is a strong case for arguing that philosophising in a collaborative manner is uniquely suited to the development of these skills and dispositions.

It is an empirical question whether practising CoPI does produce active, effective citizens who can take initiatives within their communities and societies and have the desire to improve the conditions of their own lives and those of others, and there is a kind of empirical *answer* in the media reports from pilot CoPI projects that have been undertaken with groups composed of – among others – adults and children,[1] designers,[2] senior citizens,[3] parents and children,[4] adults from mixed socio-economic and geographical backgrounds,[5] business leaders,[6] artists,[7] prison officers,[8] healthcare workers,[9] *et al.*, as well as in school and community projects with children,[10] CoPI projects with teenagers with learning difficulties,[11] and more. The observations made by different newspaper, radio and television reporters, and the interviews that they conducted with participants, provide empirical evidence that supports the argument that engaging in CoPI has the potential to transform a community.[12]

Example 1: the 1992 'Empowerment through Philosophical Dialogue' project

In 1992, while on a 'job' about a different news topic, Jennifer Cunningham was having a coffee in a canteen when she happened to overhear a small group of mothers and children engaged in a discussion about the nature of space. Intrigued, she asked if she could interview them. They proceeded to describe an experience that had changed their lives. Here is an extract from the resulting article:

> Two months ago Shirley McCafferty's children thought she couldn't read, now she's hoping to do a crash course in philosophy at Glasgow University.

Like Margaret McElhinney and Helen Burke, Shirley was inveigled on to the course from the Glasgow North Worklink project to give adults a chance to brush up basic literacy and numeracy skills.

They found themselves reading *Laura and Paul*, a story written by Dr Catherine C. McCall, a philosopher with an engaging missionary zeal about the practicality of a subject, generally dismissed as abstruse, to trigger discussion of philosophical concepts. Every discussion has its own dynamic. . . . In this group a phrase uttered in the first episode by the elder (the boy) of twin children: 'First is first,' sparked off a discussion of time and also of gender differences.

Initial inhibition soon gave way to enjoyment which spilled over into the rest of their lives. 'At first you were worried you weren't saying the right things but then you started to think about things later and we would find ourselves discussing things at dinnertime like imagination, truth, space, and God,' said Shirley.

Helen suggested that this kind of discussion was easier in some ways than social chat. 'I'm too shy to just start talking to someone, but here you say what you really think.' All three said that philosophical dialogue has had an impact on the way they deal with children. 'Kids have minds and feelings,' said Helen. Shirley added: 'Instead of telling him to go away and stop bothering me I listen to what Richard is saying.' Helen admitted she took part because she thought it would help the weans [children] with their reading and it has become known as the reading project. After all, Empowerment Through Philosophical Dialogue is not the easiest title to sell to people suspicious of education, but it describes accurately what this experiment is all about . . .

[Dr McCall] would argue that it is essential in a democracy. 'Creating conditions which allow for the emergence of both the disposition to inquire and the skills to reason empowers people in a way that simple enfranchisement does not. Enfranchisement alone will not ensure an effective democracy. But the possession of inquiry and reasoning skills empowers by enabling people – adults and children – to seek for and deal with the truth.' Fair enough, but it sounds dauntingly ambitious for areas which, like Glasgow's Possil, have become synonymous with crime and deprivation . . .

This study was independent of schools, and teachers of the children involved did not know it was going on. Some of them noticed such a difference that they called in the parents to ask if something was happening at home.[13]

(Reproduced with the permission of the Herald & Times Group)

The 'Empowerment through Philosophical Dialogue' project had brought together unemployed carers of children and the children for whom they were responsible, drawn from different areas of North Glasgow. Among the adults were: a long-term unemployed and depressed father; a grandmother looking after her granddaughter because her two sons were in prison and her daughter-in-law was a drug addict; two teenage single mothers; and a number of mothers who had never been employed. None of the adults or the children knew each other (the children all attended different primary schools in different areas). Many of the children had been identified as being 'at risk' and were failing in school. The adults in this group would never set foot in a school building, or an 'official' building of any kind, so the funders of the project provided taxis to bring them to a community hall some distance from where they lived. The adults and children were in two separate CoPI groups, although both groups used the same children's novel[14] as the stimulus for beginning dialogue. The purpose of using the same readings was to make use of the children's natural curiosity about what questions their parents had raised from reading *Laura and Paul*, and about what the parents had discussed; and conversely, the same curiosity that the parents would have about the children. Within four weeks the participants were reporting that family relationships had improved dramatically as the parents and children began to talk to each other, continuing the philosophical discussions from the CoPI sessions at home.

Although they were not selected according to this criterion, it turned out that most of the adults could not read. By the end of this short project all the adults and all the children were reading, and this alone was to transform their lives! The adults began to read newspapers and to borrow books from the library; they also began to read with their children. The children's schoolwork improved so much that teachers from the different schools that the children attended began to make inquiries. And a major change in the children concerned their behaviour. Up to this point, these children had known only unstable and chaotic lives, and their behaviour reflected this. As they began to receive attention from their parent (or grandparent), their behaviour improved dramatically.

The project funders were so impressed that they decided to raise more funds for a further project, specifically targeted towards non-literate adults. All the adults from the original project asked if they could be part of the new one; but three months later, when the second project began, only one of the formerly unemployed parents could attend. *Every single adult who had taken part in the 'Empowerment through Philosophical Dialogue' project had found work or training.* The one mother who was able to continue in the new project had a part-time job. So, the new project began with a different group of non-literate, unemployed adults. Members of the 'Empowerment through Philosophical Dialogue' project came to visit, and one young single mother explained to the new group that prior to taking part in the project, she had been too afraid to travel out of her immediate neighbourhood to find work or training.

We also heard the news that one of the children, who had appeared to be very troubled at the beginning of the project, had won the prize in her primary school for 'the most improved pupil'. Another mother had gained the confidence and communication skills to insist that her son see a paediatric specialist, and she announced to the group, victoriously, that the specialist had taken her 'wee boy off the Ritalin'!

Example 2: the 'Hawthorn' project

Similar effects from participating in a CoPI community project have been described by Susan Flockhart in her article about the mothers and children who took part in the Hawthorn project in 1994: the children began to become more reasonable, and the mothers developed confidence and skills to begin to make changes in their community.

> Where are you going when you're going nowhere? How can you tell if you're awake or dreaming? And is it raining when one raindrop fails? If you take more than sixty seconds to answer, congratulations. You've just given birth to some fine, healthy thinking – the kind of thinking, in fact, that goes on in philosophical inquiry. And if you're wondering what kind of person would get involved in something with a name like *that*, I'll tell you. Seven year old children for a start. And unemployed women from Possilpark.
>
> In a small room in Hawthorn Primary School – at the heart of an area that's been tarred as the drug and unemployment centre of Glasgow – ten mothers and 11 children came to talk, and to think. Twice weekly for six weeks, they discussed issues more commonly linked with Oxford dons: the nature of truth; epistemology; the problem of other minds. . . .
>
> But why do philosophy at all? And how can ability to discuss the nature of space help the people of Possilpark? . . .
>
> When I met them, the women in the 'Hawthorn Experiment' were convinced they could already see changes in their own confidence and behaviour – and that of their children. Brenda told me: 'My daughter used to just say, "I don't like this, or that". Now, she's started to explain herself, to say why she doesn't like something – and she quizzes me, too, looking for *my* reasons' . . .
>
> Five weeks into the Hawthorn pilot, the germ of that possibility was already there. You could see it growing, as those women talked about the way they are changing. You could hear it in Angela's voice, as she talked about a conversation with a friend who felt fatalistic when threatened by eviction. The landlords, her friend said, could do what they liked. 'I asked why,' said Angela. 'Why would you get evicted if you've paid your rent? People have rights, and you can't be evicted for no reason.' It is this search for reasons that holds the potential for change.
>
> And the questions are endless. *Why* does poverty and deprivation persist in a society that claims to endorse equal opportunity? Why should some children have to live in unhealthy environments because their parents are

unlucky enough to be unemployed? Why is educational achievement lower in areas like Possil – where local children have the same capacity to think as their middle-class counterparts?

Why doesn't our society encourage children to think? And why aren't communities given the opportunity to gain the skills that can help lead to change – and break the cycle of poverty and deprivation?[15]

(Reproduced with the permission of The Big Issue Scotland)

A month after this newspaper article was written, the women from the Hawthorn project took action against the drug dealers and addicts who were leaving needles infected with hepatitis C and AIDS in the communal landings in their buildings. Prior to the project they had been too afraid of the criminals to report them to the police, and also too wary of the police and lacking the confidence and communication skills to approach *any* authority. But having gained both the skills and the courage[16] that result from engaging in CoPI, and having formed a community, the mothers decided they would no longer tolerate their children's lives being put at risk. Two years later the local council began to demolish the slums and build new housing, partly as a result of frequent, insistent visits from mothers demanding better conditions.

Example 3: the 'Philosophy Is Fun' project of 1994–1995

Susan Lumsden describes the project as follows:

When Jean was mugged five years ago, her attacker made off with more than her money – she lost all her confidence and could no longer face work. Yet today she is running an office.

What has given Jean the strength to take up the threads of her life again is no elaborate 'new' therapy. It is philosophy. Jean is a participant in Philosophy Is Fun, a 10-week project that has recently finished in Glasgow's Castlemilk. 'It has changed my life completely,' she says. Today Jean and the rest of her group are meeting in the Castle Arms pub – to celebrate its success.

It's hard to believe an amiable group met weekly to philosophise in the pub still known locally as Bennigans, once thought to be the centre of Castlemilk's dangerous underworld.

Beneath its peaceful surface, Castlemilk has its share of division and violence. Dr Catherine C. McCall has pioneered her own brand of people's philosophy, called Philosophical Inquiry, all over the world, and was invited to Castlemilk to see if she could succeed where other attempts to break deep-rooted divisions had failed.

She has since been warned against it. Acquaintances in the community hinted she may be in some danger. But they refused to explain why. The philosophers persevered and were tolerated. This alone is being hailed as 'a breakthrough'.

Dr McCall says her brainchild can have a mediating function: 'People don't find views which are different from their own so threatening, and begin to recognise that it's fruitful to have difference.

'That's a tremendous way of preventing the kind of territorial, tribal violence that happens amongst groups of people who differ.'

Results are difficult to quantify, but there have been visible changes in groups that draw together 11-year-olds from primary schools in rival areas.

Other projects to build bridges between the groups before they go to Castlemilk High have failed, and violence has resulted. But in the Inquiry, friendships have formed. The discipline of Inquiry has many general benefits, such as building self-esteem and helping people take control of their own lives . . .

Inquiry also encourages people to persist with questions, and not be fobbed off with excuses. Especially if those questions affect their daily lives. Is it right, asks one member in the Castle Arms, that people in overcrowded accommodation should get priority on the housing list?

I get drawn into a debate at another table. 'What is homelessness?' asks Grace McKendrick. 'Are you homeless when you haven't got a house? Could a cardboard box be a home?' I can't resist any longer: 'What if you live in a house that isn't yours? If you're sleeping on a friend's floor?' This philosophy thing is infectious.

For some, the impact of Inquiry is extremely personal. Alex Brown was introduced to the Castlemilk pub group at a key stage in his recovery from a horrific car accident 10 years ago. He has had to learn to walk and talk, read and write again, and his memory has been permanently damaged.

'When I first came to the group, I was terrified,' he says. 'It was easier to stay at home, but I'm a perverse creature! I wanted the challenge.'

He goes on: 'Inquiry has given me the confidence to mix in groups, and stretched my ability to communicate verbally.' The friendly atmosphere has broken through his self-consciousness, and even helped him to laugh at his difficulties . . .

'Philosophy – I still can't spell it!' laughs Grace. 'But it's great. You should try it.'

Grace's story
I grew up in the Gorbals, I left school at 15, got married and moved to —
——, Castlemilk. The usual story. I think it all gave me a bit of an inferiority complex.

I did a weekend Philosophical Inquiry course before the Castlemilk groups started. There were people there I wouldn't normally even talk to, like lawyers and businessmen from down south.

But in Philosophical Inquiry, everybody's equal, everybody's view counts. It doesn't matter who's the best speaker. At the end of the course, one of the men actually came up and thanked me for what I'd said during the group.

I know the Inquiry has made a difference in my life, but I think other people notice it more than me. Like my daughter, who's 15. Whenever she makes a statement, I question her, and make her look at things another way.

For me the most interesting discussions were about the meanings of words. We had one about the word 'lost'. One person said: 'I was lost in Sauchiehall Street.' But someone said: 'How can you be lost if you know where you are?' Then another said: 'I lost my mother. I was lost when she died.' The same word can mean so many different things.

I'm a youth worker in Castlemilk. I think Inquiry would be great for the young people I work with. We could look at topics like drink, or drugs, and help them to see they don't have to just follow the crowd.

I've been accepted to do a day-release course in community work at Glasgow University. Me, Grace from the Gorbals, going to university! I can hardly believe it![17]

(Reproduced with the permission of The Big Issue Scotland)

The 'Philosophy Is Fun' project made a big impact on a whole community. Two adult groups met in community centres, and one adult group met in a notorious local pub. In order to provide local men with an excuse to give to their peers for why they were attending the 'Philosophy Is Fun' project, I negotiated with a national brewery to provide a free pint to everyone who came.[18] This allowed the men to tell their mates, and also the gang leaders, that they were 'only going for the free pint' and so 'save face'.[19]

With three adults' groups and four children's groups meeting over the course of a year, the effects seen in families and in the community were similar to those with the earlier 'Empowerment through Philosophical Dialogue' and 'Hawthorn' projects. The criminal gang leaders and drug barons began to lose the rule of fear that they had enjoyed for many years. Within families, relationships between parents and children improved. In the first year of the high school, violence diminished as the children from the 'mixed' CoPI primary school classes entered the school. Both children and adults made friends, for the first time, across the sectarian divide.

And there are many more examples of the way in which CoPI transforms not just individual children and adults but whole communities – too many to list and describe here.[20]

Example 4: an example from history

There is further reason to believe that collaborative philosophising leads to an improvement in society. It lies in the past. A remarkable revolution occurred in eighteenth-century Scotland, commonly known as the Scottish Enlightenment. It is credited with changing not only Scotland but the whole world.[21]

It is fairly well accepted that the economic, medical, social and scientific advances, the inventions, and the new thinking that comprised the Scottish Enlightenment were in large part the result of an extraordinary explosion of great philosophy in Scotland after the Act of Union in 1707. One reason cited for the rapid intellectual development on all fronts – beginning in the Scottish Enlightenment, but continuing into the nineteenth century – is the primacy of philosophy in Scottish universities. All Scottish students, whether they were 13 years old or 17, studied logic and moral philosophy, with the result that every Scottish scientist, teacher, minister, doctor, lawyer and many more had a thorough grounding in these subjects.[22]

Less well known regarding this intellectual explosion, however, is the role played by the philosophy clubs that were established in the seventeenth and eighteenth centuries. Across the country, merchants, farm labourers, apprentices and scientists joined philosophers, often in taverns, to form philosophy clubs, one of whose unique features was the way in which they set out to 'improve minds and society by conversation'. Rather than engaging in scholarly disputation or forensic argument, the philosophy clubs were established to work in a collaborative manner. As described in the 2005 UNESCO publication *We Cultivate Literature on a Little Oatmeal . . .* , the clubs drew

> together men with literary and philosophical tastes from all walks of life to exchange ideas and opinions.
>
> Many of Edinburgh's most important intellectual movements began with gatherings in taverns: the Tuesday Club, the Poker Club, the Oyster Club, and the Rankenian Club. The Select Society was the most important Club, welcoming members such as David Hume, Adam Smith, Adam Ferguson and Lord Kames.[23]

While royal societies and coffee clubs were established in England and on the Continent, one of the features that made the Scottish philosophy clubs unique in their time was their egalitarian nature. (Egalitarian for men, that is. Women were not admitted as members of the clubs. However, in 1717, somewhat ahead of its time, there was at least one philosophical club for women: the Fair Intellectual Club.[24]) As the UNESCO publication puts it, 'Edinburgh stood out as a city where intellect rather than social rank mattered: a place where a farmer like Robert Burns could be embraced as a member of the literati.'[25] However, philosophy clubs were established in all the Scottish cities.[26]

Many scholarly works have been devoted to explaining why this phenomenon occurred in a small, poor northern country.[27] One of the causes was Scotland's experience in the fifteenth and early sixteenth centuries. According to the *Encyclopaedia Britannica*,

As John Knox discovered during the Scottish Reformation, Scotland needed an alternative method of settling disputes, one that avoided an appeal either to the naked power of the largest warring faction or to English traditions of order and precedence . . . [T]here developed a capacity to argue from first principles rather than from precedent, analogy, or religious premises in settling disputes about the shape of religious and civil society.[28]

Scotland's unique position in having a population most of which had been literate for several generations is often thought to have been an important contributing factor both to the general egalitarianism in Scottish culture and to the specific phenomenon of the Scottish Enlightenment. As the *Encyclopaedia Britannica*[29] explains,

Knox [realised] that . . . the alternative options of first principles and argument from empirical evidence required an educated population ('a school in every parish' is the apocryphal quotation attributed to Knox).[30]

The resulting tension between arguing from first principles and arguing from empirical evidence gave the discussions and debates in the philosophy clubs a driving dynamic. Within the clubs, different and opposing philosophies and ideas were debated and discussed, and often the results were published in order to disseminate the ideas more widely.

Some historians and philosophers have found it problematic that Hume, who was a member of at least three of the philosophy clubs in different parts of the country, held such a different philosophy from that of his contemporaries. However, I would suggest that if one looks at the rules of the clubs, such as the Easy Club,[31] combined with the topics that they discussed, it is not too far a stretch to conclude that the kind of dialogue in which the clubs engaged allowed for radically different and opposing theories to be promoted at the same time.[32] The philosophy clubs discussed any and every social, scientific and philosophical problem that might arise.

The clubs also had a unique feature: they drew up rules of debate and discussion (see Appendices A and B) designed to ensure that the dialogues were conducted in a polite and respectful manner. The philosophy clubs had as their aims both the improvement of society in economic terms and the improvement of manners in social terms, beginning with their own members. Some clubs' rules outlawed the use of physical violence and blasphemy by their members both inside and outside the clubs.[33] Members could be banished if they were reported to have been fighting!

In bringing together scientists, merchants, philosophers, and so on, the philosophy clubs provided the environment for new ideas and theories to emerge from the collaborative work of their members. And I would suggest that it was the *collaborative philosophical dialogue* of the philosophy clubs that resulted in the

Scots [being] the first to link history and human nature and present man as a product of history and political environment. In arguing that the study of man is ultimately a scientific one, Scottish philosophers created what are known as the social sciences today: anthropology, ethnography, sociology, psychology, history and economics. Their interest in improving society through an understanding of human nature made an important contribution to contemporary world attitudes towards democracy, freedom and human rights. This age of philosophy is not just an episode in Scottish history: it marks a crucial turning point in the development of the western world.[34]

It should be noted that this opinion[35] – that it was the *collaborative philosophical dialogue* in which people of different professions and different strata in society engaged that provided the engine for the great scientific, philosophical, economic and agricultural revolution in Scotland – is my own, and is not necessarily shared by other philosophers.[36] However, the view that it was Scottish *philosophers* who created the ideas and theories that shaped the modern world *is* shared by many, as explained for example by Arthur Herman in his book *How the Scots Invented the Modern World*,[37] and described in *We Cultivate Literature on a Little Oatmeal . . .* :

Scotland's outstanding achievement in philosophy, particularly during the period of the Scottish Enlightenment towards the end of the eighteenth century, is one of the great intellectual contributions to world culture. Much of modern philosophy originated in the works of Scottish thinkers of that time, which influenced the whole of the English-speaking world as well as enlightened philosophical movements in Germany and France. Before the eighteenth century was over, Scotland had generated the basic institutions, ideas, attitudes and habits of mind that characterise the modern age, opening a new era in human history.[38]

There is a precedent here not only for people from different backgrounds engaging in collaborative philosophical dialogue, but for *young* people so doing: in the past, students as young as 13 studied moral philosophy and logic in Scottish universities. And there is no reason why even younger children – as young as 5 – cannot engage in philosophical reasoning, provided that they are guided by an older person educated in philosophy and logic. The benefits are numerous, both for the children and for society at large.

It is not unthinkable that social improvement, advances in technology, science, medicine, the arts, etc. might result from a return to giving primacy to a particular kind of philosophical education – an education that is philosophical in the traditional understanding of philosophy as a discipline with a rich and long history, which needs to be learned, but also an education that encourages children and young people to philosophise for themselves. And such is provided by the CoPI method.

The rules of the Fair Intellectual Club, 1717

The Rules and Constitutions of the Fair Intellectual Club in Edinburgh

We, whose Names are underwritten, being sensible of the Disadvantages that our Sex in General and we in particular labour under, for want of an established Order and Method in Our Conversation; And being ambitious to imitate the laudable Example of some of our Brethren, that make the greatest Figure in the learn'd polite World, in so far as we are capable and may reasonably be allowed, by entring into a mutual Compact and Agreement, to act for the Interest and Improvement of one another, in our Meetings; have resolved to establish a Club called, The FAIR-INTELLECTUAL-CLUB; and hereby declare our Assent, and Purpose to observe, (whilst we are alive and unmarried) The RULES and CONSTITUTIONS, which follow;

I. THAT we shall maintain a sincere and constant mutual Friendship, while we live; and never directly nor indirectly reveal or make known, without the Consent of the whole CLUB asked and given, the Names of the Members, of Nature of the CLUB.

II. THAT none shall be invited or admitted into the CLUB before her Name be proposed in it, and her Merits impartially considered, and Allowance given by all the Members to have her introduced.

III. THAT none shall be declared a Member of our CLUB, before she hath, in our Presence, subscribed her Name to the RULES and CONSTITUTIONS thereof.

IV. THAT we shall never admit more than Nine into our CLUB, whereof Five shall be counted a Quorum sufficient to act in Absence of the rest, as if the Number was compleat.

V. THAT none shall be invited or admitted into our CLUB before she be fifteen Years of Age, nor after her twentieth Year is expired.

VI. THAT altho' different Principles and Politicks shall be no Hindrance to the Admission of Members into our CLUB, being Protestants: Yet none shall presume to urge these directly or indirectly in our Meetings on Pain of Censure.

VII. THAT altho' we may, on proper Occasions, make Excursions in Commendation of the Genius and Conduct of other People; yet none shall be guilty of practising the silly Arts of Censure and Ridicule, on Pain of Censure.

VIII. THAT every Person at her first admission into the CLUB, shall entertain the CLUB with a written Harangue, and deliver the Sum of Ten Shillings *Sterling*, for the Use of the Poor, as we shall direct.

IX. THAT one shall be chosen at the Beginning of each Quarter of the Year, in our Meetings, to whom we shall address our selves when we speak, by the Name of *Mistress Speaker*, and pay all the due Respect to her that becometh us to owe, whom we impow'r to determine Differences, silence Debates, censure Transgressors, state Votes; and in a Word, to perform all the Offices that one in the Character of PRESES may reasonably be allowed to do.

X. THAT *Mistress Speaker* shall entertain the CLUB with a written Speech of her own Composure, immediately before the Election of one to succeed her in the Chair.

XI. THAT we shall elect a Secretary to the CLUB, at the Beginning of each Quarter, immediately after the Choice of Mrs. Speaker; and that she shall record in a Book, and have the Custody of the Minutes of our Management, as of all other Papers presented to the CLUB.

XII. THAT Mrs. *Secretary* shall read over the Minutes of all that pass'd in the Club during her Quarter, immediately before the Election of one to succeed her.

XIII. THAT we shall punctually attend on all the Meetings of our Club, which for ordinary are to be once a Week; and that Absents shall be censured, unless their Excuses be found to be good.

XIV. THAT whosoever refuses to submit to the Command and Rebukes of the Club pronounced by Mrs *Speaker*, shall be expelled from it, if sober Reasoning can't prevail.

XV. THAT when Death, Marriage, or other important Occurences shall in the Course of Providence, remove any Member from our Club, Care shall be taken to make a speedy Supply of her Room, lest the Club suffer, or go to nothing.

XVI. THAT we shall not be limited by our Subscriptions from making new Regulations, Additions or Alterations, for our greater Good and Improvement, from Time to Time, as we shall see Cause.

These Articles abovementioned were subscrib'd by us three, that compos'd them, before any were invited to join us. Two Weeks pass'd ere we cou'd agree in the Choice of one to be a Member: We thought we cou'd not be too cautious of admitting others into our Club, which we designed for such noble Purposes. We were ambitious of a rational and select Conversation, compos'd of Persons who have the Talent of pleasing with Delicacy of Sentiments flowing from habitual Chastity of Thought; We were eager to keep out Pretenders to Mirth and Gallantry, and all such who with constrain'd, obscene and painful Witticisms, pester People in mix'd Companies. At length we unanimously pitch'd on Three, whose Genius and Conduct were most agreeable. These we endeavoured by several honest Means to gain. The six met, according to a Paction, in my Chamber, where I, in Name of my Sisters, inform'd them of the Nature of our Club, and read over the Rules and Constitutions of it in their Hearing, to which they cheerfully subscribed.

Source: A. J. Sinclair (1996) 'The Emergence of Philosophical Inquiry in 18th Century Scotland', unpublished Ph.D. thesis, the Centre for Philosophical Inquiry, University of Glasgow, appendix D, pp. 123–124.

The laws of the Easy Club, 1713

The Fundamental Laws of the Famous Modern Society Called the Easy Club

Established in Ed^r May 12 1712

Lex 1mo

It is Resolved Statute and Enacted that the Name and designation of ye Society shall be the Easy club as most expressive of the humour of the members and Design of the Establishment. As Also That each member shall choose some Eminent Scots Author or Heroe (who is dead) for his patron by whose Name he shall be called in ye club.

Lex 2do

To prevent disorder and Confusion the Common Bane of too Numerous Assemblies and preserve ye Unanimity of the Club It is Statute and Enacted that the Number of Members shall having their determin'd abode in ye city of Edinburgh and that none shall be admitted (a) member without ye consent of the whole club and every Member before he be Chosen praeses or have a vote.

Lex 3mo

It is Resolved and enacted that ye first thing to be done at the Meeting of ye Club or a quorum thereof (which is to consist of 4 members) shall be ye choice of a praeses which shall be by the Majority of Voices (ye last praeses calling ye votes) called and No otherways when spoke to: and the better to Maintain an equality no member shall be praeses in two meetings Successively.

Lex 4to

It is Enacted that ye praeses and he only shall be address'd to when ye affairs of ye Club are discours'd of and in all such Matters he shall have a Casting Vote.

Lex 5to

Full encouragement is given to every thing that is innocently merry and Diverting but nothing that is immoral or uncivill to be allowed or tolerate[d] for ye Better order herein it is statue and Enacted that the praeses shall be absolute Judge of all Misdeanour and shall have full power to punish ye Same By pecuniary Mulcts or otherwise as he shall think fit the offender being hereby prohibite to vindicate himself after sentence neither shall the praeses have power to dispense with or alter ye Same.

Lex 6to

To prevent dispute and grudge about ye quota of Mulcts it is Statute and Enacted that if any Member shall be absent a whole meeting he shall pay one shilling Scots, or for being Sero Six pennies and if any Curse or Swear he shall pay six pennies ilk time he so offends and for lesser Misdemeanours the fine shall be six pennies and for greater One Shilling Scots The Money so forefaulted to be Collected by any Member ye Club Shall appoint to be dispos'd of as ye plurality of Members shall agree.

Lex 7to

For maintaining ye peace of ye Club it is Enacted that when any dispute or debate arise in and proves uneasy, upon ye Complaint of any one Member the Praeses shall state ye Controversy and call a Vote of Decision, Or Order the Disputants to delay their debate, or immediately Remove and decide it between themselves by force of Reason, the offenders insisting after Sentence to be declar'd impugners of the Law.

Lex 8to

The Design of ye Society being a Mutual improvement of minds by Conversation it is enacted that there be no gaming in ye club or forcing One another to drink Both being diverting from our greate design and of times provoking to an undue exercise of ye passions which is contrary to and inconsistent with our Commendable Easiness.

Lex 9mo

It is Statute and Enacted That if any Member shall be frequently or long wilfully absent from the Meetings of ye Club he shall be declared Deserter and the Same being intimate to him if he do not attend ye 1st meeting after ye said intimation and Make a Satisfying excuse the Club shall proceed to pass an Act of ejectment against him and declare his Seat in ye Club vacant. As also if any Member shall be obstinately Unneasy and Continue so, after frequent Rebukes from Master Easy any two members may bring in a bill of ejectment against him Upon which ye Club shall proceed as in ye case of ye Deserter.

Lex 10[t]

It is Statute and Enacted that no member shall bring in a stranger to a meeting of ye Club and any so doing or contemning and impugning these laws is hereby declar'd guilty of high Crimes and Misdemeanours for which he is lyable to the Censure of the Club to be punished as they shall agree.

Source: A. J. Sinclair (1996) 'The Emergence of Philosophical Inquiry in 18th Century Scotland', unpublished Ph.D. thesis, the Centre for Philosophical Inquiry, University of Glasgow, appendix C, pp. 121–122.

Notes

Preface

1 Investigating 'what is it that distinguishes people from other entities?'
2 See Chapter 4 for the full transcript of this Philosophical Inquiry with 5-year-olds.

1 Introduction

1 The full transcript of the ninety-minute dialogue with 5-year-old children is presented with accompanying explanatory notes in Chapter 4.
2 CoPI was first created and practised with university students in 1975 and later adapted for use with 5-year-old children in 1984.
3 For more about Piaget's theories on cognitive development, see Chapter 2.
4 By which I mean lecturers in education, cognitive psychologists, philosophers, teachers, educational administers, *et al.*
5 See G. Matthews, *Philosophy and the Young Child*, Cambridge, MA: Harvard University Press (1980).
6 For more, see Chapter 2.
7 Unless physically restricted.
8 The full transcript of that CoPI session with 5-year-olds is given in Chapter 4.

2 The origins and development of 'Community of Philosophical Inquiry'

1 Having spent as much time working as a stage manager in the university theatre as studying philosophy, I had watched writer-directors use improvisation exercises to generate scripts.
2 A society in Trinity College, Dublin University.
3 I was greatly encouraged to continue in this role, despite my total lack of experience, by the moral support and encouragement of my dissertation supervisor, Dr David Berman.
4 Plato, *Symposium*, ed. Kenneth Dover, Cambridge: Cambridge University Press (1980).
5 The author of that paper later published a book on children's rights, which included the expanded theories and arguments that had been generated in the dialogue at the conference.
6 I did not realise at the time how influential this philosopher was to be, and to my eternal regret I have no record of her name.
7 The Northern Universities conference was the first philosophy conference we had

attended, and we assumed it was typical. However, I was to learn later that it was anything but. Attending philosophy conferences over many years since then, I never again saw the kind of exciting dialogue that we observed there.

8   Charades is a game in which there are two teams of players. One player mimes (acts without words) the title of a book, film or play while players in his or her team must guess the title of the book, film or play.

9   This was the one and only conference that I have ever attended where middle-aged and elderly philosophers played charades – one of the features that made the conference unique in my experience.

10 For an explanation of how collaborative philosophising creates a unique type of community, see Chapter 5.

11 For an explanation of utilitarian ethics, Kantian ethics and 'egoistic' ethics, see P. Edwards (ed.), *The Encyclopaedia of Philosophy*, New York: Macmillan (1967).

12 For a discussion about the reasons for these 'effects', see Chapter 7.

13 L. Carroll [Charles Lutwidge Dodgson], *Alice's Adventures in Wonderland*, http://www.gutenberg.org/etext/19033 (1865) and *Through the Looking Glass*, http://www.gutenberg.org/etext/12 (1871).

14 See L. Kohlberg, 'The Claim to Moral Adequacy of a Highest Stage of Moral Judgment', *Journal of Philosophy*, 70: 630–646 (1970).

15 I had spent four years working in London West End theatres before returning to academic research.

16 For more detailed description of how to do this, see Chapter 7.

17 Then Director of the Institute for the Advancement of Philosophy for Children (IAPC) at Montclair State College, New Jersey.

18 Working at the IAPC in New Jersey, Lipman had written five short philosophical novels for children and teenagers: *Pixie* for 10–12-year-olds, *Harry Stottlemeier's Discovery* for 12–14-year-olds, *Lisa* for 14–16-year-olds, and *Suki* and *Mark* for 16–18-year-olds. The P4C programmes comprised the five novels with teacher's manuals that included exercises and discussion plans for teachers to use in the classroom in order to support discussion with children. For a more detailed description of the P4C programmes and approach, see Chapter 6.

19 It turned out that the first and second grade teachers knew this, but were desperate to take the graduate classes in philosophy for children, even if they were not allowed to implement the programmes.

20 Lipman's novels for children, *Pixie* (1981), *Kio and Gus* (1982), *Harry Stottlemeier's Discovery* (1982), *Lisa* (1983), *Suki* (1978) and *Mark* (1980) are all currently published by the IAPC, Montclair State University, New Jersey, USA.

21 The co-coordinator for the graduate class was a first grade teacher, Mrs Connie Bowsher, who had previously observed a visiting IAPC philosopher (Dr Michael Walley) working with older children in her school. She was convinced that something could be done for the younger children also. She believed that young children could be taught anything; the only barrier was the skill and knowledge of the teacher.

22 All the teachers attended the graduate seminars, where they were taught how to use two of the IAPC programmes: *Pixie* (for grades 4–6) and *Harry* (for grades 7–9). In the graduate class, teachers of grades 3–9 then implemented those programmes with their classes.

23 C. C. McCall, 'Some Problems with Verification in Piaget's Experimental Protocols', paper delivered to the British Psychological Society postgraduate conference (1981).

24 In the IAPC curriculum used with older children, a teacher had the resource of a large teacher's manual with exercises and discussion plans, which he or she would use to focus the discussion on the 'leading ideas' in the story.

25 I was consulting with Mrs Connie Bowsher, the coordinating first grade teacher.
26 In recent years a variation of the CoPI reasoning structure has been tried: CoPI Version2 involves three elements: '**I agree with** ———— (the name of the person with whom the speaker was agreeing) **when s/he says** ———— (repeat the point being agreed with) **because** ———— (give a reason)' or '**I disagree with** ———— (the name of the person with whom the speaker was agreeing) **when s/he says** ———— (repeat the point being disagreed with) **because** ———— (give a reason)'.
27 If twenty children take part, and each child thinks of their own idea and reason, there will be forty potential new contributions.
28 For an explanation of techniques in elicitation, see Chapter 5 on creating Communities of Philosophical Inquiry.
29 This role was crucial, and required a certain level of background knowledge as well as skill. For more detailed description, see Chapter 7.
30 From conversations with Gareth Matthews in 1984.
31 In some classes by the fourth session!
32 One of the parents who saw a change in his child was a journalist. He was so intrigued that he interviewed children in a first grade class.
33 When the children had reading time with the librarian in the school library, they would ask to 'do philosophy' with their books.
34 Figures drawn from the national California Aptitude Tests (CATs) through which all children were assessed.

3 The theoretical landscape

1 J. Piaget, *Introduction à l'Épistémologie Génétique*, Paris: Presses Universitaires de France (1950).
2 This is necessarily a simplified description of Piaget's stages. For a more complete description, see B. Inhelder and J. Piaget, *The Early Growth of Logic in the Child: Classification and Seriation*, London: Routledge and Kegan Paul (1964).
3 As argued in C. C. McCall, 'Some Problems with Verification in Piaget's Experimental Protocols', paper delivered to the British Psychological Society postgraduate conference (1981).
4 Emeritus Professor of Developmental Psychology, Edinburgh University.
5 See her classic work: M. Donaldson, *Children's Minds*, New York: W. W. Norton (1979).
6 S. Milgram, 'Behavioral Study of Obedience', *Journal of Abnormal and Social Psychology*, 67: 371–378 (1963).
7 And Popper's 'test' of science, that science proceeds not by verification but by falsification, might lead one to question the method of verifying hypotheses in empirical psychological research. See K. Popper, *Conjectures and Refutations*, London: Routledge (1963).
8 One result of this 'received wisdom' was that my 1987 and 1988 proposals for funding to research the ability of young children to engage in philosophical reasoning yielded no funds. I therefore had no option but to 'self-fund' the research.
9 The philosophical dialogue with 5-year-old children in Chapter 4 came about as a consequence of the 1988 NEH Professor's Research Seminar on 'The Concept of Child' led by Gareth Matthews. Members of the multidisciplinary seminar, who were drawn from across the United States, (strongly) recommended that I gather evidence for my claim that young children could reason philosophically, and so I began the project of transcribing the children's dialogues over the course of a year.
10 In private conversations with the author, 1984.

11 L. Kohlberg, *Essays on Moral Development*, vol. 1: *The Philosophy of Moral Development*, New York: Harper and Row (1981).

12 See A. Colby, J. Gibbs, M. Lieberman and L. Kohlberg, *A Longitudinal Study of Moral Judgment: A Monograph for the Society of Research in Child Development*, Chicago: University of Chicago Press (1983).

13 See I. Kant, *Grounding for the Metaphysics of Morals*, 3rd edn, trans. J. W. Ellington, Indianapolis: Hackett ([1785] 1993).

14 See D. Hume, *A Treatise of Human Nature*, Harmondsworth: Penguin ([1739] 1985).

15 See J. S. Mill, *Utilitarianism*, 2nd rev. edn, Indianapolis: Hackett ([1863] 2002).

16 See C. Gilligan, *In a Different Voice*, Cambridge, MA: Harvard University Press (1982).

17 In Morocco in 1971, and Jerusalem in 1978.

18 The examples also illustrate why a CoPI Chair needs to understand basic logic, as explained in Chapters 5 and 7.

19 The children also examine other philosophical topics, including the nature of consciousness, the limits of knowledge, the nature of thinking, questions of medical ethics, the nature of personhood – and more.

20 R. E. Nisbett (with T. D. Wilson), 'Telling More than We Can Know: Verbal Reports on Mental Processes', *Psychological Review*, 84: 231–259 (1977).

21 P. Wason and P. Johnson-Laird, *Psychology of Reasoning: Structure and Content*, Cambridge, MA: Harvard University Press (1972).

22 The 'language source' for such arguments would have to have been something similar to technical philosophy, which the children had never heard.

4 Philosophising with 5-year-olds

1 For more about the role of the CoPI Chair, see Chapters 5 and 7.

2 In fact, using the CoPI reasoning structure without proper training in philosophy and logic, as well as the CoPI method, can have terrible results for children! See Chapter 7.

3 The names of the children have been changed to protect their identities.

4 From 1984 to 1988 I had been using Matthew Lipman's novel for 10-year-olds, *Pixie*, with much younger children. In 1988 I began to use a draft of a new novel then being written for younger children by Lipman, *Elfie*. This was the first time the draft of *Elfie* was used, and some of the children did not realise it was a different novel and so still called the main character 'Pixie' instead of 'Elfie'.

5 More comments could be made about the dialogue, but too many would obscure the flow.

6 The names of the children have been changed to preserve anonymity.

7 For example, when working with groups of adults such as 65-year-old company directors, unemployed single mothers, artists, healthcare workers, *et al*. The CoPI Chair uses exactly the same CoPI method with any group of people of any age, in any setting.

8 K. Murris, 'The Role of the Facilitator in Philosophical Inquiry', *Thinking*, 15(2): 40–46 (2000).

9 Murris argues further that my intervention 'steers' the children away from epistemological lines in the dialogue and back towards the ethical dimensions. This is accurate, and the reason for moving towards the ethical rather than the epistemological line, both of which were present, was because we had investigated similar metaphysical and epistemological questions the day before – and part of the CoPI Chair's job is to structure the dialogue so that *new* ideas and arguments come forward.

10 At the time of Murris's writing, while the M.Phil. and Ph.D. degrees in Philosophical Inquiry were running at Glasgow University, the specific nature of CoPI was little known outside Scotland.

5 Creating a Community of Philosophical Inquiry (CoPI) with all ages

1 As understanding the origin of something is not the same as understanding its nature.
2 One needs to be trained in how to chair CoPI by a qualified and experienced CoPI trainer.
3 A minimum of twenty hours is required for a group to reach the stage of being able to engage in Philosophical Inquiry rather than discussion. Usually children will be involved in CoPI for about 100 hours over the course of a year.
4 This external realism differs from Hegel's idealist philosophy.
5 The following is, by necessity, a simplified description of a philosophy of external realism.
6 Because people are and were fallible, they made a mistake about the nature of the Earth when they thought it was flat. Even if absolutely everyone alive at the time thought the Earth was flat, thinking the Earth was flat did not make it flat!
7 For more on realism, see J. Searle, *The Construction of Social Reality*, new edn, London: Penguin Books (1996).
8 The object's presence may contribute causally to a series of events that will eventually change the weather: the 'Butterfly Effect' – a term first coined by Edward Lorenz in 1963 to describe large effects resulting from minute causes in weather systems.
9 No person or conscious being.
10 G. Berkeley, *A Treatise Concerning the Principles of Human Knowledge*, Indianapolis: Hackett ([1710] 1982).
11 K. Popper, *Conjectures and Refutations: The Growth of Scientific Knowledge*, London: Routledge and Kegan Paul (1963).
12 Many more examples can be seen in the transcript of this dialogue in Chapter 4.
13 In adult CoPI groups, participants are required to remain 'anonymous'; that is, they do not reveal their job, profession or any special knowledge or expertise they may have. This is not so much a factor with children, who have not yet acquired these properties and so are not 'defined' in any way by them.
14 For explanations of different philosophical schools of thought and positions, see P. Edwards (ed.), *The Encyclopaedia of Philosophy*, New York: Macmillan (1967).
15 Unless they are philosophically trained themselves, and even then they are often unaware.

6 Different methods of group philosophical discussion

1 Note: 'dialogue' is a subset of 'discussion': not all discussions are dialogues.
2 As there are many different ways of eliciting philosophical dialogue with groups of people, this chapter cannot look at them all. For example, since the 1990s there has been a growing international movement of philosophy cafés where members of the general public come to a café to engage in philosophical conversations directed by a philosopher, and every philosophy café is different.
3 The descriptions do not purport to be comprehensive, but rather serve as outlines that will indicate the similarities and differences between CoPI and other methods of engaging in discussion within the general field.

4 L. Nelson, *Socratic Method and Critical Philosophy: Selected Essays*, New Haven, CT: Yale University Press (1949), p. 1.

5 Ibid., p. 10.

6 Ibid., p. 9.

7 'The Socratic Discussion: An Introduction to the Method and Some Literature', unpublished notes by Karel van der Leeuw for the SOPHIA Network Meeting, 2007.

8 There are philosophical problems with Nelson's philosophy which I will not address here, as what concerns us is how his philosophy dictates the practice.

9 J. Dewey, *Democracy and Education*, New York: The Free Press ([1916] 1997).

10 The environment is understood broadly to include physical, social and intellectual environments.

11 There are some problems with this, particularly related to the nature of those needs and desires.

12 Richard Field in the *Internet Encyclopedia of Philosophy*, at http://www.iep.utm.edu/d/dewey.htm.

13 When Lipman's P4C programmes were initially introduced to schools in the United States, teachers had to undertake sixty hours of graduate training courses to learn how to implement the P4C programmes. Only professors who held a Ph.D. in philosophy taught these graduate courses.

14 In recent years some variation has developed in the P4C training models as compared with the initial provisions outlined in note 13.

15 In conversations with the author at the Institute for the Advancement of Philosophy for Children (IAPC) from 1984 to 1990.

16 One of the *Transformers* series of documentary feature films directed by Annie Paul and broadcast by the BBC in the United Kingdom in 1990 and 1991, the Discovery Channel in the United States and subsequently by many national broadcasting companies around the world throughout the 1990s.

17 However, it should be noted that different practitioners vary in the way in which they implement the ten steps, so the SAPERE approach can look very different in different classrooms.

18 See Chapter 1, note 9.

19 *Wondering* (2008), age range 6–10, and the *Teacher's Guide to Wondering*; *Wondering Adventures* (2008), age range 7–12, and the *Teacher's Guide to Wondering Adventures*; *Talking Thinking* (forthcoming), age range 9–13, and the *Teacher's Guide to Talking Thinking*; *Thinking Adventures* (2006), age range 10–14, and the *Teacher's Guide to Thinking Adventures*; *Thinking Changes* (2007), age range 11–15, and the *Teacher's Guide to Thinking Changes*; *Thinking Challenges* (2007), age range 12–16, and the *Teacher's Guide to Thinking Challenges*; *Thinking Transformations* (forthcoming), age range 13–17, and the *Teacher's Guide to Thinking Transformations*; *Thinking Philosophy* (2008) (based on philosophy Higher and A level texts), age range 14–19, and the *Teacher's Guide to Thinking Philosophy*.

7 What you need to know to chair a CoPI with 6–16-year-olds

1 For an example of why a CoPI Chair needs to understand logic, see the analysis of the underlying logical structures in the children's dialogue in Chapter 3.

2 For an introduction to logic, see M. Haight, *The Snake and the Fox: Introduction to Logic*, London: Routledge (1999). Then I. Copi, *Introduction to Logic*, London: Macmillan (1953).

3 For introduction to philosophy, see R. Scruton, *An Intelligent Person's Guide to Philosophy*, London: Duckworth (1997); E. Craig, *Philosophy: A Very Short Introduction*, Oxford: Oxford Univerity Press (2002); T. Nagel, *What Does It All*

Mean? A Very Short Introduction to Philosophy, new edn, New York: Oxford University Press (2004); S. Blackburn, *Think: A Compelling Introduction to Philosophy*, new edn, Oxford: Oxford University Press (2001); D. Dennett and D. Hofstadter, *The Mind's I: Fantasies and Reflections on the Self and Soul*, new edn, Harmondsworth: Penguin Books (1982); T. Nagel, 'What Is It Like to Be a Bat', at http://members. aol.com/NeoNoetics/Nagel_Bat.html.

4 Every CoPI student will learn basic logic and philosophy, the skills of analysing spoken language for the underlying logical structures and philosophy, the CoPI procedures, and the different materials that can be used to begin a CoPI.

5 In private correspondence with the author, August 1990.

6 See Chapter 6 for a description of the Guided Socratic Discussion curriculum and methodology.

8 Implementing CoPI in primary and secondary schools

1 However, this class had the advantage of previous experience with Community of Enquiry group discussion and Guided Socratic Discussion, both of which provide a good preparation for engaging in CoPI, so they were not typical 'beginners'.

2 Even when working with the 5-year-olds featured in Chapter 4 every day, it took about one month before most of the children had begun to master the CoPI reasoning structure.

3 Normally, most of the children in the class whose CoPI session is transcribed in Chapter 4 participated in the dialogue. However, the presence of a director, a large cameraman and a sound technician sitting in the circle with the children in order to film them, and their actions in pointing a huge film camera and sound boom at the 5-year-olds, inhibited many of the children on that occasion. So, while still spectacular, the dialogue was not as rich and varied as usual. Usually far more children would speak.

4 The age at which children begin school varies between countries. In Scotland, primary schoolchildren are usually between 4 and 11 years old, and secondary schoolchildren between 11 and 18 years old. In England, primary schoolchildren are usually between 5 and 11 years old, and secondary schoolchildren between 11 and 18 years old (but this may vary depending upon the nature of the secondary school). In many European countries, children begin school at 7 years old, and in the United States often at 6 years old.

5 Using the SAPERE approach with ten steps; see Chapter 6 for an outline of both the SAPERE approach and the GSD series.

6 This particular group of children did develop the skills of listening and waiting very quickly thereafter. There was a big difference between the first CoPI session transcribed here and the second and subsequent sessions, during which the children did not interrupt and did develop patience.

7 C. C. McCall, *Laura and Paul*, 3rd edn, Oxford: Trafford Publishing (2006), available at: www.trafford.com/4dcgi/view-item?item=18340.

8 Ibid.

9 It may be different for teenagers who are home-schooled.

10 The reading the previous week was chapter 1 of C. C. McCall, *Christine's Story* (Washington, D.C.: EPIC Publications, 2006).

Shadows were falling as Christine walked home. She wondered if John had any idea about her feelings for him. It was strange, they had known each other since Primary School but lately she had begun to feel differently towards him. 'I really didn't like the way he was when we first came to the High School,' she was thinking. 'When he started acting all tough, and getting into fights! But he seems more like himself now, as though he is more comfortable just being who he is. He actually cares about other people. He's really nothing like Dave and his gang, who hate anyone who is different from them.'

Still, she could see why some people were scared of John. John was big and he had a reputation for fighting from those years. If you didn't know him he could look scary.

She was thinking about what John had just told her on the bus: how Dave and his gang had been hanging out near the park, and would have beaten Tim up, only Tim ran right through the gang (actually knocked one of them over) because he was running away from John! John actually wanted to help Tim, not to hurt him. He had shouted after Tim only because he wanted to talk to him, but when Tim heard John shouting – he ran!

'What a messed-up situation!' Christine thought. 'I'm going to have to talk to Tim and explain that John isn't angry with him, he wants to help.'

But Christine was still worried about *how* they could help Tim without getting Tim and his family into more difficulties than they already faced.

'Maybe John's cousin is right, when she says we have to tell someone,' Christine thought. 'Tim's family need help – Tim can't go on missing school to work in place of his dad, and he shouldn't have to be looking after his little sister and a sick father by himself!'

Christine walked up the steps to her house.

'Anyway I can't lie to Mr Ross if he asks me about Tim again,' she was thinking. 'And I can't go on worrying about it – it's affecting everything. I've got to be able to sing for the school show.'

Christine's mum and dad were really proud of her getting the part of 'Sandy' in the school show. It was the lead role, and she was playing opposite Joannece. Lots of girls were jealous of her because she got to kiss Joannece, and they had to rehearse the kissing! The girls did not know that it was not real kissing. They had to learn how to do 'stage kissing', like 'stage fighting'. There was lots to learn when you were in a show.

Christine did worry a little about her dad's reaction when he saw her kissing – on stage in front of hundreds of people! They were supposed to look like passionate kisses, but Christine found that hard because she did not fancy Joannece. Even though he was very good looking.

'Well if I can't sing because all this worry is affecting my voice, it won't hardly matter that I can't do a convincing pretend kiss!' Christine thought.

9 CoPI, citizenship, moral virtue and academic performance with primary and secondary schoolchildren

1 The best-known film is the 1990 BBC documentary *Socrates for Six-Year-Olds*, which has been used throughout the world in teacher training colleges and by independent consultants.
2 See Chapter 4.
3 See Chapters 5 and 7.
4 And there are people who will offer them an easier way. But the easy way does not give the same results, and teachers in particular are frequently disappointed when they do not get the outcomes that they first saw in the film.
5 See Chapters 5 and 7.
6 Within the limits of space, it is not possible to give a full description of the results of children engaging in CoPI over extended periods of time. Such a description will be given in a further publication.
7 Each group was chaired by a graduate in Philosophical Inquiry, who had been

trained in philosophy and logic and in chairing CoPI at Glasgow University through the M.Phil. degree in Philosophical Inquiry.

8 STV News

9 The 'Philosophy Is Fun' project also generated newspaper articles and radio programmes about CoPI.

10 Too many to list and describe fully here, the community projects are described in my forthcoming book *Creating Active Citizens: CoPI with Adults and Children in the Community.*

11 The impact that CoPI has had in communities, workplaces and boardrooms, etc. (from 1990 to 2008) is the subject of my next book on Community of Philosophical Inquiry: *Creating Active Citizens: CoPI with Adults and Children in the Community.*

12 A version of the following was first published in C. McCall, *The 1991 Stevenson Lectures*, Glasgow: Glasgow University Press (1991) – a series of four public lectures delivered at Glasgow University.

13 The argument first put forward in the 1991 Stevenson Lectures and reiterated here – that adults also show deficiencies in reasoning – was taken up by Mary Midgley in letters to the editor of the *Guardian* in 1996, and later by Karin Murris in 'Can Children Do Philosophy?', *Journal of Philosophy of Education*, 34(2): 261–279 (2000).

14 CoPI participants frequently report the experience of feeling liberated through engaging in CoPI.

15 See Chapters 5 and 7.

16 This feature of having everything open to question also distinguishes CoPI from other forms of discussion and/or investigation.

17 And research has also shown that these 'skills' do not transfer into other academic subjects or everyday judgements.

18 Although the illustrations of, for example, the dynamic of dialogue in furthering inquiry, or the interrelationship of reasonableness in behaviour with reasoning skills, have been samples of Philosophical Inquiry being undertaken by children, these ideas about the nature of the dynamic, etc. hold for adult human beings too. It is human beings of whatever age, status or background who are fallible and creative and social, etc. by nature. They do not change in kind as they get older.

19 By 'fully understand' I mean that citizens understand that expert witnesses, authorities, etc. are fallible and may be wrong.

20 See Chapter 5.

21 C. S. Peirce, *Collected Writings* (8 vols), ed. C. Hartshorne, P. Weiss and A. Burks, Cambridge, MA: Harvard University Press (1931–1958). Peirce goes on to write, 'The first step toward finding out is to acknowledge you do not satisfactorily know already; so that no blight can so surely arrest all intellectual growth as the blight of cocksureness; and ninety-nine out of every hundred good heads are reduced to impotence by that malady—of whose inroads they are most strangely unaware!'

22 For a further discussion of children and citizenship in relation to CoPI, see C. Cassidy, *Thinking Children*, London: Continuum (2007).

23 I should say here that I do not think there is a clear division between character and role; I think it is somewhat of a false dichotomy. I would argue that because modern understanding does frequently divide the two, one or other aspect of citizenship is overlooked.

10 Afterword

1 For example, the 'Philosophy Is Fun' project. Features: 'The Power of Positive Thinking', *The Big Issue*, no. 55 (21 July–3 August 1995); *STV News* (2 July 1996);

'It's All in the Mind', *Record* (17 September 1998); 'Food for Thought', *The Big Issue* (1 August 2002); 'So Why Don't Sheep Shrink in the Rain?', *Sunday Mail* (6 February 2005); 'The Sun Also Rises for Our Youngsters', *Herald* (3 February 2005); 'Positive Outcome of Critical Thinking', *The Times Educational Supplement (Scotland)* (4 March 2005).

2 C. McCall, 'Design Inquiries', in *The Scottish Show 07*, Glasgow: The Scottish Show 2007 Publications (2007).

3 Featured on *STV News* (31 January 2005).

4 For example, the 'Empowerment through Philosophical Dialogue' CoPI project in Springburn, Glasgow, 1992, and the 'Hawthorn' project, Possilpark, Glasgow, 1994. Features: 'Socratic Truth in Urban Blight', *Independent* (15 July 1992); 'The Possil Philosophers', *Herald* (13 July 1992); 'Cogito Ergo Something for Everyone', *Herald* (17 February 1993); 'A Place Where Thought Counts', *The Big Issue*, no. 2 (9–22 July 1994); *STV News* (n.d., 1994).

5 The 'Scottish National Dialogue', featured in 'Facing up to the "Knowledge Economy"', *Herald Business* (30 March 1998); 'It's All in the Mind', *Record* (17 September 1998); 'Navel Exercises Floated on an Ocean of Inquiry', *Sunday Herald* (13 August 2000).

6 Featured in: 'Springing the Trap', *Scotsman* (5 April 1995); 'Let's Think Again, Deeply', *Daily Telegraph* (n.d., 1995); 'Learning the Business of Thinking Philosophically', *Herald Business* (26 February 1996); 'Laura and Paul Do Profundity', *Guardian Weekly* (8 June 1996).

7 See E. Imrie, 'Initial Aesthetic Inquiry', Glasgow: The Transmission Gallery (1977).

8 Featured on *Scottish Action*, STV (1995); 'Reasons to Be Thoughtful', *Herald* (17 June 1997).

9 'Defying the Odds with Practical Philosophy', *The Times Educational Supplement* (20 October 1995); 'Let's Think Again – Deeply', *Daily Telegraph* (n.d., 1995).

10 'Waxing Philosophical', *Herald* (30 May 1991); 'Rebuilding the Pillars of Wisdom', *Scotsman* (n.d., 1993); 'Referees at Thinking Matches', *The Times Higher Educational Supplement* (15 April 1994); 'Mum, If There Was a Big Bang, What Was the Big Bang In?', *Independent on Sunday* (12 February 1995); 'Meet the Woman Who Is Mellowing the Wildest Kids in Scots Schools . . . with Philosophy', *Sun* (12 June 1997); 'Little People, Big ideas', *The Times* (12 April 1997); 'Glasgow's Child Philosophers', *Reader's Digest* (January 1999); 'Schoolchildren Should Be Thinking Deeper, Says Philosopher', *Sunday Herald* (30 January 2005); 'Positive Thinking', *The Times Higher Educational Supplement Scotland* (10 November 2006).

11 'Discoveries on the Road to Nowhere', *Scotsman* (26 August 1993); 'Rebuilding the Pillars of Wisdom', *Scotsman* (n.d., 1993).

12 In 1992 the Head of Research of Jordanhill College visited the Hawthorn project to advise on how research could be designed to capture the wide-ranging effects of CoPI upon a community. To his knowledge, no instruments then extant could capture these effects, and so he advised using an anthropological model for research.

13 J. Cunningham, 'The Possil Philosophers', *Herald* (13 July 1992).

14 C. McCall, *Laura and Paul*, Glasgow: Glasgow University Press (1989). The second edition was used for this project. The third (2006) edition is published by Trafford.

15 S. Flockhart, 'A Place Where Thought Counts', *The Big Issue*, no. 2 (9–22 July 1993).

16 See Chapter 9 for an outline of how CoPI develops courage.

17 Interview with Grace McKendrick from Susan Lumsden, 'The Power of Positive Thinking', *The Big Issue*, no. 55 (31 July–3 August 1995).

18 The brewers wished to remain anonymous.

19 As we shall see, the phenomenon of philosophy clubs meeting in pubs or taverns was not new to Scotland.

20 As many CoPI projects have been run outside of schools and education institutions as within. These projects and their effects upon communities, workplaces and professional associations will be outlined in my forthcoming book *Creating Active Citizens: CoPI with Adults and Children in the Community*.

21 See A. Herman, *How the Scots Invented the Modern World*, New York: Crown (2002).

22 See G. E. Davie, *The Democratic Intellect: Scotland and Her Universities in the Nineteenth Century*, Edinburgh: Edinburgh University Press (1961).

23 Edinburgh UNESCO City of Literature, *We Cultivate Literature on a Little Oatmeal . . .*, 2nd rev. edn, Edinburgh: Edinburgh UNESCO City of Literature Trust (2005), p. 27.

24 See A. J. Sinclair, 'The Emergence of Philosophical Inquiry in 18th Century Scotland', unpublished Ph.D. thesis, the Centre for Philosophical Inquiry, University of Glasgow, appendix C, pp. 121–122.

25 Edinburgh UNESCO, op. cit.

26 See A. Broadie (ed.), *The Cambridge Companion to the Scottish Enlightenment*, Cambridge: Cambridge University Press (2002).

27 See, for example, ibid., and J. Buchan, *Crowded with Genius: The Scottish Enlightenment*, New York: HarperCollins (2002).

28 'Scottish Enlightenment', in *Encyclopaedia Britannica* (2008). Retrieved 16 September 2008, from Encyclopaedia Britannica Online: http://www.britannica.com/EB checked/topic/529682/Scottish-Enlightenment.

29 The *Encyclopaedia Britannica* is itself a creation of the Scottish Enlightenment!

30 As note 28.

31 See Appendix B.

32 Possibly in a manner that is similar to the way that CoPI uses difference and contradiction, where, far from being a problem, it is *because* different and often contradictory ideas and arguments are put forward that new theories emerge.

33 One can infer, from the existence of such rules, that settling differences with a sword or a knife was sufficiently common to need to be outlawed.

34 Edinburgh UNESCO, op. cit., p. 26.

35 The opinion that it was the *collaborative philosophical dialogue* in which people of different professions and different strata in society engaged in thinking about the issues of the day that provided the engine for the great scientific, philosophical, economic and agricultural revolution in Scotland requires more exposition and defence than can be given here.

36 For example, Professor Gordon Graham on *Newsnight Scotland*, BBC2 (5 February 2005).

37 Herman, op. cit.

38 Edinburgh UNESCO, op. cit., p. 26.

Bibliography

Alexander, R. (2006) *Towards Dialogic Teaching: Rethinking Classroom Talk*, 3rd edn, Cambridge: Dialogos.

Austin, J. L. (1952) 'How to Talk', in J. L. Austin (1979) *Philosophical Papers*, 3rd edn, Oxford: Oxford University Press.

Austin, J. L. (1956) 'A Plea for Excuses', in J. L. Austin (1979) *Philosophical Papers*, 3rd edn, Oxford: Oxford University Press.

Ayer, A. J. (1956) *The Problem of Knowledge*, Harmondsworth: Penguin Books.

Berkeley, G. (1710) *A Treatise Concerning the Principles of Human Knowledge*, Indianapolis: Hackett (1982).

Blackburn, S. (2001) *Think: A Compelling Introduction to Philosophy*, new edn, Oxford: Oxford University Press.

Broadie, A. (ed.) (2002) *The Cambridge Companion to the Scottish Enlightenment*, Cambridge: Cambridge University Press.

Bruner, J. (1960) *The Process of Education*, Cambridge, MA: Harvard University Press.

Buchan, J. (2003) *Crowded with Genius: The Scottish Enlightenment*, New York: HarperCollins.

Cam, P. (1995) *Thinking Together: Philosophical Inquiry for the Classroom*, Sydney: Hale and Iremonger.

Cam, P. (1998) *Thinking Stories*, Sydney: Hale and Iremonger.

Carroll, L. [Charles Lutwidge Dodgson] (1865) *Alice's Adventures in Wonderland*, at http://www.gutenberg.org/etext/19033

Carroll, L. [Charles Lutwidge Dodgson] (1871) *Through the Looking Glass*, at http://www.gutenberg.org/etext/12.

Cassidy, C. (2007) *Thinking Children*, London: Continuum Press.

Colby, A., Gibbs, J., Lieberman, M. and Kohlberg, L. (1983) *A Longitudinal Study of Moral Judgment: A Monograph for the Society of Research in Child Development*, Chicago: University of Chicago Press.

Copi, I. (1953) *Introduction to Logic*, London: Macmillan.

Craig, E. (2002) *Philosophy: A Very Short Introduction Philosophy*, Oxford: Oxford University Press.

Davie, G. E. (1961) *The Democratic Intellect: Scotland and Her Universities in the Nineteenth Century*, Edinburgh: Edinburgh University Press.

Dennett, D. and Hofstadter, D. (1982) *The Mind's I: Fantasies and Reflections on the Self and Soul*, new edn, Harmondsworth: Penguin Books.

Dewey, J. (1916) *Democracy and Education*, reprint edn New York: The Free Press (1997).

Donaldson, M. (1979) *Children's Minds*, New York: W. W. Norton.

Edinburgh UNESCO City of Literature (2005) *We Cultivate Literature on a Little Oatmeal*, 2nd rev. edn, Edinburgh: Edinburgh UNESCO City of Literature Trust.

Edwards, P. (ed.) (1967) *The Encyclopaedia of Philosophy*, New York: Macmillan.

Ennis, R. H. (2004) *Critical Thinking*, at www.criticalthinking.net.

Fisher, R. (2003) *Teaching Thinking: Philosophical Enquiry in the Classroom*, 2nd edn, London: Continuum.

Flew, A. (1989) *An Introduction to Western Philosophy*, rev. edn, London: Thames and Hudson.

Flockhart, S. (1993) 'A Place Where Thought Counts', *The Big Issue*, no. 2, 9–22 July.

Gardner, H. (1983) *Frames of Mind*, New York: Basic Books.

Gilligan, C. (1982) *In a Different Voice*, Cambridge, MA: Harvard University Press.

Haight, M. (1999) *The Snake and the Fox: Introduction to Logic*, London: Routledge.

Hare, R. M. (1964) *The Language of Morals*, Oxford: Oxford University Press.

Herman, A (2002) *How the Scots Invented the Modern World*, New York: Crown.

Hickman, L. A. and Alexander, T. M. (1998) *The Essential Dewey*, vol. 1, Bloomington: Indiana University Press.

Honderich, T. (1995) *The Oxford Companion to Philosophy*, Oxford: Oxford University Press.

Hume, D. (1739) *A Treatise of Human Nature*, Harmondsworth: Penguin Books (1985).

Imrie, E. (1977) *Initial Aesthetic Inquiry*, Glasgow: The Transmission Gallery.

Inhelder, B. and Piaget, J. (1964) *The Early Growth of Logic in the Child: Classification and Seriation*, London: Routledge and Kegan Paul.

Jackson, F. (1998) *From Metaphysics to Ethics: A Defence of Conceptual Analysis*, Oxford: Clarendon Press.

Kant, I. (1781) *Critique of Pure Reason*, trans. N. Kemp Smith, London: Palgrave Macmillan (2003).

Kant, I. (1785) *Grounding for the Metaphysics of Morals*, 3rd edn, trans. James W. Ellington, Indianapolis: Hackett (1993).

Kohlberg, L. (1981) *Essays on Moral Development*, vol.1: *The Philosophy of Moral Development*, New York: Harper and Row.

Lipman, M. (1988) *Philosophy Goes to School*, Philadelphia: Temple University Press.

Lipman, M. (1991) *Thinking in Education*, New York: Cambridge University Press.

Lipman, M. (2003) *Thinking in Education*, 2nd edn, Cambridge: Cambridge University Press.

Lipman, M., Sharp, A. M. and Oscanyan, F. S. (1980) *Philosophy in the Classroom*, 2nd edn, Philadelphia: Temple University Press.

McCall, C. C. (1981) 'Some Problems with Verification in Piaget's Experimental Protocols', paper delivered to the British Psychological Society postgraduate conference.

McCall, C. (1990) *The Concepts of Person, Self and Human Being*, Aldershot: Avebury Press.

McCall, C. (1990) 'Young Children Generate Philosophical Ideas', *Thinking*, 8, 2: 22–41. (Reprinted in M. Lipman (ed.) (1993) *Thinking, Children and Education*, Montclair, NJ: Kendall/Hunt, pp. 569–593.)

McCall, C. (1991) *The 1991 Stevenson Lectures in Citizenship*, Glasgow: Glasgow University Press. Lecture 1, 'Philosophical Inquiry with Five-Year-Olds'; Lecture 2,

'Communities of Inquiry'; Lecture 3, 'Is It Rational to Be Reasonable?'; Lecture 4, 'Reasoning and Citizenship'.

McCall, C. (1997) 'Jobs for Philosophers: Philosophical Inquiry – Origin and Development', in W. van der Vlist (ed.) *Perspectives in Philosophical Practice*, Doorwerth: Vereniging voor Filosofische Praktijk.

McCall, C. (1998) 'Everything Connected?', in P. Cam (ed.) *Thinking Stories 1*, Sydney: Hale and Iremonger.

McCall, C. C. (2006) *Christine's Story*, Washington, D.C.: EPIC Publications.

McCall, C. C. (2006) *Laura and Paul*, 3rd edn, Oxford: Trafford Publishing, at http://www.trafford.com.

McCall, C. (2006) 'Socrates for Six Year Olds: Theory and Practice', in D. G. Camhy and R. Born (eds) *Encouraging Philosophical Thinking*, Sankt Augustin: Academia Verlag.

McCall, C. C. (2006) *Teacher's Guide to Thinking Adventures*, Edinburgh: Scottish Executive, at http://www.flatprojects.org. uk/projects/c_centwesteduc/conftoearn. asp.

McCall, C. (2007) 'Design Inquiries', in *The Scottish Show 07*, Glasgow: The Scottish Show 2007 Publications.

McCall, C. C. (2007) 'Five-Year-Old Children in Philosophical Dialogue', paper delivered to The Second Enlightenment Conference, Columbia, SC, 2 March.

McCall, C. C. (2007) 'Philosophical Inquiry with Children', keynote paper delivered to Philosophy of Education Society of Great Britain One-Day Conference on Philosophy for Children, St Andrews University, 17 March.

McCall, C. C. (2007) 'Philosophising with Children', paper delivered to University of Iceland Philosophy Conference, Reykjavik, February.

McCall, C. C. (2007) 'Philosophy with Children in Scotland', paper delivered to the SOPHIA Network International Conference, Ljubljana, Slovenia, May.

McCall, C. C. (2007) 'Philosophy with Children – What is it?', keynote paper delivered to the SOPHIA Conference, University of Oporto, Oporto, 22 November.

McCall, C. C. (2007) 'Talking Thinking: Children Need Ideas', in *The 2nd Enlightenment Conference Proceedings*, Gastonia, NC: Communities of the Future.

McCall, C. (2008) 'Three Methods of Philosophical Dialogue: Differences and Similarities between Nelson's Socratic Method, Lipman's P4C Method, McCall's CoPI Method', at www.prs.heacademy.ac.uk/projects/elearning/McCall.ppt.

McPeck, J. E. (1981) *Critical Thinking and Education*, New York: St Martin's Press.

Matthews, G. (1980) *Philosophy and the Young Child*, Cambridge, MA: Harvard University Press.

Matthews, G. (1984) *Dialogues with Children*, Cambridge, MA: Harvard University Press.

Matthews, G. (1994) *The Philosophy of Childhood*, Cambridge, MA: Harvard University Press.

Midgley, D. (ed.) (2005) *The Essential Mary Midgley*, Abingdon: Routledge.

Midgley, M. (1996) 'Letters to the Editor', *Guardian*, 18 June.

Milgram, S. (1963) 'Behavioral Study of Obedience', *Journal of Abnormal and Social Psychology*, 67: 371–378.

Mill, J. S. (1859) *On Liberty*, new edn, Harlow: Longman (2007).

Mill, J. S. (1863) *Utilitarianism*, 2nd rev. edn, Indianapolis: Hackett (2002).

Murris, K. and Haynes, J. (2000) *Storywise: Thinking through Stories*, Reigate: Dialogue Works.

Nagel, T. (2004) *What Does It All Mean? A Very Short Introduction to Philosophy*, New York: Oxford University Press.

Nagel, T. (n.d.) 'What Is It Like to Be a Bat?', at http://members.aol.com/Neo Noetics/Nagel_Bat.html.

Nelson, L. (1922) 'The Socratic Method', in *Socratic Method and Critical Philosophy: Selected Essays*, New Haven, CT: Yale University Press (1949); new edn, Mineola, NY: Dover (1966).

Nisbett, R. E. (with T. D. Wilson) (1977) 'Telling More than We Can Know: Verbal Reports on Mental Processes', *Psychological Review*, 84: 231–259.

Peirce, C. S. (1931–1958) *Collected Writings* (8 vols), ed. C. Hartshorne, P. Weiss and A. Burks, Cambridge, MA: Harvard University Press.

Peters, R. S. (1977) 'John Dewey's Philosophy of Education', in R. S. Peters (ed.) *John Dewey Reconsidered*, London: Routledge.

Plato (fifth century BC) *Symposium*, ed. K. Dover, Cambridge: Cambridge University Press (1980).

Popper, K. (1963) *Conjectures and Refutations: The Growth of Scientific Knowledge*, London: Routledge and Kegan Paul.

Putnam, H. (1981) *Reason, Truth and History*, Cambridge: Cambridge University Press.

Rawls, J. (1972) *A Theory of Justice*, Oxford: Clarendon Press.

Reed, R. (1983) *Talking with Children*, Denver: Arden Press.

Rondhuis, T. (2005) *Philosophical Talent*, Rotterdam: Veenman Drukkers.

Rorty, R. (1999) *Philosophy and Social Hope*, Harmondsworth: Penguin Books.

Ryle, G. (1949) *The Concept of Mind*, new edn, London: Penguin Books (1990).

'Scottish Enlightenment' (2008), in *Encyclopaedia Britannica*, at http://www.britannica.com/EBchecked/topic/529682/Scottish-Enlightenment.

Scruton, R. (1997) *An Intelligent Person's Guide to Philosophy*, London: Duckworth.

Searle, J. (1996) *The Construction of Social Reality*, new edn, London: Penguin Books.

Siegel, H. (1988) *Educating Reason: Rationality, Critical Thinking, and Education*, London: Routledge.

Sinclair, A. J. (1996) 'The Emergence of Philosophical Inquiry in 18th Century Scotland', unpublished Ph.D. thesis, the Centre for Philosophical Inquiry, University of Glasgow.

Strawson, P. F. (1959) *Individuals: An Essay in Descriptive Metaphysics*, London: Routledge and Kegan Paul.

van der Leeuw, K. (2007) 'The Socratic Discussion: An Introduction to the Method and Some Literature', notes for the SOPHIA Network Meeting.

Wason, P. and Johnson-Laird, P. (1972) *Psychology of Reasoning: Structure and Content*, Cambridge, MA: Harvard University Press.

Index